THE ESOTERROR FACTBOOK

CREDITS

Publisher : SIMON ROGERS

Written by : ROBIN D LAWS

Artwork, layout and art design : JÉRÔME HUGUENIN

Spécial Thanks to Benoit, Effie, Gilbert, Sébastien, Simon

Map from UNOSAT
see http://unosat.web.cern.ch/unosat/asp/prod_free.asp?id=66&All=on f
or more detailed maps.

CONTENTS

ESOTERROR FACT BOOK

About This Document

The Esoterror Fact Book provides players and GMs of *The Esoterrorists* with extensive background details on the covert battle to bring about a supernatural apocalypse—and the heroic men and women who struggle secretly to stop it.

Although a small proportion of the material in this book is aimed at GMs, none of it is secret background information. Players may safely read any of it. If you are a GM, encourage your players to do so.

Background information appears in the form of Ordo Veritatis briefing materials. It presents the known facts of the setting from the point of view of the PCs' superiors. Astute reader will learning as much about the organization's spirit and culture from the style of the documents as from their explicit statements of fact.

The *Operations Manual* shows you what investigators are allowed to know about the procedures and protocols the Ordo Veritatis. Like any intelligence briefing, it omits details which would prove damaging to the group if it fell into the wrong hands.

Special Suppression Forces deals with the heavily armed commando units the Ordo sends out to deal with paramilitary and monstrous threats. It includes both background material and a section of rules material offering up somewhat crunchier rules for those who want to add detail and the smell of cordite to their GUMSHOE games.

The Enemy details the Esoterrorists themselves, as described by Ordo intelligence analysts. The chapter includes hard data and informed speculation on Esoterror funding, psychological profiles, communications and organizational structure. Briefing materials lay out what is known about ten suspected Esoterror cells and thirteen likely operatives. Players can use these sections as a operational shopping list. If you see a cell or operative you'd like to investigate, let your GM know, so she can prepare or improvise a scenario that puts you nose to nose with your chosen adversaries.

Unaffiliated Operatives profiles nine individuals who take active part in the world of supernatural ops without paying consistent allegiance either to the Ordo or to Esoterror. Some might serve as uneasy allies, while others are just as evil as your primary enemy—and less predictable.

Dread Locations discusses the membrane between this world and the Outer Dark. It describes traditionally haunted places as LSMLs: Low Membrane Strength Locations, where the wall between the mundane world and unremitting horror becomes dangerously thin. The chapter details eleven such places, from an African torture camp to a snow-swept Antarctic research station.

The book concludes with a short chapter of *GM Advice*. Players can benefit from it too, especially the section on the conceits that make a GUMSHOE game run more smoothly.

Operations Manual

Consider the following introductory precis of the full Ordo Veritatis operations manual mandatory reading for all field operatives. Read it and return it to your next Mr. Verity. The full manual will never be made available to you in its entirety. However, by channeling requests from the field through permissible operational protocols (see relevant section) you may be provided either with textual excerpts or (more likely) a succinct verbal recapitulation of Ordo policy pertinent to the situation at hand.

CASE EVALUATION

As field agents, you may wish to understand the process by which cases come to the attention of OV leadership and are conveyed to you through local handlers. Given that you are often called on to travel to an unfamiliar destination with little notice, plunge into a tactically obscure situation, and perhaps even risk your lives in pursuit of sometimes abstract goals, your curiosity is more than understandable. The following abstract attempts to answer the most common queries of field agents in this regard while omitting sensitive information which could, if intercepted, allow the enemy to divine our sources and methods.

Media Monitoring

A surprising number of cases come to our attention through simple media monitoring. Organization assets, distributed worldwide, perform Media Threat Analysis (MTA) duties, studying local and international news output available to them at their various locations. MTA officers operate singly, sending encrypted reports to high-security electronic drop sites. As Esoterror operations often involve attempts to sway or destabilize public mood, their operations are often revealed in simple news reports. Stories of interest to MTA assets include, but are not limited to, gruesome murders, abuses of official power, socially destabilizing art events and happenings, and, of course, occult activities, urban legends, and sightings of supernatural/inhuman entities.

Esoterrorist cells often piggyback on events they did not set into motion, manipulating them so as to increase public panic and spread mass dissociation. Even after an event is determined not to be of direct Esoterrorist origin, its aftermath must still be scrutinized for signs that opportunistic operations have been put into place on an impromptu basis. For example, during the Hurricane Katrina relief effort, a number of previously inactive Esoterror cells sprang into sudden motion, improvising ways to exacerbate the effects of a natural disaster and the dispiritingly inadequate official response to it. These operations included sniper attacks, the spreading of false information to deter victims from reaching the few available assistance points, and infiltrations of relief organizations for the purposes of systemic sabotage. The collective anger and anxiety generated by the failed relief response permanently damaged the membrane throughout the area. It remains weak throughout the Gulf Coast, and especially in low-income sections of New Orleans—which, for this reason, have yet to be fully rebuilt. Were it not for the efforts of three separate field action teams, dispatched to the New Orleans area in the knowledge that Esoterror cells would likely attempt such operations, the end result would have been incalculably worse. Some of our occult theorists believe that, left unimpeded, these enemy agents might well have succeeded in triggering their much-hoped for apocalyptic event. If so, the adversary has never come closer to fulfilling its nihilistic objectives.

Note that, for purposes of self-aggrandizement and recruiting, Esoterror operatives routinely credit themselves with the instigation of incidents they merely took expedient advantage of. New recruits are routinely told that the hurricane itself, an entirely natural event, was summoned by Esoterrorist ritual magic.

Massive events such as Katrina, which command immediate worldwide attention, inspire our rapid response without the need for MTA reports. Media analysts work the thousands of relatively obscure stories that daily float through the media machine, sometimes inspiring membrane-thinning cognitive dissonance in those who pause to think about

team deployment might occur on, say, a DAS of 94 or more.

Electronic Traffic Sifting

Through our high-level contacts, the Ordo monitors data flow from the electronic monitoring agencies of multiple world powers. Intelligence agencies of the major western powers, most notably the American NSA, constantly monitor worldwide communications traffic. Although the Ordo requires access to only the infinitesimal slice of it related to Esoterror activities, we arguably enjoy greater access to signals intelligence than any one of our contributing agencies. The Americans, for example, face legal limitations when listening in on their domestic communications. (They violate these restrictions in response to mundane global terror, but not to the extent that is popularly assumed.) However, we can gain access to American signals traffic through the auspices of our contacts within the equivalent agencies of the United Kingdom, France, and Canada.

As in conventional intelligence, gaining access to communications is the easy part. The real difficulty comes in sifting through vast mounds of traffic for the few tiny snippets of information worthy of further investigation. The Electronic Traffic Sifting department (ETS), a division of desk agents, uses a highly sophisticated data-sifting software program called SALAMIS to search through raw signals intelligence work product (including but not restricted to publications, emails, voice calls, and encrypted Internet traffic) for Esoterror keywords. SALAMIS' primary advantage over previous programs is its ability to zero in on clusters of words which are innocent of their own but are rarely found together outside of Esoterror communications. SALAMIS permits ETS to sift through terabytes of meaningless electronic noise to find the occasional nugget of actionable intelligence. Although intercepted communications between Esoterror operatives is always the holy grail of such efforts, telephonic and Internet material from uninformed onlookers may direct the assignments bureau to events in need of investigation.

them. They study these stories, flagging them for keywords and commonalities with past events either caused or heightened by enemy activity.

Reports are submitted in a standardized format and received by automated systems which feed them a database for macro-scale statistical analysis by a program code-named Debby Ann. Debby Ann rates potential Esoterror occurrences on a numerical scale of 1 to 100. The process by which scores are determined is at once complex and highly classified. However, even a statistical novice might infer that reports flagged by large numbers of MTAs are likelier than others to receive high scores.

Field agent teams are assigned to investigate events receiving high DASes (Debby Ann scores.) The exact DAS required to trigger an investigation varies according to field operative availability. On a slow month, a score of (to pick a number arbitrarily) 78 might prompt an operation, whereas during or after a peak of enemy activity, when fresh, mentally rested teams are at a premium,

When you, as field agents, receive especially vague instructions, or are dispatched on what appears to you to be a "fishing expedition", it is highly likely that your mission, such as it is, was triggered by ETS data. You may be dispatched on missions based on the telling presence of keywords in intercepted communications alone.

More often, keywords are used to firm up suspicions generated by more conventional means. For example, we may learn from an informant that an individual has a connection to a suspect cell of occultists. ETS then calls on its feeder agencies to monitor the suspect's communications, and finds typical Esoterror word clusters, at which point a full investigation is opened.

Ongoing Surveillance

In some instances the organization may be aware of suspected operatives or cells, or have reasonable cause to believe that a site or incident is likely to attract Esoterror intervention, while the dispatch of a full investigative team remains unwarranted. Examples of such conditions may include the following:

- Available pool of action teams has been reduced by recent heavy deployment, or by current case loads.

- Subjects or sites in question are located in hostile or neutral territory, outside of sponsoring jurisdictions.

- Level of suspicion or likelihood of enemy intervention is considered too low to justify the detail of an entire team.

- Surveillance operation is best suited to a single deep cover operative deployed over a lengthy duration.

In such cases the organization keeps the subjects and/or site under continuing surveillance. It may dispatch field agents from its Surveillance and Deep Cover (SDC) wing. (Some of you may be veterans of this department, or may be assigned to it as your fitness for duty or personal demands change over time. Agents who for family or professional reasons can no longer speed to a

distant investigation on a moment's notice may be kept in the organization to perform surveillance assignments near their homes.)

The SDC is not extravagantly staffed, however, and where knowledge of the big picture is not a prerequisite for successful surveillance (that is, most of the time), the Ordo Veritatis may hire private investigators or security personnel to conduct these duties. Such cut-outs are invariably hired under false pretenses. If you, as field agents, are required to interact with them during an investigation, you will be fully briefed on the nature of this cover story, which you will be expected to maintain.

Whatever the nature of the individuals performing the surveillance, when a report indicates an escalation of activity, a field team may be sent to the scene. It undertakes the more dangerous actions required to assemble a full portfolio of facts and, if necessary, engage the enemy directly and/or perform a subsequent veil-out.

It is remotely possible that you will encounter undercover Ordo Veritatis operatives in the course of an investigation. Standard procedure dictates that they not reveal themselves to you, except to preserve the lives of friendlies and innocents or to forestall disastrous mission failure. Under certain scenarios, the cover identity of a long-term undercover operative (such as an infiltrator into an Esoterrorist cell) may be deemed of greater import to our overall mission than the result of any single investigation. In such cases, the undercover operative may maintain his *bona fides* by failing to cooperate with you, or even actively obstructing your aims. Where possible, however, he will covertly assist you. You are urged in the strongest possible terms to avoid the negative example of several past field agents, whose aggressive tactics led to injuries or deaths for our deep cover operatives.

Informant Reports

Another branch of Ordo Veritatis desk officers maintains a worldwide network of informants. These include academics, journalists, law enforcement officials, members of the intelligence community, and participants in occult sub-cultures.

Some are aware of the nature of the Esoterrorist threat. Others are cultivated by deception and believe themselves to be serving some other agenda. In the developing world, many act as agents of other intelligence organizations, and provide information to the Ordo via their handlers in such agencies as the CIA, SIS, or DGSE. Certain informants report directly to Ordo Veritatis handlers stationed throughout the world. Others file reports electronically and never, after the establishment of the initial relationship, interface with any of us in person.

Informants are typically provided a list of persons or a list of incident types, and are instructed to alert us in the event of any unusual activity.

Protection of informants and contacts is a matter of the highest priority. When dispatched to conduct an investigation, you will not meet the informant(s) who triggered it, except where absolutely necessary. In the vast majority of cases, you will simply be presented with their testimony as part of your initial briefing with Mr. Verity. It will be stripped of any identifying information. Only where such contact is unavoidable will you be permitted to meet directly with contacts. Where the contact is unaware of our organization and its agenda, you will be supplied with sufficient background to preserve the deception.

Contacts may place themselves in danger to gain information for us. The insertion of an investigative team into an ongoing situation may exacerbate such risks, as Esoterror conspirators lash out at possible informants. Where our own undercover operatives willingly accept the concomitant hazards of their duties, informants are to be regarded as civilian volunteers, deserving of maximum protection. Unless otherwise ordered, assume that the safety of civilian contacts is as important, if not more so, than the successful completion of your mission, whatever that may be.

INVESTIGATION

The uncovering of salient information is the core of your mission. Always ask yourself:

- What has gone on here?

- Who is responsible for it?

- Where can I find them?

- How can I stop them?

Always remember the cardinal rule of investigation, as laid out by your instructors in your very first training sessions: *if you don't know what to do next, go find more information.*

Conducting Interviews

It is a rare case which does not hinge on information gathered verbally from witnesses, suspects, and sources. Strong interview technique is pivotal to quick and efficient progress through an investigation.

It takes time for a group to find its interviewing rhythm. Until then, you may find it difficult to open subjects up, and have trouble determining what to ask. Before entering into an interview, start by reviewing what you know, or can reasonably surmise, about the subject. Ask yourself what the subject is likely to know. Finally, ask yourself what you need to know in order to move forward.

Rely on your improvisatory instincts to move you through rough spots in any interview. Almost any interview will shift under your feet as you discover more about the subject. It will show new lines of connection to the interviewee and/or establish additional facts requiring follow-up. Even so, the practice of pre-interview conference will give you a strong starting point from which to improvise as the conversation develops.

Do not be afraid to grant momentary advantage to a hostile witness. If you make a seeming mistake, don't get flustered. Find a way to capitalize on it by luring the subject into a false sense of confidence or security.

Motivation To Talk

Before you can gather information from a subject, you must motivate them to open up. Ask yourself what a subject might want from you. If they want nothing from you, identify a tactic to convince them that they do. An interview is a negotiation, in which you trade something—for example emotional validation, information, or cessation of threat—in exchange for the facts you need.

Although interpersonal skills are your primary tool in any interview, don't forget the usefulness of professional contacts and shared interests. An art historian may respond more favorably to your command of her subject matter than to flattery or appeals to bureaucratic procedure.

Opening Gambits

Getting the subject talking is only half the battle. Now you have to ask the right questions. You may have already set forth a line of questioning in a quick pre-interview conference with fellow investigators. If so, by all means follow it.

Often, however, you'll have an inkling that a subject has something to tell you, if only you can work out what on earth to ask. When stumped, default to one of two modes: narrative or confirmatory.

Narrative Openers

Use the narrative opener when the information you seek is an account of some past event. Start simply by asking the interviewee to recount his or her experiences in regard to the case. Impel them to tell you a story.

- "Tell me what happened up in the old mill."

- "What led you to open the door and discover the body?"

- "How did you discover the ruins, Professor?"

- "How did you come to be friends with Mr. Smith?"

If opened in this way, the subject will often supply a groundwork of facts to work from, which you can then review, asking specific questions to elicit more detail in the areas that concern you.

The narrative approach serves as a good measure of witness honesty. Most people talk in anecdotes if allowed to ramble on. Subjects who tightly limit answers generally have something to hide. Although witnesses have many reasons to lie, many of which won't pertain to your case, the discovery of those reasons can induce greater candor.

Subjects are often reluctant to admit to inexplicable or supernatural experiences. To proceed, they need your tacit permission to admit to experiences that others will regard as crazy. As you will not be trying a case in a court of law, you may feel free to pose leading questions. Rather than asking them if something strange happened, introduce this as an already accepted fact and then ask them to fill in the details:

- "Something weird happened to you that night. What was it, exactly?"

When encouraging witnesses to open up, retain plausible deniability for the veil-out. When you explicitly assure a witness that demons really are invading his corn field, it becomes infinitely harder to later convince him that he was under the influence of a leaked industrial chemical.

Confirmatory Openers

When you're fishing for information without knowing exactly what you need from a witness, it is often useful to start by asking them to confirm what you already know.

- "We're told the traffic lights blink strangely at night. Is that right?"

- "Did you know that Miss Greene stopped attending classes last semester?"

Give the witness chances to confirm or deny the facts you put before them. Often a correction or amplification will start you on the chain of questions leading to the central nugget of information the witness has for you.

At the very least, repetition of the main facts of the case helps to cement them in your own mind.

This mode helps you to lull hostile or deceptive witnesses by making them feel that they're not giving anything away. It is emotionally safer to merely comment on a pre-existing narrative.

Getting the Facts

Once you have the subject talking, your next challenge is to gather all of the facts important to the case, even though you may not know what you're looking for. When interviewing, it is always useful to refer to your notes. Maintain a list of the central unanswered questions before you in the case, revising as necessary as you gain more information. If you reach a point where you feel that the witness has more to offer, but you're stumped for a question, consult this list to get you back on track.

Zero in on statements that don't gibe with what you've already been told. Your current witness may be lying or mistaken, or may be honestly correcting someone else's misstatement. Inconsistencies may result from simple witness error, which is all too common even among professional observers. Often, however, they provide the key to your mystery.

The challenge with an honest, cooperative witnesses is to separate the incidental facts from the probative ones. Honest witnesses are often eager to please and provide too much information. Often they substitute incorrect conclusions for a spare description of the basic facts. When dealing with an overly gregarious or chatty source, you must work to keep them on topic without hurting their feelings and causing them to withdraw from you.

Reluctant or deceptive witnesses will provide terse or evasive replies. Some deceivers pretend to be friendly and loquacious, burying you in excess data. Turn this to your advantage. The more such sources say, the more likely they are to trip themselves up by uttering an inconsistency.

Watch witnesses for signs of evasion or dishonesty. These show that you've hit a sore spot. By pressing these buttons, you can often prompt a useful revelation, or find the leverage to force more truthful answers.

Interviewing In Stages

Sometimes you must interview a subject several times to get the full truth. You may not be sufficiently deep into the case to know which questions to ask. Inconsistencies with other witness statements may warrant further exploration. Facts discovered subsequent to an interview may give you the leverage you need to force later admissions.

When returning to a witness, ask yourself if the original investigator is best suited to the second interview, or if another team member should spell him or her off. If a strong rapport has already been established, build on this relationship. Do likewise if a useful sense of fear or intimidation has been cultivated. If, on the other hand, the witness responded poorly to the first mode of approach, send in a new investigator to take the opposite tack. By splitting the interview into stages, the use of the classic "good cop/bad cop" technique, familiar to anyone who's ever watched a cop show, becomes less apparent.

Repeat interviews tend to offer diminishing returns, so strategize before returning to a witness. Remind yourself what he knows, what he seems to want, and what the weaknesses or inconsistencies in his account may be.

Maintaining Cover

At first glance, the task of keeping your true purpose and organizational allegiances secret while prying information out of witnesses and officials may seem daunting. Indeed, it is vital both to your security and that of the order that you stick closely to your cover identities. However, you will find that in practice it is surprisingly easy to project an image of false authority.

Every investigator is in essence a con man. This is as true for ordinary homicide detectives as for Ordo Veritatis assets. Con stands for "confidence." Act as if you unquestionably possess the authority to ask questions and gather evidence, and nine out of ten civilians will instinctively accept you. Those who do not tend to be troublemakers, criminals, and eccentrics—people who are either disinclined to seek official redress for their grievances, or who will be disregarded by traditional authorities.

The longer you remain in an area, the greater the likelihood of attracting unwanted suspicions. Thus it is in your interest to dispense with a case as quickly as possible. Minimize contacts with suspicious witnesses.

Multiple impostures help to confuse matters. Even if already in a cover identity, you may want to pose as yet another fictitious person while bracing a problem witness.

Lay the seeds of misinformation with such individuals. It is often to your advantage to allow them to think that they're onto you, while in fact you're convincing them that you belong to some other shadowy covert agency.

Credentials and Official Liaison

When investigating in the industrialized democracies where the Order enjoys a firm foothold, you will often be provided with special credentials identifying you as officers of a police or intelligence agency appropriate to the case. Those of you with suitable professional backgrounds will be credentialed as actual officers or agents. Others will be granted supplementary clearances as special consultants.

You have been trained in the cultural and bureaucratic apparatus of relevant agencies, such as the CIA, FBI, Military Intelligence, Secret Service, and their counterparts in other signatory nations. Project confidence that your credentials are valid and you will not be prevented from going about our business. Although you can expect grumbling resistance from the officers or investigators you displace, they will not impede you in your mission. If you do, it may be a sign of Esoterror infiltration of the agency in question. This in and of itself may constitute a crucial clue into the mystery at hand.

When embarked on a credentialed investigation, heed this motto: *assume wide latitude, and it will be granted.*

Handling and Controlling Physical Evidence

Your relationship to evidence is different than the law enforcement or intelligence agencies to which you may be credentialed. The police seek to bag and tag legally secured evidence to clear its later use in a court of law. Intelligence agencies gather information, often secretly and sometimes illegally, to increase their knowledge base. You gather information extra-legally in order to eventually misrepresent and destroy it. The terms of your liaison with public agencies allow you ultimate custody of all physical evidence. Use their lab facilities but your technical abilities to process and analyze all such evidence. Never allow it to be entered into the agency's system. At the end of the investigation claim all of it, in order to proceed with your veil-out.

The terms of your detail to an agency explicitly allows you such evidentiary control. Any prolonged pushback against these terms may indicate the presence of Esoterror assets.

HOSTILE CONTACT

There comes a time in any investigation when a sweep of a dark basement for clues turns suddenly and gut-churningly into a combat with the denizens of the Outer Dark. Apart from the general tactical skills you have probably learned from either our trainers, or those who taught you to fight in your everyday capacities, certain special operational requirements pertain to situations of hostile contact.

Priorities

Your priorities in any hostile contact situation are, in order of importance:

- To protect lives of non-hostile civilian personnel..

- To protect the lives of your Ordo Veritatis comrades and of other non-civilian personnel (police, soldiers, intelligence agents.)

- To contain or destroy the creature, preventing it from doing future harm.

- To suppress knowledge of the creature's existence.

- To capture hostile humans for interrogation and possible incarceration.

Establishing A Tactical Hierarchy

Investigations are collaborative affairs, where consensus leads to good conclusions and parallel efforts crack problems faster than a strictly hierarchical approach. Combat situations are the opposite: they occur too quickly for discussion and require lightning-fast coordination. Designate a tactical hierarchy at the beginning of each investigation. (If embarking on a new investigation with the same personnel as the last one, you may assume that the previous tactical hierarchy remains in place until you choose to alter it.) A tactical hierarchy is a list of all team members, arranged in order from the most suitable leader to the least.

Good tactical leaders show coolness under fire, are strongly perceptive, and well versed in skirmish tactics. They may or may not be the group's most skilled combatants. Often it is best to send the physically toughest men forward into the fight, while keeping the tactical leader back from the fray. He can then occupy a vantage point allowing for an encompassing view of the entire fight, from which he can issue orders.

In a fight, the investigator who, among those present at the scene, is first-listed in the tactical hierarchy becomes the tactical commander. He issues orders to advance or retreat, and, where appropriate, to execute useful maneuvers.

Tactical Withdrawal

The most important command your tactical commander can issue is the one calling for an an orderly retreat. Investigators may find themselves outmatched in the presence of Outer Dark Entities (ODEs.) Where creatures are in a containable location, such as a basement, cavern, or building, or are resident in a lair or habitat they are apt to return to, it is often best to retreat after damaging first contact. Withdrawal allows the group the opportunity to attack on its own terms, with adequate equipment, and perhaps armed with SMD (Special Means of Dispatch; see below.) Creatures do not warrant equitable treatment or a fair fight. They wish to exterminate you and you should feel the same way about them. Don't fight bravely, fight cleverly.

Withdrawal is contraindicated where it would violate other priorities as listed above. If creatures are apt to escape from their present location to reveal themselves to the wider world, or where retreat would free them to prey on innocents, the tactical commander must perform a risk-benefit analysis. Investigators must be ready to lay their lives down for the protection of non-combatants or broader preservation of the membrane—provided that within their potential sacrifices lies a reasonable prospect of success. Pyrrhic victories are admirable; uselessly suicidal gestures rob innocents of whatever aid you would otherwise be able to extend to them.

Special Means of Dispatch

Some supernatural entities are distinguished by a special means of dispatch (SMD), a weapon or attack type which is either necessary to kill them, or does dramatically greater damage to them. In a case where you suspect creature activity, especially where the entity does not conform to a known type, be sure to include in your information-gathering any indication of its SMD

SMDs may vary across creature sub-types. For example, vampires of bearing the rt/st genotype (of Eastern European descent) shrug off damage unless struck in the chest cavity with wooden weapon, while vampires of the rt/so genotype (of South American extraction) are vulnerable only to throat injuries or decapitation.

Where discretion allows, it is permissible to break communications silence to seek SMD information from the order's central databanks. The research efforts of teams like yours allow us to continually refine and update our knowledge of SMDs.

Fortunately this refinement is not a continual upward movement toward better knowledge. ODEs and ODISes (Outer Dark Influenced Subjects) may transcend biological limitations to undergo a process of magically-based rapid evolution. Up until 1989, it was possible to render a bleeder corporeal by spraying its ethereal manifestation with a fine saline mist. Then, beginning with OPERATION CANISTER (November 17-24, 1989, Brentwood, TN), this proved ineffective. Nor was this a localized exception; it hasn't it worked on any other bleeder since.

THE VEIL-OUT

Successful veil-out completion is essential to membrane preservation. In the wake of a wide-ranging investigational phase and messy, disturbing extirpation phase, the difficulty of a veil-out may seem daunting, even demoralizing. However, it is essential to remember this:

Hardly anyone really wants to know the truth.

Denial Is A Survival Mechanism

All of us live, from day to day, in denial even of life's mundane horrors. We all know that we are one day going to die—probably from a debilitating, painful and prolonged disease. Worse, we know that all of our loved ones are going to die, too. The prospect of their loss is much harder to bear than our own nonexistence. If we spent our days dwelling on this terrible truth, we would be unable to function at all. Instead, we are protected by a powerful and necessary sense of denial, allowing us to file this information away in the back of our minds and go about our business. This defense mechanism is so universal that it can only be explained as a necessary adaptation for survival. Those who lack it suffer from diagnosable mental illnesses, such as depression. Some have argued that the human impulse toward religious faith is a manifestation of this genetic adaptation, that it originated in order to comfort us in the fact of inevitable mortality. (*Note*: The Ordo Veritatis takes no official position on the ultimate veracity of religious belief, except to note that in no investigation we have ever taken part in has positive intercession from divine beings been reliably observed.)

Whatever its origins, this impulse to deny awful truths serves as the greatest ally of an investigator in pursuit of a veil-out. At some instinctive level, our species knows about the Outer Dark. At the same time, the unconscious understands the dangers of bringing this awareness to the surface. Esoterror seeks to disable these mental defenses, as part of its war against the membrane.

This suggests an intriguing possibility: that the

membrane itself is a manifestation of massed human consciousness, a literal psychic wall of denial between us and a realm of insanity.

It also explains why the insane and emotionally disturbed are more likely to encounter ODEs; they are rendered vulnerable by their weak connection to the membrane.

At any rate, the membrane itself appears to act as our confederate as we re-edit the truth to enable this sense of denial.

In other words, people will believe a surprising amount of nonsense, even that which contradicts the input of their own senses—if it conforms to what they want to believe. What they *must* believe, in order to survive as a species.

This makes your task somewhat easier. Consensus reality does not demand an airtight alibi. Plausible deniability is all it takes.

Constructing Cover Stories

Plausible deniability starts with a cover story. Begin by asking yourself: "What is the most likely mundane explanation for the events we're about to veil out?"

A second consideration is the outrageousness of the cover story itself. Remember that it is not only overtly supernatural events that weaken the membrane. Events that makes life seem surreal and inexplicable also harm it, though to a lesser degree. So, given a range of plausible and achievable veil-out options, pick the explanatory narrative that seems the dullest and least noteworthy.

Case study: An unremitting horror entity known as a giggler feeds on the trauma of sexual molestation victims. It helps guide members of a pedophile ring to the troubled kids who frequent a drop-in center in a vice-infested downtown area. The giggler is mystically tied to the center by a child murder committed on the site in its previous incarnation, as a massage parlor. After the children are victimized, they see the giggler;

it manifests as a creepy demonic clown. An Ordo team investigates, identifies the nature of the haunting, and exorcises the giggler by discreetly setting fire to the shelter, destroying its connection to the mundane world. Now the lead investigators debate various possible veil-outs.

Investigator Emily Costas proposes explaining the clown sightings as the actions of a human leader of the pedophile ring who, like John Wayne Gacy, liked to entice victims by donning circus gear.

Her colleague, Bruno Hunter, points out that the clown-pedophile connection will in and of itself seem lurid. Tailor-made for tabloid headlines, it will sow fear, disturbance, and cognitive dissonance. Better to drop the clown angle altogether, saying that the kids developed an urban legend about a killer clown to mask their distress at being targeted by an abuse ring.

Denying the existence of the abuse altogether might cause less damage to the membrane, but would prove inhumane and unethical. Such a tactic would damage the victims by denying their experiences. It would also require that the Ordo disappear a number of mundane pedophiles, violating our ethical guidelines.

Cajoling Witnesses

Witnesses to the supernatural events of the case pose the central threat to your cover story. Step one in most veil-outs is to identify the surviving witnesses and enlist them in confirming the cover story when approached by media outlets and civilian authorities.

Many witnesses traumatized by Outer Dark manifestations will be only too happy to assist. Most want to forget and deny the upsetting, unbelievable events they witnessed. They may not only willingly agree to lie for you; they may anxiously seize on your story as the truth. Reinforce this impulse wherever possible: a witness who believes the cover story is even more effective than one consciously concealing a horrible actuality.

Witnesses who perceive you has having performed a service or favor for them yield their cooperation easily.

Others may be convinced with an appeal to authority and/or the greater good. Explain that agency you work for wants to avoid public panic. This has the added advantage of being true, except that you'll be naming the organization you are credentialed to, not the Ordo.

Sadly, some witnesses are harder to convince— especially those to whom you've developed a hostile relationship in the course of the investigation. These will require persuasion. Convince them to help you now using the same interpersonal techniques you employed to wring information from them. Lay on the charm, appeal to procedure, offer reasurrance. Intimidate scumbags as necessary. Figure out what they want and make a deal.

> *Case study: Having saved the drop-in shelter kids from the giggler, investigator Emily Costa convenes them together, privately. First she announces plans to rebuild a better drop-in shelter on the site of the one that burnt down. (This effort is secretly Ordo-funded.) Emily engages them by telling them that they'll be consulted in the design of building the new center. However, if they make themselves seem crazy by describing what they saw, the bureaucrats will have an excuse to remove them from the process. The kids, who have no desire to share their dark experiences, readily agree to Emily's proposed cover story.*

Using the Media

In the global war against Esoterrorism, no battlefront is more strategic than the mediasphere. A tactically failed Esoterror operation becomes a strategic victory for the enemy when it is able to spin news events to increase the sense of a world spinning out of control. Likewise, a Veritatis response that takes a heavy toll on the organization can nonetheless become a net positive when we are able to utilize the media to reinforce the idea of a stable and ordered existence.

Some members of the media are conscious participants in the struggle for the membrane, serving either Esoterror, or working as our assets.

The majority, however, are neutrals. As with witnesses, think of your interactions with them as negotiations. Understand what they want, and show them how you are in a position to grant it.

Reporters for media outlets big and small are overworked, deadline-driven and suffering from severe cases of information bombardment. They need to churn out material that grabs audience attention, and do it quickly. Despite the popular stereotype, few reporters revel in the cheap sensationalism of weird tabloid stories. (Cheap sensationalism of celebrity culture is another matter, which is why Esoterror is so interested in exploiting denizens of the B-list.) Journalists tend to view stories of human deviance, gruesome murders, and paranormal events as a humiliating necessity of the profession. Their fear of failing to deliver a juicy story to their editors exists in a fingernail-gnawing balance with the terror of humiliation that comes if they fall for a hoax. As you pitch the mundane version of a story to reporter, play on these two impulses of fear and shame.

Certain reporters are swayed by other means. Journalists dependent on official sources can be threatened with loss of future access. Many television talking heads are insecure egotists who can be braced with a little strategic flattery. Police beat reporters tend to be pro-cop. Expect them to respond favorably to requests to suppress particular details, if you make a convincing case that doing so assists law enforcement.

That said, the universal currency when asking for a new spin on a story is other publishable information. Bargain with reporters by offering them stories of more solid provenance than the supernatural angle you wish to suppress. No matter how debased his current beat, any journalist dreams of the big investigative scoop that exposes malfeasance or leads to positive social change. During the investigative phase of your operation, keep your eyes open for non-occult secrets which may serve as bargaining chips in later dealings with journalists. When bribing journalists with this sort of information, be careful not to damage the reputations or livelihoods of blameless third parties. It is one thing to prove that a public servant is on the take, but quite another to out a closeted celebrity whose secrets harm no one.

Case study: In her coverage of the drop-in center story, local newspaper reporter Alana Hornaday has on a couple of occasions mentioned the predatory clown figure feared by the at-risk kids. After the center burns, investigator Bruno Hunter approaches her and asks her not to stigmatize the center's clients any further by continuing to cite this element of the story. Instead he gives her something bigger to chew on — documents recovered by the team during the investigation showing that center staffers were diverting needed renovation funds into an alderman's vanity project.

Counter-Reliables

Certain fringe media outlets or personalities are so discredited that any story they carry automatically loses credence by association. We designate such media assets as counter-reliables. In the case of a counter-reliable, you want the journalist to run the true story — or a disreputable version thereof. Although it's always safest to salt your information with easily-debunked factual errors, you can often count on such individuals to add their own distortions and wild speculation to the mix. If a reputable journalist is about to run with a damaging story, get a counter-reliable to scoop her.

Another advantage of the counter-reliable is the ease of planting stories with them. Their lack of discrimination in regard to sources allows you merely to slip a manila envelope under a doorway, rather than going to the risk and trouble of a face-to-face encounter. The more dodgy and enigmatic a source, the greater credence a counter-reliable will grant it.

The Ordo media affairs department runs an active disinformation campaign dedicated to the care and feeding of counter-reliables. By covertly providing fringe journalists with bogus stories and then debunking them, this team slowly converts potentially dangerous media representatives with occult or paranormal interests into useful counter-reliables.

Stalwart counter-reliables include:

- Night time talk radio host Jack Toll, whose program, *Tolling the Hours,* has obsessively covered UFOs, faith healing, conspiracy theories, and the weirder side of cryptozoology since 1987. Although Toll maintains a pose of neutrality on the validity of the paranormal, he encourages his regular roster of cranks and loonies to float outrageously bizarre theories and predictions. His show's coverage of astronomical anomalies (an side-effect of the Esoterror plot busted in OPERATION ORPHAN) led indirectly to the mass suicides at the Doomhaven cult compound in 1997.

- Juanette Ruiz edits the long-running digest-sized paranormal magazine *Destiny*. With the *Weekly World News* tabloid sadly out of business, *Destiny* now serves as America's most highly circulated counter-reliable publication. Ruiz is not herself a believer, but a savvy editor with a sharp sense of her audience and a constant need for half-credible new material.

- Nathan X (a.k.a. Nathaniel Gleibhauser of Thornhill, Ontario), blogger and moderator of Paraforum, an Internet discussion site where crazed credulity rules. Nathan often spontaneously aids us in veil-out activities by seizing on early press accounts of Esoterror operations, to which he adds a layer of wild speculation. His quick responses, as disseminated through the blogosphere by his readers, then become mixed up with the truth, solidifying it into easily-debunked urban legend.

Friendly Media Assets

Many past and former investigators are still employed as journalists and assignment editors. Other colleagues serve the Ordo in an auxiliary capacity. These Friendly Media Assets (FMAs) can aid you in their civilian capacities by slanting, burying, or reassigning stories during your veil-out procedure. The availability of FMAs to assist you in your veil-out will be communicated to you by Mr. Verity during your initial briefing.

Ideologically Allied Media Assets

Some figures are by intellectual disposition supportive of Ordo aims, even though they are completely unaware of our existence or the value of their efforts. These we call IAMAs, or Ideologically Allied Media Assets. The vast majority of these are skeptics and debunkers who disbelieve completely in the existence of the occult and seek to counter any report that reeks of what they consider to be gullible nonsense.

IAMAs must be handled differently than FMAs. When approaching the former, you cannot hint at the existence of the organization or your true purpose in seeking their aid. Instead maintain the pretence of a fellow materialist/rationalist outraged by the bunkum and hoo-hah. Decry the eternal gullibility of mankind as you slip them the false leads that will discredit claims of the supernatural.

Consistently useful IAMAs include:

- Henry "Hank" Noone, pipe-smoking, tweed-jacketed editor of *Debunk!,* a glossy magazine devoted to rationalism. Amid its pro-atheist, libertarian content appears a steady stream of anti-paranormal investigative journalism. Noone's magazine often tees off of noted counter-reliables like Jack Toll and Nathan X (see above), completing the circuit of disbelief.

- Erin Westervelt, righteous young activist and founder of the media pressure group the Media Disinformation Awareness Network (MDAN.) Westervelt and her small band of college-age hyper-rationalists tirelessly hound media sources who credulously report on paranormal, New Age, and junk science topics. Their pressure tactics yield a surprising number of retractions.

Countering Enemy Media Assets

Unfortunately, the enemy also has its assets in the media industry. Some are primary Esoterror operators, using their platforms to spread membrane-degrading memes and sentiments. Others are minor assets operating in a support capacity. Their job is to take the supernatural activities that occur during primary operations and use the media lens to magnify their impact. Where known EMAs (Enemy Media Assets) are active in a given area or sphere of influence, you will be supplied with their profiles as part of your pre-operational briefing. You may discover them in the course of an investigation. Needless to say, the effort of identifying EMAs is an ongoing one. Any evidence you uncover to this end should be conveyed to your Mr. Verity during debriefing.

EMAs are unlikely to yield to persuasion or blandishment. If you approach an EMA whose status as such is unknown to you, he may pretend to cooperate, only to blindside you with a membrane-destructive story. For this reason it is crucial to assess the honesty of media contacts whose assistance is rendered too readily.

To counter an EMA, you must undermine his credibility and that of his story. To this end, you can:

- plant evidence which contradicts his story

- arrange for witnesses to lodge ethics complaints against him

- go over his head to friendly or neutral editors and gatekeepers

- give a wildly exaggerated story to a counter-reliable, undermining it by association

- arrange for the EMA to be ridiculed or critiqued on valid but unrelated grounds

Laying Groundwork

Investigative teams need merely lay the groundwork for a successful veil-out. Once debriefing has occurred, follow-up efforts will be performed by a specialized Media Outreach Team (MOT.) As these teams are tasked to uneventful psychographic activities, they are rarely confronted by armed enemy agents or ODEs. In rare circumstances, they may meet resistance, calling for an investigative team to be detailed to the case. This may be the team that investigated the original case, or a new team, as expedience dictates.

CODE OF ETHICS

The Ordo Veritatis is dedicated above all to the protection of mankind. Agents pledge to defend human life and dignity. These goals cannot be attained unless all of our operatives, including investigative agents, adhere to a strict code of ethics.

Raw recruits often assume that, as a secretive, quasi-governmental organization, we employ ruthless means to achieve our all-too necessary goals. Nothing could be further from the truth. Assassination, torture, and other offenses that shock the conscience are not only inherently immoral—they weaken the membrane. Fear, intimidation and dismay are the handmaidens of Esoterror. Forced by necessity to operate in secret, we cannot allow our lack of accountability to turn us into abettors of our enemies.

Ruthless and criminal actions by the forces of good are significantly more harmful to the membrane than the offenses committed by those already dedicated to evil. The creatures of the Outer Dark feed on the psychic energy given off by a slide into moral degeneration. Your small act of corruption might expose the world to greater supernatural danger than a harrowing murder committed by a conscienceless psychopath.

Assassination

The Ordo Veritatis does not as a matter of policy endorse the practice of assassination. Cold-blooded murders do greater damage to the membrane than killings in self-defense, by several orders of magnitude.

In rare instances, the assignment desk may determine that an assassination is the only conceivable means of forestalling a much worse membrane breach. Only then is a warrant of exigency issued permitting what is in general strictly forbidden.

Without such a warrant and the accompanying explicit mission instructions, field agents are to, under no circumstances whatsoever, practice assassination or cold-blooded killing of any human subject.

Assassination and ODEs

Different ethical rules apply to ODEs, who are not human and lack the capacity for moral choice. They are literal expressions of evil, given flesh and substance, and summoned to a world where they do not belong. It is entirely permissible to attack them with intent to kill, and to do so in a manner that minimizes an agent's exposure to danger.

Where it is established beyond a reasonable doubt that an apparent human subject has been parasitized or irrevocably possessed by an ODE (is an ODIS), it is then permissible to treat the subject as one would any other monstrous being. The host has, for all intents and purposes, already been killed, by the entity. In this instance, you are merely granting the victim his or her final rest.

Apprehension, Rendition, Lethal Force

Rules against assassination are not to be construed as a prohibition against lethal force in all operational circumstances. You are however enjoined to employ the minimal force necessary to safely achieve your mission objectives, which include the collateral protection of innocent lives. Where possible, use non-lethal force to stop or restrain hostiles who are not known or suspected Esoterrorists.

In your mission briefings, you will be told if we wish you to apprehend a given Esoterrorist for interrogation. If this is the case, you may use lethal force against him only where absolutely necessary in self-defense or the defense of others. Strive at all costs to subdue him, so he can be rendered to one of our secret facilities. When you have secured

the subject, send an encrypted SMS message to a prearranged, untraceable number. A rendition team will supply coordinates for a pick-up—often your present location—and the subject will be taken off your hands within twenty-four hours. Needless to say, it is crucial to defend your site of makeshift detention from enemy rescue efforts until such time as your rendition relief appears.

By default, however, we prefer it when Esoterror operatives arrange for their own demises. Housing imprisoned Esoterrorists until the end of their days is a costly and hazardous undertaking. Ordo prisons are kept small to reduce the chance of exposure. Although you must not kill in cold blood, many enemy operatives conveniently prefer to go out in a blaze of glory than to face the humiliations of interrogation and imprisonment. You may always use lethal force against enemies employing it against you.

This is not to say that you may goad others, especially not adversaries unaffiliated with Esoterror, into attacking you in order to justify your use of lethal force against them. Your extra-legal enforcement powers must be used with utmost judiciousness.

Post-Rendition Veil-Out

When the Ordo arranges for the apprehension and permanent detention of a suspect, the investigative team will be tasked, as part of its veil-out procedure, to disguise the subject's disappearance as an explicable and minimally distressing event. As with the veil-out of supernatural activities, you must devise the plausible story most likely to survive the follow-up efforts of unsuspecting loved ones, relatives, business associates and (if the subject is a public figure) the press. Typical approaches include faking the subject's death or voluntary disappearance. Especially in the former instance, make sure to script fictional demises to cause the least amount of distress and attention. For example, a supposed death from illness is less membrane-damaging than an accidental one, which is turn preferable to death by negligence or intentional violence. When arranging disappearances, a little evidence goes a long way. Searchers must be convinced that the subject has voluntarily departed, but not given enough clues to his whereabouts to mount a search exposing the veil-out.

Interrogation Techniques

Given the implacable animosity that Esoterror operatives evince towards civilization as we know it, and the often sadistically murderous techniques they use to bring about its end, the temptation to do harm to them once they are helpless and in our custody is all too understandable. This impulse must be resisted at all costs. The practice of torture weakens the membrane. This is why supernatural occurrences are more frequent and more powerful in lawless or authoritarian jurisdictions than in the western world. The effect is found both when public acceptance of torture rises, and when torture is practiced in private. In his classified research document *Ritual Implications of Harsh Interrogation*, Ordo social scientist ASH TRIANGLE convincingly argues that this effect can be attributed to the similarity of both intent and action between summoning rituals and torture-based interrogation.

Accordingly, all Ordo operatives are proscribed from employing the following techniques: waterboarding, stress positions, sleep deprivation, exposure to temperature extremes, prolonged sensory interference (including both deprivation and excess stimulation, for example the playing of deafening or disorienting sounds or music.) As should go without saying, more obvious means of inflicting harm, suffering, and the fear of death are also forbidden.

Instead, specially trained interrogation teams employ soft psychological means (SPM) over a long period of time. These may include trickery, intimidation, and the establishment of emotional dominance, but just as often involve the slow winning of a subject's trust.

Morgan Lee's comparison of results gained through SPM versus the harsh techniques used prior to our discovery of torture's effects on the membrane shows that intelligence gathered in the current manner is twelve times as reliable as the brutal old techniques.

Veil-Out Ethics

As mentioned in the relevant section of this operations manual, agents performing veil-outs are expected to respect individual and community dignity. Do not create cover stories which impugn the reputations of innocents, or expose them to psychological trauma or emotional suffering. Do not, falsely or otherwise, harm the reputations of the innocent.

It is permissible however to dispense rude justice to serious malefactors, whether or not they are knowing servants of the enemy.

Warrant of Exigency

Violations of Ordo ethics may be undertaken only under the terms of a Warrant Of Exigency, an addendum to one's mission briefing authorizing extraordinary action.

Should you encounter a situation in the field that seems to require an ethical violation, stop, rethink, and search for an ethical alternative. If there truly seems to be no way forward but to commit a violation, make an emergency contact to Mr. Verity. He will relay your request to the assignment desk, which will take swift action to either accept or decline your request for a Warrant of Exigency. 78% of requests are ill-judged and therefore declined. They may be refused without comment, or with an alternate suggestion for handling the obstacle without ethical transgression.

The So-Called Ticking Clock

Beginning students of situational ethics often pose a scenario known as the ticking clock. In this hypothetical scenario, the agent has no time to call for a warrant of exigency. He must act now, committing an ethics violation, to forestall a much worse catastrophe. Should he commit the act, or allow himself to be stymied by red tape?

The answer is that you must wait, or suffer disciplinary charges before a review board (see below.) Punishment for unauthorized ethical violations may include imprisonment in a secure facility for the rest of your natural life.

Now decide: is this ethical violation so necessary that I am prepared to sacrifice the rest of my life for it, just as I might by throwing myself into the maw of a rampaging ODE?

If you are not prepared to make this sacrifice, the catastrophe is not as great as you want it to be. Find an ethical means of achieving the desired outcome.

Treason

By far the most serious ethical violation is treason, intentional cooperation with the enemy to damage the organization, reveal its secrets, harm innocents, or damage the membrane. The Ordo differs from conventional intelligence agencies in that willful betrayal and defection are extremely rare. Where mundane spies are prone to an eventual belief that all ideologies are equal, our operatives rarely lose sight of the stark contrast between themselves and the minions of the Outer Dark.

Where agents turn against the Ordo (or, in internal parlance, "go dark"), it is much more likely to be the result of severe psychological disorder than willful betrayal. These all-too-frequent cases fall outside the bounds of standard ethical violations and are are a matter for Psychiatric Metrics (see p. 22.)

Review Board

We are proud to say that the vast majority of our agents, knowing the moral and metaphysical consequences of transgression, honorably navigate their ethical obligations. On a very few occasions, however, it becomes necessary to discipline agents for violations.

This poses a difficult challenge to an organization such as ours. We are not an ordinary employer, capable of meting out minor punishments such as demotions or fines. The high degree of secrecy necessary to our operation renders us vulnerable to disgruntled employees. Mere dismissal is not a viable option. Therefore we are forced to subject serious or repeat violators of the ethical code to extremely draconian punishment: indefinite, possibly permanent, incarceration.

Charges may be lodged by an agent's teammates or Mr. Verity. Your investigative work may be monitored by a follow-up team. These are randomly detailed to a certain percentage of cases as a matter of routine. Should strong evidence of malfeasance be found during follow-up, the team head refers charges.

When a charge is preferred, an initial three-person ad hoc committee is formed from active members of the assignment desk. This preliminary review group (PRG) may summarily dismiss charges on one or both of the following grounds:

- charges are deemed to be of insufficient gravity

- evidence of violation is too scant

The seriousness of the only disciplinary measure available to us severely discourages frivolous use of the review board process. It may also be determined that the alleged offense stems from loss of conscious volition due to a severe psychological disorder. In this instance, the case is referred instead to an emergency psychiatric evaluation process called a 101 Board (see "Psychiatric Evaluation.")

Where the PRG determines that the charges are both serious and well-documented, a full review board is convened.

This consists of a three-judge panel, drawn from former investigators. In the ensuing quasi-judicial process, the accused may argue in his own defense, or appoint another member of his investigative team to serve as his advocate. The latter option allows greater dispassion and tends to get better results. An advocate for the prosecution is appointed by the PRG. Where charges were preferred after a follow-up investigation, the head of the follow-up team often serves as prosecutor.

The prosecutor calls witnesses and places evidence before the panel. Defense may cross-examine witnesses during this phase. When the prosecution rests, the defense may exercise the option of presenting additional witnesses. These may in turn be cross-examined by the prosecutor. Proceedings are less formally determined than criminal trials in western democracies. Judges may ask questions of either defense or prosecution advocates at any time during the proceedings, and may interrupt to question witnesses directly. After defense rests and closing statements by both advocates are made, the judges retire to deliberate. Only on a unanimous guilty verdict is the investigator relieved of his or duties and moved from temporary to permanent incarceration.

Proceedings and deliberations are recorded on video and, in the event of a guilty verdict, automatically reviewed by a five-person appellate team made up of active-duty Ordo leaders. They may vacate the verdict on a simple majority, returning the investigator to active duty.

Details of our system of imprisonment for wayward agents are for obvious reasons beyond the scope of this operations manual. It is hardly a secret that the facility bears the code name Camp Slumber. One might also deduce that its incarceration regime is conducted in a maximally humane manner, so as to prevent damage to the membrane.

PSYCHIATRIC METRICS

The enemy's chief weapon against us is not the bullets of its operatives or the ethereal claws of its summoned creatures, but madness. Of all unplanned losses to investigative ranks (not including retirements and reassignments), by far the largest proportion can be attributed to psychological traumas. Where 4% of agents are convicted of ethical violations, 7% killed in action and 30% physically disabled in the line of duty, 59% of agent losses come about as a result of psychological trauma and induced mental illness. Given this danger, the Psychiatric Metrics department maintains all possible diligence in its efforts to prevent and ameliorate agent mental illness.

Unplanned Losses to Investigative Personnel

Ethical violations

Killed in action

Physically Disabled

Psychologically Disabled

All investigative personnel are trained to take proactive care of their own mental health, and that of their teammates. Seek the therapeutic counsel of our psychiatric providers as part of every debriefing. If you suspect that you or others are suffering from PTSD or other long-term effects of contact with the Outer Dark, report symptoms and seek treatment.

Although it is your responsibility to tend to your mental health, and that of your colleagues, we recognize that even trained professionals may fail to seek help voluntarily. The self-reliant, warrior personality type required to perform the hair-raising missions of the Ordo is also, ironically, the most likely to conceal signs of mental disorder, and to delay treatment for same. The line between necessary stoicism and dangerous denial can be razor-thin.

To this end, the Psychiatric Metrics department practices a regime of preventative vigilance, calling in agents for frequent, routine psych evaluation. The exact nature of our testing procedures is kept confidential, to prevent agents in denial from circumventing our processes of diagnosis. Under constant refinement, our techniques far exceed the diagnostics of conventional psychiatry. Agents who have been with us for any period of time will recognize some of the techniques: verbal therapy, word pattern recognition, image reaction, cognitive testing, and anti-deceptive measures.

Agents noted to be suffering from warning signs of debilitating mental illness are pulled from field rotation for treatment.

Due to these rigorous procedures, agents are rarely permitted to sink slowly into psychological disability between missions.

This reverses a trend pertaining as recently as 1992, when psych disabilities were evenly spread between long term deterioration and rapid spirals into madness occurring within the span of a single investigation. At that time psychiatric discharge represented a full 72% of unplanned personnel losses within the investigative unit. Raw numbers of agents in the other loss categories remains flat, meaning that improved measures of the Psychiatric Metrics department have greatly cut agent losses over the last decade and a half.

Reporting Procedures

Report any incidents of psychological distress or trauma during your post-mission briefing with your handler. Your Mr. Verity will then refer you to the Psychiatric Metrics department, which will then conduct a diagnostic interview. From there you may be recommended a course of therapy, either in-house at an Ordo facility or through an affiliated contractor.

If you feel that you require therapy or evaluation at any time, send an encrypted text to the psychiatric SMS number provided in your intake kit. Use the code provided there for a self-report.

You are required to alert your debriefer to any suspicions you may have that your fellow teammates require a psych evaluation. Do not feel that you are betraying your comrades by doing so. To collude in an effort to deprive a teammate of needed psychiatric aid represents the true betrayal.

Should you, on post-briefing reflection, come to feel that you have failed to alert the order to a comrade's possible emotional or cognitive distress, use code protocol B from your intake kit to send an SMS to psych services.

Available Counseling

Psychiatric contractors, often former investigators with mental health backgrounds, are cleared for non-operational secrets. You may freely discuss with them the existence of the Outer Dark and the general nature of your encounters with it, leaving out identifying details such as places, times, and of course the cover identities of your teammates.

Treat your contacts with affiliated therapists as operational secrets. Do not inform non-cleared personnel, including civilian friends and loved ones, of their identities. Revelation of their Ordo affiliations could lead to reprisals against them, and penetration of our support network.

101 Board

Agents are placed on permanent or temporary psychiatric disability as the result of a procedure called a 101 Board. A 101 Board is convened under the following circumstances:

- During inquiry into a possible ethics violation, the review board process determines that the subject may be acting under the influence of a mental disorder.

- During debriefing, an agent's actions on mission seem to indicate a serious psychiatric disorder.

- The agent displays symptoms of psychiatric disability during his or her civilian life, up to and including a violent crime or act of self-harm.

- In mission, an agent's comrades report symptoms of disability, including violence or self-harm. An agent extraction is performed; a 101 Board is convened after remaining agents complete their mission.

A 101 Board consists of three Ordo psychiatric professionals. Where safety permits, they interview the subject in an informal, comfortable, but secure environment. They may meet with the patient for up to three days. After this period, they make one of the following determinations:

- Patient is mentally healthy and may be returned to active duty.

- Patient may return to active duty after treatment.

- Patient is permanently unfit for duty and must be retired on psychiatric disability.

- Patient is not only unfit for duty, but a danger to himself or others. The agent is remanded to secure Ordo psychiatric hospital (Installation Spaniard) until he is no longer at risk of violence or self-harm. He is then retired on psychiatric disability. This determination is known as a Ruling 90.

- Patient's erratic behavior is not due to mental illness, but is instead attributable to possession or infestation by ODEs. A tactical euthanasia team (TET) is called in to immediately and safely speed the agent to his or her final rest.

The latter two determinations require unanimous verdicts; all others can be arrived at by simple majority.

On humanitarian grounds it is sometimes necessary to commit the subject of a Ruling 90 to a non-secure civilian facility. This might, for example, allow the patient to benefit from visits by friends and family. The more patently delusional the subject, the less operational risk this decision imposes. His claims of encounters with malign demonic entities on behalf of a worldwide altruistic cabal will seem merely delusional. Patients treated by doctors who believe their experiences to be hallucinatory are, however, less likely to recover. This choice is therefore contraindicated except where the agent is judged to be incurably insane.

COMMUNICATIONS

One advantage we maintain over the enemy is in the comparative sophistication of our communications intelligence. Through our connection to civilian intelligence agencies, we enjoy significant access to global communications intercepts. The enemy, thankfully, gains only sporadic access to such resources. This communications gap should not breed complacency! Certain of the creatures at the enemy's disposal are able to read not only the thoughts and desires of their victims, but to pluck information from modern communications. For this reason we exercise extreme operational care during missions, keeping paring contacts with Mr. Verity to the barest possible minimum.

ETS Requests

Unfortunately for the field agent, the wide buffet of communications data available through Electronic Traffic Sifting (see p. 6) does not extend to real-time intercept requests from investigators. The need to conceal our operational within the NSA and its sister agencies requires us to send our requests to them in a sluggish, roundabout manner. On occasion we will be able to supply you with communications intercepts in mid-case. If so, the governing circumstances, including the number and nature of permissible contacts, will be supplied to you by Mr. Verity or found in your briefing pack. If no such mention is made, any electronic surveillance is made on your own initiative.

Note that the Ordo's ethical guidelines are

unconcerned with privacy issues, insofar as they relate to Esoterror operations and suspects. As always, you are forbidden to use information as a weapon against innocents and neutrals. You are free to conduct whatever electronic surveillance operations you deem necessary for the completion of your investigation.

You may also use the false credentials we supply you with to request that liaison intelligence or law enforcement agencies supply you with their relevant work product. As always, it may become necessary to marshal your persuasive powers to circumvent inconvenient procedural rules.

Maintaining Radio Silence

To maintain operational security, investigators are discouraged from contacting Mr. Verity or home base except in situations of extreme urgency. Almost all of these are requests for extraction:

- An agent or civilian has suffered a life-threatening supernatural injury, the nature of which cannot be revealed to civilian medical responders; extraction required.

- An agent has undergone a psychotic break so severe that his ability to maintain order secrets in the face of civilian psychiatric questioning is compromised; extraction required.

- An enemy agent has been captured; rendition required.

By default, investigative teams are chosen for their ability to display independent initiative and are expected to resolve questions on their own, in keeping with the policies enumerated in this ops manual. You have been selected on the basis of a demonstrated capacity for independent problem solving and are expected to exercise it. Do not look to Mr. Verity for additional guidance or assistance as an investigation unfolds.

On certain missions, you may be given permission to contact Mr. Verity for support according to a predetermined protocol. For example, he may be able to arrange a single wiretap for you, after you determine which of three possible suspects in a community is an Esoterror dupe. If this is the

The Chitterer Transcript

The following is an excerpt from an interrogation of an Esoterror operative (here codenamed COVEN) regarding the entities we call chitterers. At this stage of the interview the subject had become generally cooperative, but resistant on certain key issues.

INTERROGATOR: When our agent spotted you on the Canal Grande and called in for an extraction team, there was a sound on the line. A rasping, clicking noise.

COVEN: Must have been Italian intelligence. Their wiretapping equipment is very outdated. If they put in half the effort they devote to espresso machines—

INTERROGATOR: We have a tape recording of the sound. Do you want me to play it for you?

COVEN: [Demeanor changes rapidly.] No.

INTERROGATOR: You know what it is.

COVEN: Yes.

INTERROGATOR: Tell me.

COVEN: I can't. It will get inside my soul.

INTERROGATOR: You're safe here.

COVEN: Not from that I'm not.

INTERROGATOR: Have you seen one of them?

COVEN: [Laughs.] It isn't plural, you doomed motherfucker. I shouldn't even be thinking about it. You bastard. You're making me picture it. Drawing it in.

INTERROGATOR: It can't get through these walls.

COVEN: Don't you get it? It's already inside me. And now it's inside you, too!

COVEN was found dead in his cell the next morning. An autopsy revealed that his heart had been boiled from the inside, as if by a microwave device. The interrogator was later placed on permanent leave (with treatment) after a routine interview with Psychiatric Metrics revealed a sudden, barely controlled impulse toward necrophilia.

case you will be provided with a special number to make the contact when you have reached the appropriate point in your investigations.

For reasons explained below, communications from the field should, whenever possible, be conducted by SMS message. You will be provided with untraceable phones containing contact numbers and software to quadrilaterally auto-encrypt any texts sent to those numbers.

The Watchers Watched

What the enemy lacks in signals intelligence it can sometimes make up for with the aid of supernatural servitors. Information on these demonic watchers is scant; gaining data on them is a top priority. We do know that agents have sometimes heard indistinct, profoundly unnerving background noises while making voice calls. Later enemy actions suggested that these calls had been subject to a security breach. The noises have occurred on supposedly secure lines, defeating our toughest electronic anti-detection measures. The mid-1990s operations MYCOSIS, BIOPSIC, and LAMINATE are thought to have failed due to the presence of these uncanny listeners. All told, eleven field agents were killed or disabled during the three missions. Moreover, desk operatives receiving communications during these cases subsequently experienced psychotic symptoms. One became a family annihilator, killing his wife and three young children before turning a shotgun on himself. Others remain hospitalized to this day.

Researchers have given the entities responsible for this surveillance and contagious madness the preliminary name of "chitterers," based on the clacking, insect-like noises overheard on the lines they tap.

For reasons we have yet to pinpoint, chitterers mostly appear on communications from the field to headquarters, and rarely between agents in the field. We speculate that the original ritual that summoned them to our plane somehow specified the Order itself as a target or anchoring force. How they are gathered or marshaled by the enemy remains a mystery. They appear only in cases involving high-level Esoterror leaders. As it is impossible to know in advance which investigations touch on such figures, we are obliged to maintain radio silence on all missions.

The existence of an occult listening protocol poses a daunting challenge our researchers have yet to resolve. We must find a way to neutralize it without ourselves resorting to magic.

RECRUITMENT

Before you were recruited as an Ordo investigator, you were identified by a member of the organization as a possible candidate. Without your knowledge, desk officers conducted a thorough background check. We accessed your bank records, checked your credit history, traced your Internet usage, and compiled a thorough dossier of your relatives and associates. One or more investigators on inactive-duty status performed further inquiries in person. Their activities included, but were not necessarily limited to, contact interviews, direct observation of your daily routine, and electronic surveillance[1].

The exact org chart involved in your approval for active-duty status lies beyond the purview of an investigator's ops manual. Suffice it to say that the process is rigorous, and has never led to the accidental recruitment of a double agent.

Recruit Scouting

Now that you have been through it yourself, your main relationship to the recruitment process is as a talent scout. While engaged in operations, you will have many opportunities to observe civilians engaged in law enforcement, intelligence, journalism and information-gathering activities. Many will be members of liaison agencies to which you are temporarily credentialed.

Others may be following a parallel investigative track to your own. Although your immediate priority will be to co-opt or neutralize them, you may notice that they possess many of the same skills and traits that led to your own recruitment.

Recruits needn't come from conventional

---

1 As any seasoned investigator could easily surmise, supplementary monitoring surveillance of this nature may occasionally take place, on a strictly precautionary basis, even after agents attain full active-duty status.

agency backgrounds; we have happily recruited academics, antiquarian booksellers, arms dealers, clergymen—even criminals. You yourself may fit one of these nonstandard profiles. Determined foes of Esoterror come from all walks of life.

When you spot a potential recruit, discreetly gather his or her contact information. Elicit the subject's attitudes toward the perils of terrorism and the rewards of duty. Evaluate if possible the potential candidate's problem-solving skill set and courage under fire.

During the debrief phase of your mission, inform your Mr. Verity that you have scouted a possible candidate. You will be provided with a form JS-2. Compile it at your leisure, using the information gained during the mission. Then scan it and upload it to the secure FTP site listed on the form.

The next time you meet this individual, it may be as a colleague.

Doubling and Tripling

On a few occasions our investigators have commenced this informal preliminary stage of the recruitment process only to discover that the target is in fact an Esoterror asset placed on the scene for the purposes of deep-cover penetration. If red flags occur, it may be a coincidence—or it may suggest that the entire case you're investigating is a ruse to bring a mole into contact with you.

Where possible, maintain the illusion of ignorance regarding an apparent would-be mole's Esoterror connections while in the field. During debrief, alert Mr. Verity that you have a potential Mockingbird situation. File a form MA-3 with full details of your dealings with the possible double agent. An Ordo counter-intelligence team will be detailed to reel the target in, for interrogation and, where possible, reorientation as a triple agent.

Uninformed Friendlies

On certain missions you will encounter Uninformed Friendlies (UFs), individuals who fight the forces of Esoterror without full knowledge of their overall scheme and the increasing fragility of the membrane. As you interact with them, you will need to balance the information and operational it causes cognitive dissonance, leading people to question the foundations of their reality. A folk healer engaging in ritual treatment among the people of his remote jungle village does no harm to the membrane, provided that his culture already accepts his workings as effective and admirable. In such a cultural context, we have no cause to suppress his activities. In fact, our attempt to destabilize or discredit such a person would itself be membrane-negative, as it would seem disturbing and surreal to his community.

This is not to say that supernatural effects cannot damage the membrane in a social context where belief in magic is widespread. Most such societies believe in good and bad magic, the latter being considered sorcery or witchcraft. The practice of evil magic clearly arouses dismay and social unease, and thus weakens the barrier between realities.

Further, magical rituals which exert obvious effects far beyond the norm engender cognitive vertigo, also harming the membrane. Most tribal healers, for example, produce their effects through a combination of belief (a powerful placebo) and folk remedies. If one was suddenly able to reattach an arm, that effect would destabilize the local sense of reality. Membrane damage occurs even though the patient's recovery of his limb is seen as a positive outcome.

The number of societies where magical acts do not create a sense of fungible reality has dwindled rapidly throughout the decades of the twentieth century.

Even in contemporary, industrialized societies, reactions to apparent acts of magic vary. It is possible for fake magic to weaken the membrane, and for genuine supernatural effects to go unnoticed—depending on the perceptual frame in which they occur.

In the church of San Gennaro in Naples, priests display, on a bi-annual basis, a vial of dried blood supposedly belonging to their patron saint. It contents are made to liquefy in front of worshippers. The devout believe in the literal reality of the miracle. Skeptics say it's a trick, and that the untested substance isn't blood. Our tests

support they can provide you against the dangers they pose via their ignorant and possibly counterproductive methods.

UFs can damage the membrane by:

- practicing authentic magic

- increasing public belief in magic, whether through authentic practice or trickery

- publicizing Esoterror operations and/or supernatural forces

- engaging in activities that will serve as fodder for sensationalistic media coverage

- causing suffering and psychic torment, or enjoying the suffering of enemies, thus damaging the membrane

Magic and Social Context

Note that the apparent practice of magic is only a threat to the membrane in social contexts where in the vicinity confirm that the event carries on year after year without harming the membrane. It already fits into the governing preconceptions of believer and skeptic alike. If Esoterror attempted to somehow disrupt or subvert the ceremony, we would of course have to intervene. Without such enemy involvement, we make no effort to prevent this visual metaphor of faith. Nor do we particularly care whether the miracle occurs spontaneously, or is helped along by the priests. It affirms preexistent reality conceptions, and thus preserves the membrane.

Although these distinctions can seem dauntingly convoluted if dissected too thoroughly, they fortunately boil down into two simple rules:

> 1. Don't suppress socially acceptable folk magics.

> 2. When you use magic to fight Esoterror, Esoterror wins.

Support and Recruitment

Certain UFs might serve as exemplary agents if properly recruited and trained. During the mission at hand, guide them toward support tasks that do not damage the membrane. Do not encourage them to take risks they would not otherwise embrace. If they propose using potentially destabilizing magic, use your persuasive talents to convince them otherwise—without revealing the true nature of our organization, or the existence of the membrane.

Attempts to turn the power of the supernatural against the foe are always counter-productive. Supernatural rituals powerful enough to be of use against Esoterror targets are invariably of Outer Dark origin. UFs employing them are probably furthering the aims of an Esoterror cell, perhaps as unwitting pawns in a struggle between rival enemy factions.

An apparent exception occurs when acts of benign folk magic appear to suppress ODEs. Some creatures display vulnerabilities to the display of amulets, charms, or to other quasi-ritual acts—like the decapitation of a vampire. The magic here is inherent to the creature and not to the object to which it is vulnerable. Shooting a lycanthrope with a silver bullet is not membrane-negative magic. These are all examples of Special Means of Dispatch (SMDs); see p. 13.

A UF who proves open to your guidance while still demonstrating the initiative required of a good agent should be recommended for potential recruitment.

Neutralizing Unmanageable Subjects

UFs who resist adjustment, holding firm to ruthless or sorcerous tactics, must be neutralized by minimally unethical means. Often it is sufficient to discredit the subject so that he or she is characterized as a nutty fringe character in any ensuing media reports.

In extreme cases, an enemy of Esoterror whose methods pose serious risk to the Outer Dark barrier is objectively indistinguishable from an Esoterrorist and must be treated as such. Apprehend the subject and call for an extraction squad. The subject is then imprisoned in a secure facility until such time as he can credibly demonstrate that he is no longer a threat to the membrane.

AGENT REPLACEMENT

During any operation, you must be prepared for casualties.

Extraction Protocols

For reasons of operational continuity agents are expected to remain on mission in the wake of injuries which do not completely impair their ability to proceed. Agent replacement is risky: it may expose both the investigative and extraction teams to enemy attention. As such, it is not to be called on frivolously.Only when agents are incapacitated by physical or mental injuries are you to call for extraction. To do so, use your provided untraceable cell phone to send an SMS message to the number provided. The number changes on a regular basis, so make sure that you are using the phone given to you by Mr. Verity for the mission at hand. Instant updates may change the number during an operation; calls for extraction can only be made from provided phones.

Extraction teams arrive under appropriate cover. In urban areas they typically arrive as paramedics, police, or firefighters. Wilderness extractions are made under the cover of coast guard, park service rescue teams, or reserve or active duty military units. The nature of the cover chosen depends on local availability; where we are blessed with a choice, we pick the least remarkable option.

We field two types of extraction teams: RO (rescue only) and SSF (special forces.) The latter team is capable of transport only and unable to defend against hostile action. SSF extraction supplies as a heavily armed commando response, capable of whisking you from a scene with extreme prejudice. Though they can fight their way through surrounding enemies if need be, their primary mission will be to get you (and any other targets you designate) out of danger. They will pursue fleeing enemies only if they pose an exceptional danger to innocents, or if they can be finished off with little-to-no additional risk.

By default, expect an RO extraction team to come for you. In most missions, there will be no cavalry to save you—merely a mop-up crew to haul your wounded back to the nearest securable medical facility.

ETA for extractions varies by location. In a large urban area under the jurisdiction of a first-world member nation, arrival can occur in as little as fifteen minutes. Remote areas may take up to six hours. In neutral jurisdictions, average duration between an extraction call and team arrival is one hour for urban areas to twelve for remote territories. In hostile or lawless regions, remoteness works in your favor: it's easier to drop into an undefended wilderness than to smuggle a recovery team into a city center swarming with secret police.

Wherever you are, poor weather conditions can prevent swift extraction.

Certain missions rule out extractions and renditions altogether, or impose severe restrictions on them. You will be informed of these operational obstacles during your briefing.

Reinforcements

When an incapacitated agent is removed from a case, assignment desk determines whether reinforcement is indicated, or if the mission should continue with its reduced roster. Generally, the later in the mission the extraction occurs, the less likely it is that a replacement will be inserted into the team. A dead or permanently incapacitated agent is always replaced, as are agents with skill sets crucial to mission completion.

On occasion agents have made de facto field recruitments, bringing an uninformed friendly or liaison from a civilian agency into an investigation in place of an incapacitated agent. Although this practice is officially frowned upon, we are forced to acknowledge that several of our best operatives were brought into the Ordo on precisely this basis.

COUNTER-SURVEILLANCE

As you go about your investigations, it is essential that you at all times observe counter-surveillance protocols. These prevent both your exposure, and that of the organization you serve.

The secrecy surrounding our organization is not only a matter of operational security. We must of course keep our identities and tradecraft hidden from the enemy to protect us from attacks and penetration. Unlike ordinary intelligence agencies, however, we must also conceal our existence and purpose from the general public. Revelation of our mission would deal a severe blow to membrane integrity!

You must therefore be prepared to conceal your activities not only from the foe, but from mundane observation, particularly by pesky media types.

There Is No Org Chart

You will note that there is no organizational chart in this operations manual. As investigative agents, the command structure of the Ordo, and its various constituent departments, are a matter of only abstract concern to you. Esoterror torturers understand that you know little of our internal operations. We intend to keep it that way.

One can certainly conclude from the document at hand that we field special forces, extraction teams, and place some agents on permanent or station duty in high-activity locations.

We also maintain a large staff of desk officers, working at a number of secret bases. These include researchers, scientists, interrogators, signals analysts, psychologists, and corrections officers. It does not take a master of deduction to assume the presence of a sizable corps of support staffers performing the unglamorous tasks that keep such a large infrastructure in motion. All are trustworthy and highly vetted.

As investigators, you will interact only with your handler, Mr. Verity, and perhaps with members of extraction teams. At the end of each assignment, Mr. Verity performs a debrief. Expect debriefs to occur in hotel conference rooms, rental office spaces, and other blandly anonymous temporary venues. Schedule permitting, we stage these near the site of your investigation, before you return to civilian life. Otherwise they debriefs take place in your home town. In extraordinary circumstances, you may be pulled into an actual base for this information exchange. If so, you will be blindfolded during transit, so that no ODE can pluck the installation's location from your writhing brain.

Your Mr. Verity may vary from one mission to the next. Mission handlers are assigned on a random rotating basis. Draw no conclusions from the continued presence of a single Mr. Verity in your Ordo lives, or the lack thereof. Engage in pleasantries if you must. Be aware that Mr. Verity has been trained to respond to small talk with details from a completely fictional cover identity.

Meetings with Ordo appointed psych evaluators and therapists occur under like circumstances, as do 101 and Review Boards.

Your Comrades Are Fictional

During each of your missions, you and your teammates will be supplied with cover identities, complete with all necessary accompanying credentials. These include badges (where needed), security clearances (ditto), plus credit cards. We provide wardrobes matching your covers and fill your wallets with fake family photos.

Underlying these artificial identities is another set of fake selves. You are also provided with a second set of cover names to use with your teammates. These are your permanent Ordo appellations (POAs.) They resemble your true selves, but are distinct in detail. If you're a book seller from Toledo named Charlotte Fong, your POA will present you as Eugenia Chan of Solon Springs, Wisconsin.

This way, if one of you is taken by the enemy and tortured or mind-raped, you can only provide only extremely general information about your comrades.

For this reason, team members are strongly discouraged from sharing details of their personal lives with one another. Some investigators stick to a curt, just-the-facts approach to colleague interaction. Others delve more deeply into their artificial POA identities, making up personal details to chat about.

Whatever happens on an Ordo investigation, stays on the Ordo investigation.

Investigators must be so close to their teammates that they can depend on one another in life and death situations, anticipating one another's thoughts. At the same time, they know only a false version of you, and you know only the same of them. This paradoxical interplay of trust and deception can prove emotionally destabilizing over the long run, sometimes leading to signs of dissociative disorder. Report any difficulties to your therapist or during routine evaluation by Psychiatric Metrics.

Some agents have historically responded to the stresses of POA secrecy in particular and the agent's secret life in general by entering into romantic and/or sexual relationships with other teammates. Such behavior is strongly discouraged, on the grounds that it causes tension within a team. It is not technically forbidden, however. We urge you to curtail such consolations if they begin to compromise unit cohesion and mission completion.

You Are Being Watched

With the notable exception of the the chitterer (p. 27), Esoterror at this time appears to wield no significant supernatural means of surveillance.

They have however been known to monitor investigators by conventional means. Esoterror does not appear to subject our agents to general counter-intelligence protocols. This absence of effort must be attributed to lack of resources, rather than an abundance of scruples.

However, where they are operating and have personnel to spare (which is not always the case) they may stage ad hoc counter-intelligence operations to neutralize investigative teams.

When in public, conduct yourselves as if you are being watched. In private, perform routine sweeps for electronic surveillance before speaking candidly. Maintain high encryption of all Internet activity.

Use your credentialed status to disguise your activities. If you're operating as an FBI agent, behave in a manner consistent with that cover. When you must depart from that behavior, exercise caution and watch for watchers.

Station Duty

A select few agents are assigned to station duty, in which they conduct long-term operations within a specified territory. Exposing themselves and their loved ones to heightened risk, they live and work in the area they patrol.

Certain stations may be manned by single operatives only, who liaise with investigative or SSF teams as they are posted to conduct particular operations.

Areas particularly rife with enemy activity warrant the appointment of entire permanent teams who manage all investigations against local adversaries. Station appointments are generally open-ended. When certain conditions are met, station teams are tasked with the creation of mop-up plans. With the aid of other investigative and SSF teams temporarily assigned to an umbrella operation, the station group sweeps up all identified enemy assets, conclusively ending Esoterror activities in the designated area for the foreseeable future.

OCT Status

A station duty assignment is made when assignment desk personnel, subject to the approval of higher leadership, designate a locality as possessing OCT, or Ongoing Complex Threat, Status. The locality is most often a large metropolitan area. On occasion ongoing station status has been attached to rural counties, sectors of exurban sprawl, or small nation-states. Factors leading to an OCT designation include, but are not limited to:

- The apparent presence of a numerically large or heavily resourced Esoterror cell or cells operating within an area.

- Analysis suggests that greater information on overall enemy operations can be assembled by allowing a cell to operate under close monitoring by station agents.

- Indications that leaders of aforementioned cell or cells are individuals of high influence, against whom operations may not be undertaken until conclusive evidence of their Esoterror involvement is gathered.

- Esoterror operatives are heavily protected or possess considerable retaliatory potential, rendering immediate action against them unwise until station agents can investigate and neutralize these defensive/deterrent capabilities.

- Locality coincides with one or more areas of weakened membrane, leading to frequent incursions from entities of the Outer Dark.

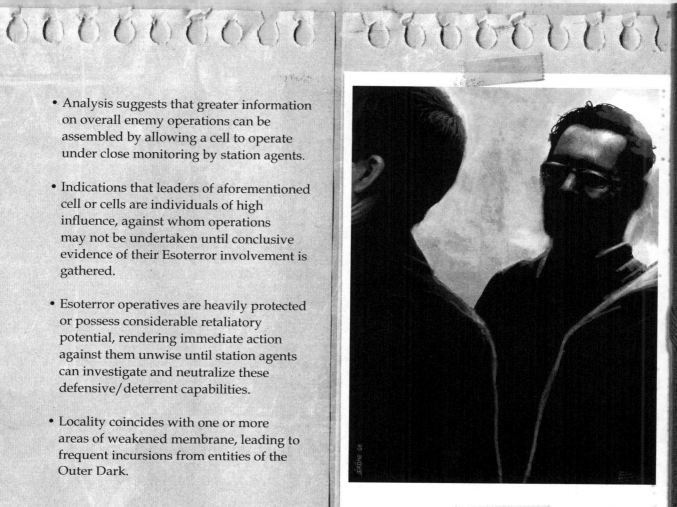

Candidate Selection

Station duty requires a special breed of agent. When assembling teams for station duty, an ad hoc recruitment and assignment desk committee looks for the following personal traits:

- High comfort with long-term assignment. Candidates must display excellent stress management techniques. In contrast to the short term nature of most OV assignments, here the agent is on call 24/7. Enemy surveillance is presumed to be constant and could at any moment lead to hostile contact.

- Superior skill at double life maintenance. Candidate must be able to operate under deep cover, keeping true assignment secret from friends and family. The penalty for exposure is steep—civilian relatives, co-workers and casual acquaintances may be put in danger by enemy counter-ops.

- Specialist knowledge of designated area. Agents must be quick studies, able to rapidly acquire strong degree of area expertise. Where possible, natives of designated area are chosen. Lifelong familiarity with an area grants assets an immediate ability to blend in, speak the language, recruit informants, and spot anomalous activities suggesting Esoterror actions in progress.

Demands On Private Life

At first glance it may appear that the ideal station agent is one without a significant outside life. Efficiency studies have shown the opposite—that the archetypal obsessive loner is prone to excessive operational risk, mental breakdown, and suicidal ideation. In extreme cases their own solitude and terrible knowledge lead to membrane corrosion, perpetuating the cycle of supernatural interference station assignment is meant to curtail.

Healthy relationships with civilian family and friends are essential to the long-term psychological outlook required of the successful station agent. However, as stated above, the proximity of one's support circle to the enemy operatives and uncanny phenomena may lead to crisis. Agents must be prepared for enemy actions against their loved ones. Drill them in evasive techniques and self-defense, without revealing the nature of the threats you're training them to flee. During periods of high threat status, it may be possible to request protective surveillance from local law enforcement or other unknowing OV assets. These resources are not infinite and must be drawn upon only when necessary.

Although we wish it were otherwise, the harsh truth is that such precautions have been known to fail. In such circumstances, the organization supports your efforts to recover your loved ones. It also provides counseling to traumatized survivors, using techniques which both provide emotional succor and protect bystanders from mind-searing contact with the Outer Dark.

However, one must always keep in mind the purpose of any Esoterror feint against agents' loved ones. They intend to apply leverage to the order so that they may conduct their operations unmolested. Station agents must be prepared to make the awful choice between the safety of family members, and the fate of humanity as a whole.

Should the worst case scenario come to pass, the names of your dearly beloved will be inscribed, after suitable and solemn ceremony, on the Wall Of Fallen Innocents. This memorial is located at an undisclosed Ordo Veritatis headquarters, to which you will be secretly borne for the duration of the service.

Establishing Long-Term Cover

Station agents will be provided long-term cover identities allowing them to operate with maximum flexibility in pursuit of their covert goals. Given your possible preexisting ties to the community and need to surround yourself with a personal support network, it is likely that you will operate under your actual birth identity. However you will be supplied with a work assignment or other credentials permitting you to spend the bulk of your time on investigative activities. Agents need

only apply a token effort to the putative duties of their cover identities. Cover duties relate to your career and educational background and skill sets. Common examples include:

- Assignment as a student, mature or otherwise, to an institution of higher learning.

- Provision of a "do-nothing" job at an OV-friendly corporation or small business.

- Establishment of a credible-seeming self-employment or freelance situation. Examples: art appraiser, book dealer, independent journalist or photographer.

- If you are already an officer of a local police force, you are assigned to a vaguely defined task force allowing you to perform self-directed investigations while filing the occasional sheaf of unread paperwork.

- If you are already the owner or operator of a business, OV assets will support its operations while you concentrate on investigations.

- In some circumstances, the entire team will be established as employees of a shell company, such as a limousine service, paparazzi group, or private detective agency. Bounty hunting companies, in jurisdictions where these are supported by law, serve as excellent shadow companies.

Self-Directed Investigations

When a new station team is established, it will be provided with a one-time briefing by its designated Mr. Verity. It will thereafter receive such intelligence dispatches from case evaluation as circumstances warrant. However, the team is from inception onwards expected to generate its own assignments. Armed with whatever dangling leads it acquires during its initial investigation, the team must systematically peel back the organizational layers of its target Esoterror cell or cells. It conducts its own miniature, localized version of the case evaluation process, monitoring media, placing wiretaps, cultivating informants, and establishing stake-outs of suspected enemy strongpoints. A station assignment reaches its endpoint when it has acquired enough data to call for a mop-up (see below.)

To aid in self-directed assignment generation, agent teams are provided with the latest copy of a powerful software package known as CASIE (Case Analysis Schematic Interpretation Engine.) CASIE accepts input from local media, statistical studies, and electronic communications data to find unsuspected connections between apparently innocuous facts, indicative of possible Esoterror activity. Although only one in four CASIE leads points to genuine enemy action, the value of its hits more than compensates for the routine legwork involved in eliminating its false positives.

Adversary Mapping

Station agents are expected to roll up any operations posing a direct and immediate threat to the life or well-being of the community. Enemy schemes of less imminent peril can be permitted to continue, in the hopes that agent surveillance will yield information allowing for the identification and apprehension of entire cells. To this end, you conclude each discrete investigation, after any required veil-out procedure, by adding to your adversary map, a speculative org chart identifying the apparent relationships between Esoterror operatives. Those agents experienced in police or intelligence work will recognize this procedure from their efforts against organized crime or espionage networks. An investigation may be considered a success if you are able to add one or two names and photos to your ongoing adversary map. Not every operation need end in your training a hail of bullets on a slime-dripping minion of the madness realms.

Your ultimate objective is the assemblage of a more or less complete adversary map, with special attention to its top leadership. Often you will have been assigned to station duty to find definitive proof that certain highly placed individuals are in fact knowing supplicants of the Outer Dark. This proof need not be of the standard necessary to secure convictions in a court of law. It must

convince our high patrons in the complex of western nations that the named individuals are bad actors who must be removed from the scene post-haste.

Cynics may observe that certain western leaders have recently demonstrated an high degree of credulity regarding intelligence reports, and reason from this statement that their evidence must only appear suggestive. No argument could be more counterproductive. The Ordo has won its record for accuracy not over the lifespan of any one government or administration, but over a period of decades. Further, our patrons are often predisposed against accusations leveled at persons they regard as their own peers. We must always be right.

Mop-up must always be justified.

Adversary map as physical prop

A physical representation of the group's adversary map can serve as a powerful focus for your station series. As the group adds to it each week, they see their progress through the storyline visually represented. The map serves as a recap of past sessions and suggests new directions to move in.

To create an adversary map, you'll need a corkboard, whiteboard, or similar surface you can store intact between sessions and add to over time. You'll need pins or tape to fix them to the board, along with tape or string to mark out the connections between suspects.

Prepare for each session by finding photographs, either from your own collection or grabbed from the Internet, of people who can "play the roles" of the various conspirators.

Using the images of recognizable actors permits an instant visual shorthand. Player knowledge of the actor's defining roles factor intuitively into their understanding of the supporting character he represents. A picture of Christopher Lee will summon a different set of associations than one of Ray Winstone, for example.

Familiar faces may, on the other hand, introduce a feeling of fictionality. They may inspire players to joke or make meta-references that break the fourth wall. Completely unfamiliar faces evoke a sense of documentary realism. Enhance this by subjecting photos to distortion techniques. Use image software effects to remove color, blow out contrast, blur focus, or add filters to create a video effect. Ordinary people in the distant background of photos seem suspicious, as if under surveillance, when singled out into headshots and blown up from a small pixel size. Bad shots you would otherwise discard are perfect for this purpose.

The Lettuce Man

Jane Doe #1
Hotel Extortion

John Doe #1
Surveillance

Rafe Snell
The Bag Man

Leonid Semnyov
Fixer / Guns

Eero Akelund
Architect
Ley Lines ?

Prof. Simeon Resler
Translator (Devoured ?)

Gaz Whystun
Muscle

Undercover Infiltration

Successful adversary mapping may prove impossible without an inside view of enemy operations. For this reason a station team may find it imperative to insert an undercover operative inside an Esoterror cell. This may be achieved by two primary means:

- turning a current Esoterror operative into a double agent

- creating a false identity for an OV

operative and arranging for his recruitment into the cell under surveillance

Needless to say, great peril, especially for the turncoat or infiltrator, attends to either approach. Undercover operations are second only to bug hunts in their agent mortality rates. The high quality of intelligence gleanable from such an arrangement justifies even extreme risks.

Cell Busting

Mop-up timing may occur at your leisure, subsequent to the gathering of a decisive piece of evidence that persuades the leadership to sanction the series of simultaneous raids needed to take out your target cell.

Circumstances may force your hand, however, requiring a sudden call for an emergency sweep. Niceties of intelligence and influence are swept aside should you uncover an impending Esoterror event of potentially game-changing magnitude. Here you communicate via usually forbidden express channels directly to your Mr. Verity, making the case for the seriousness of the threat.

Whether the timing of your mop-up is calculated or reactive, it is likely that station team members will be the best suited to supervise crucial and dangerous elements of the final sweep. If you have undercover assets inside the Esoterror cell, for example, you will be urged to leverage them in bringing about a fast and efficient conclusion to the operation.

Station team members will be required to lay out a veil-out plan for any mop-up. Accordingly, they are advised to plan the final wave of apprehensions so that they fold neatly into their predigested cover story.

Running a Station Duty Series

By default, *Esoterrorists* series are episodic. The characters drop into a new situation, solve the problem, and go home, until the next scenario beckons and the cycle repeats itself.

A station duty series allows you to introduce an ongoing continuity to your game, in which the events of each scenario fold into an overall narrative arc. The characters achieve incremental victories against a shadowy and formidable Esoterror cell. Eventually the arc reaches a final climax with a pulse-pounding takedown episode.

Start your series by asking your players if they want to be dispersed through the community in separate cover occupations, or gathered together as part of a single front company, like a detective agency or bounty hunting crew. Have them tailor their characters and sources of stability to these roles.

The first scenario introduces the suspected big fish against whom the team must cautiously proceed. (Over the course of your series, he can turn out to be the main antagonist, or merely a diversionary figure concealing an even worse villain.) The team gets to know the secret supernatural world behind the mundane exterior of their assigned location, and brushes up against the outer layers of the Esoterror conspiracy.

Further scenarios might be GM-driven mysteries, or improvised investigations spearheaded by players as they follow up on past leads. Over time, and with careful note-taking, you can build an interconnected cast of supporting characters, including not only enemies but allies and neutrals. With PCs' friends and family in close proximity to the action, you can introduce soap opera elements to your storyline—not to mention the occasional high-tension kidnapping ~~just in time for sweeps week~~ to ramp up the dramatic stakes.

The local character of the station determines the mood and theme of your game. The easiest choice is to use your home town as the characters' base of operations. An exotic choice lends variety and a sense of danger. A station duty series set in Moscow, Kabul, or Baghdad's Green Zone will have a much different feel than one placed in Boston, Leeds, or Calgary.

NON-AGENT ASSETS

As circumstances warrant investigators may be made aware of non-agent assets. A non-agent asset is an individual who renders occasional aid and support to the order without being a full-time field operative, desk officer, or administrator. Although non-agent assets most often prove useful during the veil-out, their services may assist you at any point in an investigation.

Where a liaison with a non-agent asset is deemed operationally fruitful, you will be given contact information for the NAA in question. You will also be informed of their status as an infield or outfield agent.

Infield assets are in the know, aware of the Esoterrorists and the threat they represent. They know that by helping you they're abetting benign international conspiracy called the Ordo Veritatis. Most infield assets are ex-desk officers or field operatives retired from active duty.

Just because you're dealing with an infield asset does not mean you should be fully forthcoming with information. Assume that they have not made full recruitment status for a reason. Many were passed over for consideration due to red flags that cropped up during background vetting. The enemy has had much better luck infiltrating our NAA network than that of our full agents. No matter what their status, be suspicions of NAAs who ask questions.

Outfield assets are dupes who believe they serve some other cause close to their own hearts. When dealing with them, you must maintain the pose of being agents of this other, possibly fictional, organization. If they know of Esoterror or the supernatural, you will be apprised of this in your briefing materials. In most cases they are not, and you must avoid all mention of the true nature of the struggle.

NAAs may be of any background. You will most likely deal with NAAs of the following types:

Press and Media: Skilled at information gathering and gifted with an instinct for the stories the

public is predisposed to believe, reporters make themselves useful both during the investigation and in the veil-out. Outfield assets believe you to be agents of secretive law enforcement or intelligence agencies, and expect exploitable scoops in exchange for assistance. Naturally most of the stories you feed them will be verifiable but fabricated.

Police: Rely on law enforcement NAAs for information. Except where commanded by infield assets, call on them for operational assistance only when there is no chance of an encounter with patently uncanny forces.

Military: Useful in sweeps and mop-ups, military NAAs will almost always be infield assets, who can be counted on to quietly stage their operations under the veil of maneuvers or strikes against conventional terror targets.

Deal carefully with outfield Intelligence NAAs; they play the same game we do, and are trained to double- and triple-think their contacts. Infield agents are often desk officers who move seamlessly between the Ordo and a civilian or military agency. Either sort is most useful as a font of unsourced yet reliable information.

Nearly any other government agency may yield helpful NAAs. Esoterrorists exploit natural disasters; we have salted emergency response agencies throughout the western world with friendlies. Government meteorologists can help spot unnatural weather patterns.

Academics and scientists serve on various Ordo advisory boards, aiding us as we continually refine our media analysis algorithms and data mining protocols.

In the developing world, members of aid agencies and other NGOs often prove the best source of unbiased information about prevailing political and social conditions. They can help school you in the complex etiquette of bribes and graft needed to navigate through high-corruption societies. Exercise caution: Esoterror often recruits among the dispossessed, and itself penetrates NGOs.

Where lawlessness runs riot, the role of authority is usurped by the criminal underworld. Even in the developed nations mafioso may enjoy access to information and *materiel* forbidden to mundane officials. Trust them as far as you can throw them; they are almost never infield assets. When dealing with them, you may be called upon to pose as criminals yourselves. Such contacts are best handled by team members with their own history of shady connections. Investigators conforming to this profile have internalized the internationally recognized non-verbal language of criminal negotiation.

Occultists come in several varieties: those who study belief in magic as a social phenomenon, and those who practice what they falsely consider to be efficacious ritual sorcery. (As scarcely bears repeating, the only magic that works at all emanates from beyond the membrane, and is inevitably malign.) Either academics or deluded "white magicians" may be aware of the Outer Dark/Esoterror as a dangerous force. They can achieve this degree of understanding without

being aware of our organization. You may find them useful as providers of scuttlebutt from the local "magick" scene.

Some would-be sorcerers know of the madness realm and hope to traffic with it. As these are potential Esoterror recruits, we never use them as NAAs.

Special Suppression Forces

Investigative teams act as the operational backbone of the Ordo Veritatis. Certain assignments, however, require the exercise of extraordinary paramilitary force. These tasks are given over to units known as Special Suppression Forces (SSF). SSFs are comprised of highly trained special forces operatives. Recruited for their backgrounds in unconventional warfare, members of SSF teams primarily include active duty and reservist military officers, employees of contract security firms, and covert field operatives of various Western intelligence agencies. They sweep up nests of ODEs, engage in counter-terrorism, conduct counter-sortilege activities, and practice counter-intelligence against the enemy. They may also be called upon to conduct Dangerous Environment Operations, performing standard OV forward team missions in war zones and lawless regions where paramilitary capability becomes an indispensable element of task completion.

MISSION STATEMENT

SSF teams act as the hard, armor-plated edge of the Ordo Veritatis. When the cold war between the guardians of mankind and the agents of the Outer Dark turns hot, we call on them. A member of the SSF is trained to plan exquisitely, to hit swiftly and decisively, and to leave behind no evidence of his actions. He must maintain strong unit cohesion within a group of fellow fighters he may see once or twice a year, and whose real names he may not know. SSF officers must protect the secrecy of the organization, destroy their targets, and protect the innocent, in that order. Although expected to protect the lives of their teammates and of themselves, these objectives remain secondary. An SSF team may find itself as the last line of defense preventing irremediable tearing of the membrane between life as we know it, and the howling nihilism of the Outer Dark. When given the choice of defending the world or saving himself, he knows that he must unflinchingly choose the former.

RECRUITMENT

SSF members are brought into the organization by members of the Recruitment Branch (Paramilitary Division), a special branch of the Recruitment Branch. RBPD members are embedded among Western military organizations and to a lesser extent other armed forces around the world. They may also serve in intelligence agencies or private enterprises, including mercenary firms, arms dealers, and various entities occupying nebulous positions between private and governmental.

They maintain a constant lookout for individuals bearing both the characteristics of standard Ordo field agents[2], plus a high degree of training in unconventional warfare, counter-intelligence, and black operations. Recruits are drawn from special forces, counter-intelligence operatives, and contract employees of private security firms such as Wackenhut and Blackwater. Potential recruits are placed under surveillance for a period of up to a year, during which their psychological profiles are carefully assessed by the RBPD. Ninety per cent of potential candidates are rejected at this point, a number that has increased from 78% in 2000. (Increase of active military engagement by Western forces in Iraq and Afghanistan has taxed the pool of potential recruits. Many must now be rejected due to lingering ill effects of their mundane combat experiences. These have already subjected them to post-traumatic stress syndrome and related dysfunctions resultant from active combat duty.)

The remaining 10% are approached in the field by RBPD officers, often after their mundane duties place them into peripheral contact with Esoterrorist operations. Prospective candidates may be assigned to several missions under auspices of their usual superiors or employers before full scope of Outer Dark incursions is made

---

2 To reiterate, those qualities include high intelligence, investigative skills, pronounced psychological resistance, skill at deception, trustworthiness, ability to assimilate the existence of the supernatural, and possession of a strong support network of friends and family.

apparent to them. Provided that their actions continue to reflect their suitability for the mission, a full approach is made. Information is provided on the nature of the struggle, and an offer of OV membership and SSF duty extended. Only 2.3% of applicants refuse. These disappointing few are subjected to a veil-out procedure in which they are convinced that the recruitment attempt was an elaborate psy-ops experiment on the part of their superiors, which, by rejecting, they passed with flying colors.

TRAINING

The extent to which additional standard paramilitary training is called for is then determined during a series of meetings between subject and recruitment officer. Typically the recruit is already well-prepared on this front — this is why he has been approached — but if there are gaps in his resume, arrangements are made to send him to friendly training facilities to fill them. The recruit's mundane skill set is burnished in friendly but non-aware facilities, requiring the adoption of a cover story and, on certain occasions, a covert identity.

Recruits also report to Base Camp Fantasia, an undocumented military base on ██████ ████████████. There they are trained in techniques of unconventional warfare specifically pertinent to supernatural targets. Through a mixture of course work and battlefield simulation, they learn the vulnerabilities and tactics of thirty-seven known Outer Dark entities. They learn where vital organs are located, which weapons are ineffective against which targets, and how to bolster resistance against their most common psychic attacks. Other techniques taught include:

- target determination in common circumstances, for example what or who to shoot at first when you burst into a ritual in progress

- operating with compromised senses and/ or communications equipment

- protocols for dealing with supernatural contagion. At what point *do* you kill your zombie-bitten comrade?

LIAISON BETWEEN UNIT TYPES

Operational security imposes barriers between investigate units and their SSF counterparts. Investigators can take better advantage of their capabilities by observing liaison protocols.

Calling In SSF Support

The order fields few SSF units, relative to the number of active investigative teams. As many of them are active-duty military officers or security contractors, they are relatively difficult to extract from their non-Ordo assignments. Request for immediate SSF insertion into a crisis at hand are therefore subject to withering scrutiny. The Ordo assignment desk must weigh the dangers posed by threats posed by investigative teams. Their primary criteria is the breadth of the physical and psychological threat at hand. The personal safety of investigators is at best a tertiary concern when SSF assignments are made. They are expected to be able to handle themselves in confrontations up to and including the tactical challenges typically handled by a police SWAT team.

SSF units are dispatched to handle military-level threats and mop-up missions. It is easier to field an SSF team for mop-up duty, for example clearing nests of creatures, because such threats are often not time sensitive, allowing for the quiet assembly of a team without alerting uncleared officials in their day-to-day organizations.

In other words, investigators can't count on SSF teams to sweep down and take care of standard-issue dangers for them. Only in near-apocalyptic circumstances should one send a request for SSF assistance in mid-investigation and expect them to relieve you of the risks associated with it.

Command Chains

The command structure of an SSF unit is malleable, changing from mission to mission. Like investigators, each member is expected to think autonomously while coordinating with others for maximal mission success. For liaison purposes, an SSF team leader is appointed on a per-mission basis. The assignment desk matches the capabilities of the rotating team leadership post to the challenges of the case.

SSF team members are in no way under the command of an investigative team requesting their assistance on a case. Although they will generally follow the lead of investigators, who may suggest overall objectives for the SSF team, they jealously guard the right to make their own tactical decisions. All team leaders are instructed not to waste SSF resources by allowing their operatives to needlessly risk death or injury. They are within their rights to decline requests from investigators when they feel that the main team does not fully require their assistance.

Conversely, SSF teams are trained not to interfere in the investigative aspects of a case. They leave the fact-finding component of a joint mission to the clue-sniffers. Where they choose to seek information at all, they focus on the gathering of actionable operational intelligence.

Ameliorating Mission Clash

The order strives to eliminate the counterproductive inter-departmental rivalries that afflict many of its mundane counterparts. Investigators and SSF units alike are strongly urged to park territoriality at the door. Coordinated missions work best with a strong division of labor, where the SSF units fulfill their mission types and let the investigators investigate.

MISSION TYPES

SSF missions fall into the following five categories.

Bogey Hunt

A bogey hunt is a mission aimed at the extermination of supernatural creatures, most notably escaped or summoned denizens of the

Outer Dark. Often when one nest is uncovered, examination of residual evidence leads to additional lairs, or to the Esoterror operatives who brought them into being.

Challenges in bogey hunts include:

- shielding civilian personnel from danger

- preserving general ignorance of the supernatural

- encountering new and evolving forms of Outer Dark entities with previously undocumented powers.

Counter-Terrorism

Counter-Terrorism missions are aimed directly at Esoterror operatives themselves. Often an SSF team is assigned to bring about the dissolution of a recently uncovered cell by any means necessary. These means include but are not limited to military raids, sabotage directed against installations and (in exceptional cases) assassination. Naturally the requirements of self-defense sometimes regrettably necessitate the killing of operatives the assignment desk would prefer to see captured alive.

Unlike investigative operations, counter-terrorism actions often occur without the cooperation of local intelligence and law enforcement. The challenges are those of any aggressive covert action against terrorists of the non-occult persuasion: maintaining secrecy, avoiding civilian casualties, and quickly departing from a jurisdiction after mission objectives have been achieved.

Infiltration and Disruption

Covert infiltration and disruption missions send SSF forces to conduct covert operations against Esoterror cells, cut-outs, allies, and dupe organizations. Unlike Counter-Terrorism missions, these operations leave their target groups intact but compromised. Typically the SSF team must identify an enemy installation, reconnoiter it, plan an insertion, and complete a task, and depart unnoticed. The task might be the removal of data or artifacts, the planting of a bug, the insertion of disinformation into a database, or an act of subtle sabotage.

A counter-terrorism mission to place a timed bomb in an enemy base might be seen as a combination of the two mission types.

Counter-Sortilege

Counter-sortilege operations seek to disrupt sorcerous activities. These most often involve raids on rituals. Other missions of this type include attacks on sites of malign energy, reorientation of ley lines or other membrane-affecting natural features. The chief challenge in a ritual disruption is timing—strike too early and many potential participants escape your net. Strike too late and the entities arrive.

Dangerous Environment Operations

On occasion a mission of the sort typically handled by a standard investigation team will require activity in a war zone or lawless region. As these theaters of operation are highly hazardous even to well-trained civilians and are best navigated by persons with a military background, they are often deemed DEOs—dangerous environment operations. They are then assigned to SSF teams able to defend themselves under battlefield conditions, and whose military perspective will likely have a bearing on the mystery at hand.

Dangerous environment designation changes as geopolitical shifts warrant. Areas currently under DEO determination include Iraq, Afghanistan, northern Pakistan, Somalia, and Chechnya.

Extra-Crunchy Combat

The following section consists of rules text, and should not be considered an excerpt from an in-world document.

With its focus on investigation, GUMSHOE keeps its combat rules stripped-down and simple. Some groups may prefer an additional level of tactical choice and special case modeling provided by the following optional rules. Though well suited for a SSF series, they can be used in any iteration of GUMSHOE. Use them only if a clear majority of your group clamors for them. In many groups, one or two vocal tactics fans cry out for extra crunch, while the rest quietly dread it. If you add these options to play and find that they slow down action sequences, because you have to stop to remember the rules or for any other reason, feel empowered to remove them again. Macho fetishism for nuts 'n' bolts combat detail can be an important factor in evoking the spirit of a special forces campaign, but it's not as important as keeping the combat fast and furious. If a player designed his character based on the availability of a combat option you intend to remove, allow him to redistribute his build points.

Admit these combat options to your game on a case-by-case basis. You may feel the need for Called Shots without wanting to open the door to Techno-Macho Utterances, or vice versa.

To keep things simple, you can rule that no character can invoke more than one combat option per round—you can't attack recklessly and then try for a multiple attack, for example. Then again, the types of players who like lots of crunch in their combat are the ones who like to wring maximum benefit from the system by finding powerful combination effects.

Combat options can be added to other GUMSHOE games with a heavy accent on fighting. References to the Fleeing ability do not apply to *The Esoterrorists*.

Though extra-crunchy by GUMSHOE standards, these optional rules don't break from the narrative emulation mode of the game to present detailed simulations of real-life armed combat. Groups jonesing for that degree of crunchiness, or accustomed to old school cause-and-effect reasoning, may want to consider a hybrid approach. Take GUMSHOE's investigative abilities for the fact-finding portions of the game, but handle general abilities by grafting on the crunch-heavy modern military system of your choice. Candidates for hybridization might include *GURPS*, D20 Modern, or *Twilight 2000*.

Automatic Weapons

To keep the story moving and its main characters alive at least until the climax arrives, the action genre treats automatic weapons fire as much less deadly than it is in real life. Characters either remain pinned down by suppressing fire (which is realistic) or routinely outrun lines of machine gun fire (which is not.) Important characters are much less likely to be hit by automatic fire than they are by single firearm shots. Minor thugs, guards and henchmen are more likely to be hit by autofire.

The following optional rules allow for a more detailed treatment of automatic fire. It still models genre, not reality.

If you score a hit with an automatic weapon, and the GM has no narrative reason to prevent you from making an easy kill, you may then spend Shooting points to do additional instances of damage to him, at a rate of 1 instance of damage per 2 Shooting points spent. Damage is assessed after you decide how many extra instances you want to pay for.

Blake, raiding the compound of a Miami narco kingpin, uses a light automatic weapon to opens fire on a guard. He makes a Shooting test against his Hit Threshold of 3, spending 2 points to augment his roll. He rolls a 5, overcoming the Hit Threshold. Blake's player, Alex, decides to spend 4 points to purchase another two instances of damage. He now

RAPID Refreshes

General pool points in GUMSHOE function not as a simulation of any real-world phenomenon, but as a dramatic conceit—they measure each PCs' share of spotlight time.

Thus you can feel free to accelerate refresh rates when the underlying dramatic rules of a series or scenario change.

In an SSF game, everyone is assumed to equally competent in the combat arts. They are not competing for specialty time against characters using other general abilities. Everyone is expected to shoot and scuffle in multiple combat scenes over the course of a scenario—often with little downtime between scenes.

To keep characters alive and competent seeming, make the following adjustment to refresh rates for Shooting and Scuffling only. At the beginning of any new fight sequence:

- Characters with positive Health pools refresh all points.

- Hurt but conscious characters refresh half of their points.

- Seriously wounded but conscious characters refresh one quarter of their pool points.

- Unconscious characters refresh no Health points.

The GM decides what constitutes a dramatically distinct scene. A brief break while combatants regroup or a second wave of reinforcements creeps up doesn't count as a new scene. As a rule of thumb, a dramatically distinct fight scene takes place in a fresh location or after more than an hour has passed without exchanging blows or shots with the enemy.

In other words, rapid refreshes change pool points in Scuffling and Shooting so that they no longer measure the number of cool combat things you can do over a series of interconnected scenes, but rather the number of cool combat things you can do during a single fight.

Applying similar logic, other scenarios or series frames assuming heavy use of another general ability by all PCs should allow rapid refreshes of that ability. For example, a supernatural homage to the film *Ronin* might revolve around frequent car chase scenes, requiring rapid Driving refreshes.

rolls three damage dice, getting a 5, a 3, and a 6, reducing the guard's Health by a total of 14 points. This takes the guard from 2 to -12 Health, leaving him dead. Blake has paid a total of 6 Shooting points for the entire exchange, taking his Shooting from 21 to 15.

If additional dramatically unimportant enemies stand within 3 meters of your first target, you may spread out your additional instances of damage between these additional targets.

Blake bursts through a door and finds the kingpin cowering behind a sofa, with three submachine gun toting goons waiting in front of it, shoulder to shoulder. Alex makes a Shooting test against the middle goon's Hit Threshold of 3. He spends 1 point on the test,

rolls a 4, and hits. He may now pay 2 points apiece to do additional instances of damage to his initial target, or to the guys standing on either side of him. With 14 shooting points left, Alex chooses to hit each of them twice. Having already scored the first hit, the remaining five cost him a total of 10 points. He rolls three pairs of damage dice, getting a 3 and a 5 against his main target, a 3 and a 5 against the guy on the left, and a 5 and a 2 against the guy on the right. Each goon had 2 Health. Now the main target and guy on the left are both at -6 (seriously wounded), and the guy on the right is hurt, at -5 Health. The GM rolls Consciousness rolls for all three, failing each time. They all pass out, bleeding out on the palazzo's fine marble flooring..

Health Ratings For Minor Foes

When choosing Health ratings for dramatically unimportant foes, don't worry about simulating their relative robustness in comparison to the general population. Focus on how many hits they ought to be able to take before dropping, according to dramatic logic. If you want a thug who falls to a single burst of automatic fire, give him a Health of 1 or 2.

(This advice applies to all GUMSHOE iterations.)

If you score a hit with an automatic weapon, and the GM finds it dramatically unsuitable to allow extra damage, the target takes only one instance of damage, as usual.

If a PC is hit by an automatic weapon by a goon, henchman, or other unimportant character, he takes only the usual single instance of damage. This restriction vanishes if players start to count on it. Saying "He can't hurt me much, he's only a henchman," should lead to a swift and bloody comeuppance.

> *The three goons open fire on Blake. Although they're carrying Uzis, they're not important enough to the narrative to qualify for additional instances of damage should they hit.*

When a PC instead takes an automatic weapon hit by an important enemy, the GM may spend the enemy's Shooting points to do additional instances of damage, at a rate of 3 points per instance, to a maximum of three extra instances.

Genre conventions surrounding automatic weapons of earlier eras are somewhat different; for period games, use the Rate Of Fire rules in *Trail Of Cthulhu*, p. 65.

Called Shots

In certain situations simply hitting an enemy isn't enough: you need to get him in a particular spot. You may need to hit a creature in one of its few vulnerable locations, blast a detonation trigger out of an Esoterrorist's hand, or sever a feeding tube currently draining a comrade's blood.

To specify the location of a hit is to make a called shot. Called shots are harder to make than ordinary strikes. If you're Shooting, the target is smaller than the enemy as a whole. While Scuffling, you forfeit the opportunity to take opportunistic shots when your opponent lets down his defenses against you.

When taking a called shot, you specify the desired location of the strike. If you are trying to achieve an effect other than damage to the opponent, specify this now. The GM decides whether this is a likely outcome of such a hit. If it is clearly not a likely outcome, and your character would logically know this, the GM warns you in advance, so you can do something else instead.

Some creatures exhibit partial invulnerability can only be damaged by hits to particular body locations: certain creatures go down only with head shots. A sulphurous entity from the Outer Dark may require a shot to its tiny third eye. In this case you are only trying to do damage to the creature and do not specify an additional effect.

The GM then adds 1 to 4 points to the target's Hit Threshold, depending on the additional difficulty entailed. Use the following table as a guideline. Body locations listed in italics are for creatures; others assume a human of ordinary size. Hit Threshold modifiers for ordinary body parts of extraordinary creatures are left as an exercise for the GM.

With the new Hit Threshold determined, you then make a Shooting or Scuffling test, as per the standard rules. If you succeed, your specified effect occurs as desired.

If you struck an ordinary person in a vital location (head or chest) with the intention of doing greater damage to him, add +2 to the damage. (This can't be combined with a Point Blank shot, which is

Desired Location	Modifier to Hit Threshold
Large carried object (rocket launcher, laptop computer, backpack)	+1
Tentacle, more than 24 cm thick	+1
Torso	+1
Chest (if attacker is facing victim)	+2
Gut	+2
Head	+2
Tentacle, 12 - 24 cm thick	+2
Hand	+3
Tentacle, 0 – 12 cm thick	+3
Weapon or other hand held object	+3
Eye	+4
Chest (if victim faces away from attacker)	+4

already assumed to hit a vital location.) If, after this damage is dealt, the victim is already Hurt but not Seriously Wounded, you may then pay an additional 6 Shooting or Scuffling points (whichever applies) to reduce the target to -6 Health. If the target is already Seriously Wounded you may then pay an additional 6 Shooting or Scuffling points (whichever applies) to kill the target outright.

Partial invulnerability: Blake Santos is faced by a Chernobyl zombie, which can only be taken down by a head shot. His player, Alex, announces that he's going to try to shoot it in the head, in hopes of wounding or killing it. The Chernobyl zombie's Hit Threshold is 2. Hitting the head imposes a +2 modifier to that, for a final Hit Threshold of 4.

Now that the Hit Threshold has been determined, the fight unfolds normally.

Desired effect: Later, Blake faces Omar Blanck, an Esoterrorist agent carrying a remote control for a sarin gas bomb. "I want to shoot it out of his hand, blasting it into a million little pieces," says Alex, declaring a called shot. Brenna assigns the +3 Hit Threshold modifier for a handheld object to Omar's Hit Threshold

of 4, for a new Threshold of 7. Alex spends 5 points to modify his die roll for the Shooting test. He rolls a 6, for a final test result of 11, more than enough to overcome the higher Hit Threshold. Therefore, he gets the result he wanted: "The remote flies from his hand, irreparably shattered!" narrates the GM.

Vital location: Omar flees. Angered that he was willing to subject hundreds of subway passengers to the horrifying death of a nerve gas attack, Blake decides to aim for his head as he dashes for an escalator. His intention is simply to do additional harm to his target by hitting him in a vital location. This increases Omar's Hit Threshold to 6. Alex spends 4 Shooting points for a modifier to his roll. He rolls a 4, for a final result of 8. He hits Omar in the head. The damage from his light firearm is +0. Alex rolls a damage die, getting a 6. This drops Omar, who was hit earlier in the scene, from 2 to -4 Health. Omar is now hurt; Alex can spend another 6 points to drop him to -6 Health, making him seriously wounded. He does so. The GM decides that Omar topples at the brink of the escalator, a bullet lodged in his brain.

Critical Hits

When your raw die roll on an attack attempt is a 6, and your total result after pool expenditures are taken into account exceeds the target's Hit Threshold by 5 or more, you score a critical hit, rolling two instances of damage and adding them together.

Blake , escaping from an Esoterrorist torture complex, punches a guard, whose Hit Threshold is 4. His player, Alex, spends 3 Scuffling points on the attack, then rolls a 6, for a final result of 9. This exceeds the Threshold by 5, allowing a critical hit. Blake deals damage equal to two punches, with a -2 damage value. He rolls a 5, for a modified result of 3 damage, and a 6, which modifies to 4 damage. The guard loses 7 Health, going from 5 to -2.

If PCs can score critical hits, their dramatically important enemies can, too.

Evasive Maneuvers

By going evasive , you can opt to fight defensively, decreasing both your chance of being hit and your chance of hitting anyone else. For every 2 Athletics or 4 Fleeing points you spend, your Hit Threshold increases by 1, for a maximum increase of 3. When you try to hit anyone else, their Hit Thresholds against you increase by 2 for every 1 point your Hit Threshold increased. While evasive, you duck, weave, backtrack, and otherwise concentrate on not being hit. Announce that you're going evasive at the beginning of your action for the round; doing so does not cost an action itself. The effects last until the beginning of your next action, at which point you can renew them (provided you can afford the cost.)

Badly pressed and running out of Scuffling points, Blake attempts to fend off a clootie while waiting for other members of his team to thunder down the corridor to his rescue. His player, Alex, declares evasive action and spends 4 Athletics on a 2 point Hit Threshold increase, taking Blake's threshold from 4 to 6. The clootie's Threshold increases (against Blake's attacks only) from 4 to 8.

Extra Attacks

By pushing yourself, you can attempt more than one attack by round, provided that your *rating* in the ability you're fighting with is 12 or more.

Scuffling: After reaching or exceeding your opponent's Hit Threshold, you may spend 3 Scuffling, plus 2 Health, to immediately launch a second attack. The Scuffling points are not applied to your roll; they are the cost of the extra attack. However, you may still spend further points to boost that test result.

Blake Santos grapples with a possessed sales clerk in a department store invaded by the Outer Dark. She's bitten his ankle, tearing an alarming chunk out of it. He responds by kicking her in the face. After spending 2 Scuffling, he rolls a 1, just barely meeting her Hit Threshold. He rolls 4 for his damage die, which, with a kick doing -1 damage, reduces her Health from 6 to 3. She's still not far enough away from his ankle for his taste, so Blake

decides to take a follow-up shot at her. His player, Alex, pays 3 Scuffling and 2 Health — the latter being less than he thinks he'll suffer if she gets another bite. He then spends another 3 Scuffling to boost his attack result. He hits her, reducing her from 3 to -1 Health.

Shooting: After reaching or exceeding your opponent's Hit Threshold, you may spend 4 Shooting, plus 1 Stability, to immediately launch a second attack. The Shooting points are not applied to your roll; they are the cost of the extra attack. However, you may still spend further points to boost that test result.

Blake returns fire against a demonic floorwalker holed up in the sporting goods section, hitting him with a shotgun blast. "He reels back, bleeding, stunned... then seems to recover, drawing a bead on you," narrates the GM, describing the possessed employee's successful Consciousness roll. Reasoning that another shot might finish him off, Blake's player, Alex, decides to buy an extra attack, paying 5 Shooting and 1 Stability. He then pays another 2 Stability to add to his Shooting result. Alex rolls a 6, for a final result of 8. That's a hit. He does 6 points of damage, seriously wounding the clerk.

If you have already launched an extra attack this round, the cost for yet another attack equals is multiplied by the total number of attacks you've already dealt.

Having already taken two attacks, a third attack to finish off the clerk would cost 8 Shooting and 2 Stability. Judging this too high a price to pay, Alex declines the chance.

Creatures who attack more than once per round pay no price for the privilege. They cannot gain extra attacks on top of that by spending points. In extraordinary circumstances, where dramatically appropriate, the GM may allow intelligent creatures who normally get one attack to use the extra attack rules, provided that they are also available to players. As NPCs lack Stability ratings, extra firearm attacks simply cost them 6 Shooting points.

Feints

When engaged in a Scuffling contest with an opponent, you can put him off guard with a series of false blows meant not to do harm, but to maneuver yourself or others into a better position against him for future blows. Forgo an attack against your opponent. You then may spend up to 3 Scuffling points to reduce his Hit Threshold by the number of Scuffling points spent. His Hit Threshold remains lowered until the end of your action in the following round. A target currently suffering a reduced Hit Threshold due to one feint can not have it further reduced by another. Feints are most effective when multiple PCs battle a single tough opponent.

Blake Santos and Aparna Dhawan fight kickboxer-turned-mutant Anaconda Jackson. As his Hit Threshold is a daunting 7, they've been making only costly headway against him. Blake elects to feint against him. He forgoes his next attack to instead spend 3 Scuffling to reduce the Hit Threshold by 3, to 4. Aparna then spends 2 points on her Scuffling to hit him. She succeeds, dropping him from 12 to 11 Health. Anaconda hits Blake, taking him from 8 to 4 Health. Blake then spends 2 Scuffling points on his follow-up attack, for a result of 5. He takes Anaconda from 11 to 8 Health. Now that Blake has completed his action, Anaconda's Hit Threshold goes back up to 7. But now Aparna decides to feint...

Grenades

A grenade is a thrown weapon with a damage modifier of 2. It can be accurately used within a range of fifty meters. Characters use Athletics to throw grenades, checking their rolls against a Difficulty equal to the target's Hit Threshold.

If a grenade attack overcomes the target's Hit Threshold, the target suffers up to three instances of damage. The victim can nullify one instance of damage by spending 4 Athletics points and two instances by spending a total of 6 Athletics points. These expenditures represent extraordinary actions to minimize harm done by the grenade. They can, for example, be described as:

- leaping away from the blast radius

- ducking behind cover

- batting the grenade away

- catching the grenade and throwing into a convenient hole, pond, or bucket of water.

In an open environment, other characters within three meters of the grenade suffer one instance of damage, which they can avoid by spending 4 Athletics points.

In a contained environment, such as a vehicle, trench, or small room, all other characters within three meters are subject to three instances of damage. They can avoid one instance by spending 3 Athletics points and two instances by spending 5 Athletics points.

Where multiple characters stand to be damaged by a grenade, one of them can leap on it by making a Difficulty 5 Athletics test. This is available as a free action taken during the grenade-thrower's round. Only one character can attempt to jump on a given grenade. If more than two characters want to try, only the one with the highest Athletics *pool* gets the opportunity. Resolve ties by giving the grenade-jumping privilege to the PC who, in the GM's judgment, has had the least spotlight time during the current session. A successful jumper takes four instances of damage, none of which can be nullified through the expenditure of Athletics points. No other characters take damage.

If a grenade attack fails to overcome the target's Hit Threshold, it lands in a spot between the thrower and target. All characters within 3 meters of this spot must pay 4 Athletics, or suffer one instance of damage.

Martial Arts

Characters with a Scuffling rating of 8 can specify that they are trained in one or more martial arts. Once per fight, their players may gain a 4-point Scuffling refresh by uttering a brief, evocative narrative description of his or her elegantly bone-crunching moves:

> • "With a flowing Kata Gurama, I try to sweep him up onto my shoulder and down to the pavement."
>
> • "Using my krav maga training, I target the back of his knee with a pivoting, angled kick."
>
> • "Remembering the sweat and humidity of that sweltering Bangkok gym so long ago, I summon up all my strength to tag him with a ferocious cross jab."

At the GM's discretion, especially poetic or believably obscure descriptions may fetch a 5-point refresh.

These utterances needn't be improvised; players can prepare key phrases in advance, then adapt them to the situation at hand.

New Investigative Ability: Military Science
Ability Type: Academic

You are a student of warfare, probably trained as such in a military academy. This expertise includes a knowledge of military history, strategy and tactics, and the weapons, technologies and engineering techniques of the battlefield. You can:

• identify uniforms and insignia

• identify an unknown military or paramilitary force by examining the weapons they use

• deduce a soldier's training and assignment history from his demeanor and use of slang and jargon

• spot weaknesses in an enemy's fortifications or tactics

• use Military Science as an interpersonal ability to gain the trust and cooperation of military and paramilitary personnel

Although especially suitable for SSF campaigns, this ability could be added to any contemporary or near-contemporary GUMSHOE game.

Non-Lethal Weapons

In GUMSHOE, non-lethal attacks never take an opponent out faster than standard combat. Otherwise players will have their characters simply knock their enemies out and kill them in cold blood, which is unsympathetic and out of genre. Thus tasers and stun guns work less effectively in the game than in real life.

NO TASERS (OPTIONAL RULE)
Although tasers exist in the world, they are not used by OV operatives. A string of incidents in which victims suffered fatal heart attacks after overzealous taser use have led to stringent operational restrictions. In one case, taser use empowered a supernatural creature. (This emulates the treatment of tasers in the source

material. In real life they might arguably be a life-saving non-lethal technology. Because they make action sequences boring and short, popular fiction occasionally puts them in the hands of bad guys and their minions, but does not give them to the heroes. Sympathetic characters use holds, punches, and/or threats of gun violence to subdue recalcitrant suspects.)

These weapons are ineffective against nearly all supernatural creatures.

Jumping In

Provided you have not yet acted during the current round, you may Jump In, spend 4 Athletics or 3 points Shooting or Scuffling at the end of any other character's action to take the next action. If you spend Shooting points, you must then make a Shooting attack. If you spend Scuffling points, you must then make a Scuffling attack.

> Blake and Aparna fight on the arctic ice against Trond, a bestial Nordic occultist. The order of action is Aparna, Trond, Blake. Aparna is hurt and out of Scuffling points; she tries to kick Trond and fails. It is now Trond's turn to act. Blake's player, Alex, decides to Jump In. Because he is going to use Scuffling to hit him, he has to spend Scuffling points. His Scuffling drops from 10 to 7. He now goes before Trond. Until changed, the order of action becomes: Aparna, Blake, Trond.

You may also Jump In at the end of a round, making yourself the first character to act in the new round.

Where two characters want to Jump In at the same time, PCs take precedence over GMCs. If two PCs want to act first, precedence goes to the one who arrived closest to start time for the current session.

You may forgo your alloted action during a round, then jump in at any later point at no cost. In this case you are voluntarily moving yourself back in the order of action.

Reckless Attacks

By fighting all-out, taking no precautions against being hit yourself, you can increase your chances of hitting your opponent, and your chance of being hit yourself. Spend 1 Athletics to decrease both your and a chosen opponent's Hit Threshold by up to 3 points. The minimum Hit Threshold achievable through a reckless attack is 1. Your opponent's Hit Threshold decreases only against you, but your decrease occurs against all potential opponents. The decreases last until the beginning of your next action, at which point you can renew them by paying another Athletics point.

> Confident that his men will flee if their commander is taken down, Blake fights recklessly against the mercenary leader El Olor. He spends 1 Athletics point and decides on a 2-point decrease. El Olor's Threshold decreases from 3 to 1, but only against Blake's attack. Against his comrade, Aparna Dhawan, the jefe's Hit Threshold remains 3. However, El Olor's thugs strike at Blake as if his Hit Threshold is 1.

Sniping

If you have a Shooting rating of 8 or more and are armed with a long gun equipped with a scope, you may decrease the Hit Threshold of a target for a single Shooting attack by taking at least one round to aim . If the target is aware of your presence, his Hit Threshold decreases by 1. If he is unaware of your presence, it decreases by 2.

Special Weapons Training

If you have a Shooting rating of 8 or more, you can spend 4 build points to grant yourself Special Weapons Training in one particular make of firearm: for example, a Walther PPK, .357 Desert Eagle, or Heckler & Koch USC carbine. (When taking this option during character creation, these build points must come from your budget of general build points.) In your hands, this weapon increases its damage by 1. A light firearm carries a damage value of +1, while a heavy firearm is +2. This applies not only to the particular weapon you own, but to all other weapons of that exact make. If you have special weapons training in the Fabrique Nationale P90 and your own weapon is confiscated by Taliban tribesmen, the replacement weapon you later acquire from a CIA contact in Islamabad still provides you the enhanced damage rating.

You may take Special Weapons Training in one light and one heavy firearm.

Support Moves

If your Athletics rating is 8 or more, you may perform support moves. In a support move, you use your action to execute an Athletics maneuver, which then places one of your comrades in a superior position against an opponent. Describe, in exciting detail, how you intend action to either improve your comrade's position, or degrade an opponent's. If your suggestion seems plausible, the GM clears you to make an Athletics test. Although your GM can adjust Difficulties according to described circumstances, you usually test against a Difficulty of 4. If successful, you allow your comrade to add the difference between your result and difficulty to a Shooting or Scuffling roll against the designated opponent. If the comrade fails to attack that opponent as his next action, the benefit is lost.

In the Peruvian mountains, Blake finds himself pinned in a narrow crevasse as a gelatinous plague demon attempts to melt his face. Aparna, higher up on the cliff face, is out of Shooting points but wants to assist her comrade. Her player, Cecile, describes a support move: "I rappel down and kick a loose chunk of rock so that it caroms off the thing's head!" The GM rules that this is possible and not extra difficult (though dangerous — if Aparna fails, she'll have to pass a second Athletics test or fall and hurt herself.) Cecile adds 3 to her Athletics roll of 6 for a final result of 9. The creature attacks Blake, reducing his Health from 11 to 5 as the flesh of his skin puckers and fizzes. Now it's Blake's turn to act; he may apply a bonus of 5 (the difference between Aparna's difficulty and result) to his roll. He spends a Scuffling point of his own, for a total bonus of 6, and rolls a 1, for a result of 7. This is just enough for Blake to overcome the creature's very high

Hit Threshold and score 6 points of damage with his machete.

Suppressing Fire

If you are armed with an automatic weapon and have a Shooting rating of 8 or more, you can lay down suppressing fire, preventing opponents from crossing a line drawn by your weapon's bullets. Although creating a line of suppressing fire prevents you from hitting your opponents, it also prevents them from firing directly at you. It is most useful for preventing enemies from advancing or pursuing.

When you first lay down a line of suppressing fire, make a Shooting test against a Difficulty determined by the approximate length of the line you're drawing. The line must be within your weapon's range. Increase the Difficulty of crossing the line by spending extra Shooting points on the test.

Length of Line	Difficulty
Alleyway	3
Road (1 lane)	4
Road (2 lanes)	5
Road (3 lanes)	6

You may then maintain the line of bullets with no further effort, provided you do nothing else, for either 2 rounds (if using a pistol) or 5 rounds (if using a machine gun.) Once this period elapses, you must take an action to reload, dropping your suppressing fire for one round. Then you must retake the test.

Opponents can see the line of fire; only the reckless or desperate will try to cross it.

To cross an established line of suppression fire requires an Athletics test with the result of the gunman's suppression fire test as the Difficulty. On a failure, the character suffers an instance of damage for the weapon type and falls back to his previous position on the far side of the fire line. If he succeeds with a margin of 0 to 4 between result and Difficulty, he crosses the line but suffers an instance of damage. On a margin of 5 or more, he crosses the line without taking damage.

As his comrades rush a rescued kidnap victim to safety, Blake stays behind on a Central American street to delay his former captors. He lays down a line of suppressing fire across the mouth of the alleyway he expects them to emerge from. Spending 3 Shooting points against a Difficulty of 3, Blake's player, Alex, rolls a 1, for a result of 4. This is enough to lay down a line of fire across the alleyway.

The lead kidnapper, Juan, is controlled by a demonic spinal parasite called a chowk, who cares little for his host's survival. It sends Juan through the suppressing fire. The GM makes an Athletics test, spending 3 points on the attempt, and rolls a 4, for a final result of 7. This overcomes the Difficulty, which is Blake's result of 4, by 3 points. This is enough to cross the line but not enough to avoid damage. Alex rolls damage for his heavy firearm; Juan loses 6 Health from a bullet hit.

By acting in tandem with other team members, you can increase the size of your line of fire, and keep the bullets flying when one of you has to reload.

Techno-Macho Utterances

Rules aren't the only way to create an atmosphere of gun grease and cordite. Adopt this rule if you want to keep the combat rules simple while giving your resident gun bunnies a taste of the fetishistic combat detail they crave.

Once per fight, a player with a Shooting rating of 8 or more can gain a 3-point refresh in that ability by uttering a brief narrative description of his or her actions redolent with Clancy-esque detail:

- "The rubber recoil pad of my SAIGA SWAT shotgun bounces against my body arm as I come through the door blasting!"

- "I sit at the bunker, waiting, scope trained on the doorway, my M4A1 kitted out with all the custom blessings the SOPMOD can bestow."

- "As I fire one of its trademark bursts of the HK UMP, I take a deadened, existential solace from the soulless blankness of its polymer casing."

At the GM's discretion, a techno-macho utterance may provide a 4-point refresh when it is so impenetrably jargon-filled that other players recoil in awe at the utterer's ballistic enthusiasm.

In the deployment of techno-macho utterances, advance preparation is no vice. Players should feel free to script out lines of suitable dialogue, perhaps on index cards.

RUNNING AN SSF SERIES

Special Suppression Forces can appear as gung-ho GMCs who appear as recurring characters in a standard *Esoterrorists* series, bringing in the big guns to mop up problems uncovered by the PCs' investigations.

You might also run an alternate *Esoterrorists* series in which the PCs are all members of an SSF unit. This game is heavier on fighting than the standard series type, but does not entirely discard the investigative aspect at the heart of the GUMSHOE system. Instead, it changes the nature of what is investigated. Its distinctive scenario design formula places the focus on finding intelligence granting tactical advantages in upcoming fights.

Scenario Design

A typical *Esoterrorists* scenario consists of a trail of clues which often leads to a fight at the end, and may include one or two minor and avoidable violent incidents of antagonist reaction along the way. Often the fight at the end can be turned over to unknown confederates or avoided through clever play.

An SSF scenario always includes fights, which are not meant to be avoidable. Where the standard team's job is to find out what's going on and maybe call the cavalry, here the PCs are the cavalry. Investigative scenes become the connective tissue between fight sequences.

As SSF missions start where standard ones leave off, it's perfectly acceptable to start *in media res*, with a fight in progress. Or they can begin with a briefing. For example, they might review the case notes of a supporting character investigation team, getting the skinny on the bogeys they've been assigned to mop up.

The information they have available to them decreases throughout the scenario. They begin with a full dossier on their first fight. Once they finish it, they find a core clue leading them to one or more investigative scenes, which leads them

to a second fight. They enter this battle with less prior information than they had for the first. Then they find another core clues, leading to another sequence of investigative scenes, which in turn leads to a final fight, where they know even less and face their greatest threat so far.

Where a standard scenario is often about who did it, or what happened, the mystery being solved here is generally: where do we go next, what do we kill when we get there, and how do we kill it?

Investigative sequences can be easier to solve than a standard scenario, but need not be.

If you run an extended SSF series, you'll want to shake up the scenario formula given above. Do this as soon as the players become sufficiently familiar with it to find scenarios predictable. A paramilitary scenario might turn into a more standard investigation midway through. Another scenario might be an extended series of chase/survival sequences in a hostile environment. A war zone adventure might force the group to temporarily abandon their bug hunt to fight against equally deadly mundane bad guys. You might stage a crossover episode, in which the group starts by playing investigative characters, then switches to their SSF guys for a final confrontation.

Tactical Fact-Finding

When designing fight sequences, build them around opportunities to apply investigative abilities to the battlefield. These opportunities can occur during interstitial investigative sequences, or during the fights themselves. In keeping with the acronym-heavy spirit of a paramilitary series, these opportunities are called TFFBs, for Tactical Fact-Finding Benefits.

In your scenario notes, describe each TFFB by listing:

- the investigative ability used to gain the advantage

- the action required to find the information

- the tactical circumstance under which the benefit comes into play

More Fighting, More Refreshing

Where a typical *Esoterrorists* scenario features a few minor scrapes and perhaps one major battle at the end, an SSF scenario may feature three or more serious fights per case. Enable the PCs to survive these by permitting refreshes of Athletics, Shooting and Scuffling between each fight.
To qualify for these refreshes, a character must engage in downtime.

- They must spend at least four hours of quiet relaxation in a restful environment, free from the reasonable expectation of further combat. (If they find themselves with a fight suddenly on their hands, they lose their chance at a refresh until it is resolved and all the criteria here are fulfilled again.)

- Any characters who lost Health during the previous fight must receive Medic treatment, regaining at least 1 Health point in the process.

- Any characters who lost Stability since the last period of downtime (or beginning of the current scenario) must undergo Shrink treatment, regaining at least one Stability point.

A character's failure to receive Medic or Shrink treatment prevents him from refreshing, but not his teammates.

- the nature of the benefit

Although the most obvious ability to yield a TFFB is Military Science (p. 11), the standard investigative abilities can also yield plenty of useful information.

- Interpersonal abilities can wring valuable tactical data from allies, witnesses, shady middlemen, prisoners, and enemy operatives.

- Natural History might provide terrain intel.

- Textual Analysis could find hints on fortification weaknesses in a captured personal journal.

- Ballistics hints at the sophistication of the weapons the team can expect to face.

- Cryptography cracks the tactical information in encoded enemy communications.

- Electronic Surveillance, after an Infiltration exercise, might secure a floorplan of the site to be raided.

These clues may be garnered in a scene previous to the fight in which they become relevant. Alternately, the players may get the chance to gather a clue in the middle of a fight.

Sometimes they get the benefit simply by taking part in the battle. On other occasions they may have to do something to trigger the benefit—kill the opposing unit's leader, blow up a support column, set a communications jamming device in place.

Benefits of tactical investigation may take the following forms:

- Refreshes: one or more team members gains a refresh of a set number of pool points in a designated ability or abilities; points that would put their pools higher than their ratings are ignored. Refreshes are best used when the benefit's triggering circumstances occur in mid-fight, and when the benefit is abstract and hard to quantify.

- Temp points: one or more team members gains pool points in a set number of pool points in a designated ability or abilities. Temp points can cause pools to exceed a character's ratings. At the end of the scene in which they are granted, the pools of temp point recipients drop by the number of temp points gained. Temp points are best used for situations of broad and abstract benefit, where the PCs enjoy an advantage from the outset of the armed conflict.

- Difficulty adjusts: The Difficulty of a specific action decreases for the team, or a team member, or increases for an enemy or enemies. The most obvious example is an decreased effective Hit Threshold for one's enemies, or an increased effective Hit Threshold for oneself. Changes in difficulty can apply to many circumstances; Hit Threshold adjusts best reflect positional advantages, where the team members are better able to conceal themselves from incoming fire, or force enemies to expose themselves to it.

- Enemy pool reductions: When the benefit's triggering circumstance comes into play, the team's enemy loses a particular number of points in one or more pools. Pool reductions are best used to reflect a change in battlefield conditions putting the team's targets at a sudden and dramatic disadvantage.

- Surprise: The team is able to begin the fight with one or more rounds during which the enemy is unable to return fire or perform other actions. This applies to situations where the team is able to leverage tactical information to suddenly launch an attack against unprepared adversaries.

Some situations may warrant a combination of advantages—an enemy pool reduction plus a number of temp points, for example. Be prepared to substitute more appropriate benefits when creative players wring different and unexpected tactical circumstances from their tactical fact-finding.

In a standard *Esoterrorists* scenario, an opportunity to enhance later tactical success with an investigative ability generally requires a spend, because it confers an advantage that is only tangential to the solution of the central mystery. In an SSF campaign, the acquisition of tactical advantage *is* the central mystery. Here they should not require spends. In fact, as the whodunnit aspect of their adventures is secondary, you may decide that the acquisition of other intelligence of broader interest to the Ordo Veritatis, but unrelated to the essential war-fighting mission of the SSF unit, is accessible only via investigative spends.

Fact-Finding and Combat Sequencing
Prevent tactical fact-finding during a fight from slowing the action to a crawl by integrating it with the turn sequence.

Right before the fight, each player gets the chance to query a single investigative ability. When an appropriate ability is named, the GM supplies the tactically beneficial information. Invoking a particular ability yields all information arising from it; there is never any benefit to repeating an already-used ability. Facts found are usually free, though the rare example providing an extraordinary tactical benefit may require a spend. If so, the GM invites the player to make the spend; players do not have to ask if spends are available.

Except in odd circumstances where it is possible to meaningfully interact with enemy combatants while they're trying to kill you, interpersonal abilities are typically of little use in mid-fight fact-finding.

Each player also gets to invoke another ability at the top of each action during the fight. Drawing on an investigative ability does not cost an action. Players should spend their off-turn time picking the ability they want to use. GMs are within their rights to rule that player who dithers over his ability choice can't attempt tactical fact-finding that round. They should not penalize them by also skipping over their combat actions, or making them more difficult.

Some pieces of information may be gained through more than one ability. As players may feel less disappointed to get no information from an ability than to duplicate someone else's revelation, you may wish to omit repeated clues.

For an example of in-combat fact-finding, see the SSF adventure "Operation Whirlwind Reaper," p. 130.

Example TFFBs
After the team discovers the enemy's jungle shanty, they can use thermal imaging equipment and Electronic Surveillance to locate their camouflaged generator. If, in battle, they lob a grenade onto the generator (Athletics test, Difficulty varies between 2 and 5 according to how close the grenadier is willing to get to it, exposing himself to enemy fire) the insurgents are plunged into darkness, increasing unit members' Hit Thresholds by 2. Unit members suffer no corresponding disadvantage, assuming they wear their night vision goggles.

Note the triggering action (using thermal imaging equipment), ability (Electronic Surveillance), tactical circumstance (using a grenade on the generator) and benefit (decreased enemy Hit Thresholds.)

Having found blueprints to an enemy safehouse, the group may look for weak points using Architecture. If so, they discover signs of a Roman catacomb underneath it. If they attack through the catacomb, they can, on a 2-point Explosive Devices spend, blow a hole in its ceiling—which is the Esoterrorists' floor. The targets come raining down into the catacomb, injured and unready, their Health pools reduced by 4 apiece, ceding the team one round of surprise.

The triggering action is the decision to look for weak points, the ability Architecture, the tactical circumstance is blowing the catacomb floor, and the benefit is the lowered Health pools plus one round of surprise.

Using Impersonate to mingle with peripheral members of an southern Iraqi death cult, a unit member can discover that the group's leader calls himself Abu Ubeid, and that he can be recognized by his hulking, ursine physique. When they engage his cultists, the team can gain 6 free points apiece, to be divided as they like between Shooting and Scuffling, when they kill Ubeid, demoralizing his followers.

Triggering action: asking the right questions of the death cultists; ability: Impersonate; circumstance: killing the leader; benefit: free points.

Training Flashbacks
Flashbacks to training and briefing provide a fun way to convey information to the players as if their already characters know it. This allows you to jump into the scenario and skip the usual overdose of introductory exposition.

In early fight scenes, especially those conducted *in media res*, training flashbacks can allow you to provide TFFBs to players without putting them through prior investigative sequences. These might grant benefits for free, simply to add interest to a fight scene, without an ability use or triggering action.

You might begin a session with a bogey-hunt encounter against a new creature of your creation, the multi-headed Vornath Excrescence. As the action begins, enemy agents already lie dead on a dusty alkali plain, having fallen to the unit's blazing guns. Now the team has to deal with the creature the Esoterror assets summoned. Having set up the scene with a bang, you flash back in time to a briefing at Camp Fantasia, in which a lecturer describes the Vornath Excrescence as a carrion feeder with a taste for human spinal fluid. Flashing back to the battlefield, the players are now given a chance to realize that the creature wants to feed on the corpses of its slain summoners. By standing aside, they prompt the entity to turn its back to them as it plunges its suckers into the dead men. They then get a reduction in its Hit Threshold and a round of surprise against it.

Alternately, it might occasionally be dramatically appropriate for training flashbacks to require abilities and thoughtful use of triggering actions. The later in the scenario a training flashback occurs, the more the players should have to work for its benefits.

The Enemy

Since its inception as a movement, Esoterror has proven itself a slippery and ever-evolving enemy. At times its actions appear to be consistent with a coherent, if distributed, organization inching toward a common goal. Other evidence suggests that it is nothing more than a loose confluence of dangerous lunatics, frequently working at cross-purposes. One top analyst (codename TALLOW MONORAIL) has described it as a Schrödinger's conspiracy, in that our efforts to observe it motivate its members to alter its structure.

With that word of caution, it is possible to make certain general statements about the nature of the foe, as it is currently configured.

FUNDING

By the standards of international terrorism, Esoterror is a well-funded operation. For every dollar raised and disbursed by the largest and most influential conventional terror group, the Al-Qaeda network, Esoterror gathers ten dollars. (These figures may be somewhat obscured by Esoterror penetration of the increasingly beleaguered AQN. Analysts surmise that as many as 23% of AQN expenditures are now diverted by Esoterror moles to serve the agenda of the Outer Dark.)

Conventional terror raises much of its money from small donors, funneled through front organizations including radical religious institutions and phony charities. Esoterror enjoys no comparable source of grass roots support. Its funding comes in large bundles, handed over by a small handful of wealthy donors. These monies travel around the globe through a laundering network of unparalleled elusiveness. Esoterror financiers appear to operate multiple money-funneling pathways in parallel to one another. When we bust one, redundant cash pipelines remain intact and flowing.

We have identified over one hundred high net worth individuals who we suspect of participation in the Esoterror sect. For every name on the list there are probably four we have yet to uncover. Esoterror disinformation campaigns muddy the water by planting evidence against honest individuals, including our governmental and elite patrons.

Other major sources of funding include conventional terror and crime syndicates infiltrated by Esoterror. Monies extracted from these organizations by embezzlement or extortion also flow into enemy coffers. Any person placing an illicit bet, purchasing an illegal drug, or availing themselves of the services of a prostitution ring may be unknowingly tithing a portion of the proceeds to the Outer Dark.

Although the adversary can raise funds with ease, it faces a bottleneck in disbursing them to its operatives, thanks to our monitoring efforts. When we pinpoint the location of an ongoing Esoterror operation, we then task an electronic forensic accounting team (EFA) to track all large or unusual disbursements coming into it through conventional financial networks. In response to our vigilance, Esoterror has learned to pre-fund its cells before any major operation likely to attract EFA attention. As a result of is that cell leaders are rarely able to access significant new funds after we target them for investigation. If they have not requisitioned equipment, secured safehouses, or arranged for reinforcements prior to your arrival on the scene, you can be reasonably certain that they will be unable to marshal them during the course of your investigation. Only by leaving physical bundles of cash via dead drop can the greater organization reliably refill an operational unit's drained coffers. As this entails a high degree of risk and exposure of additional cells, Esoterror engages in it only in the rarest of cases.

Any sign of ad hoc cooperation from other cells, financial or otherwise, should be regarded as indicative of a high-yield enemy operation — possibly one of apocalyptic import.

PSYCHOGRAPHICS

The academic desk officers assigned to our Psychographic Profiling Unit (PPU) face the daunting task of finding the logic underlying the twisted actions of the functionally insane. All high-profile Esoterror actors can be regarded as psychopathic in the classic sense of the term. They gratify their desires and ambitions without moral compunction, unrestrained by pangs of conscience. However, for investigative purposes, it may prove fruitful to divide their operatives into various psychopathic sub-types.

PPU analysts stress that these categories are useful for investigative purposes only, as a tool in determining the motivations, emotional breaking points, and potential future actions, of Esoterror suspects. They possess little if any diagnostic or therapeutic utility. Keep them in mind as you seek the right button to push during an interrogations or interview.

Note also that many individuals will possess qualities of multiple categories to various degrees. Where one set of traits dominates, you will want to determine which profile is most applicable. In cases of weak or mixed motivation, the interviewer may get positive results using the verbal triggers for any applicable category.

Dominant

Esoterror operatives exhibiting the dominant personality type are motivated by the desire to exercise power over others. Dominant types seek the top positions in large hierarchies. They may strive to head nation states, multinational corporations, unions, or institutional churches. Once installed in these positions, they attempt to enlarge their authority, either by widening the reach of their organizations or removing checks on their power. There is no position so modest that a dominant-type psychopath will not seek it—if only as a stepping stone to greater things. Dominants of more modest achievement might head small businesses, municipal governments, or condo residents' boards.

Dominants follow Esoterror believing, often correctly, that their network of illicit contacts will aid them in the acquisition and maintenance of power. To them the conspiracy, in all its occult ruthlessness, serves as the ultimate contact network.

Once in a position of authority, the dominant invests heavily in the status quo. His efforts to bring about an apocalyptic membrane rupture may take on a perfunctory quality. Others imagine a post-catastrophic world in which their authority is further elevated. They imagine themselves ruling over the miserable survivors from their massive thrones of human bone.

Due to the type's unrelenting pursuit of authority, any Esoterror cell including a dominant is likely to be led by that individual.

Verbal triggers: Dominants respond positively to flattery and negotiation, and negatively to bureaucracy and intimidation.

Submissive

The submissive type exists in a mental world of extreme self-abnegation and seeks reassurance in unquestioning obedience. He is attracted to Esoterror as a harshly paternalistic authority willing to make all of his choices for him. Submissives thrive on difficult missions and a flagellating sense of sacrifice. They project unresolved feelings toward withholding or psychopathic parents (often of the dominant personality type) onto their Esoterror masters and the high demons of unremitting horror. A submissive seeks to prove himself to the symbolic parent by ably performing his Esoterror duties to. Perversely, he is gratified more by failure and its resulting punishment than by success and praise, which can never fill the yawning chasm at the center of his psyche.

Submissives are the organization's flunkies and minions. If they mistakenly gain authority by rising within the conspiracy to the level of their incompetence, they become anxiously self-destructive, desperately hoping to be cut down to size. At first blush, this dynamic might seem advantageous to our aims. Ironically, it brings its own set of dangers. A submissive in full self-sabotaging mode can cause great collateral damage. He may recklessly violate the group's core secrecy principals, endangering the public with open manifestations of the supernatural. The results of these dramatic cell implosions can be fiendishly difficult to veil out.

Though supposedly servile, submissives can be high-maintenance lackeys, requiring constant attention from their co-dependent authority figures. In some dysfunctional Esoterror cells, it is the incessant demands of the allegedly inferior partner that spurs the dominant to action.

Verbal triggers: To crack a submissive, transfer his instinctive servility from his Esoterror masters to you, then employ intimidation or basic interrogation techniques. Beware triggers that treat him as an desirable individual, such as flattery or flirting, or which seek to reassure him. These induce cognitive dissonance, prompting the subject to become uncommunicative.

Cipher

Ciphers' childhood identity formation remain incomplete, leaving them listless and unmotivated until they come into the orbit of a strong personality. Left to their own devices, they want little for themselves except to secure very basic needs and to pass the time.

Outwardly, the behavior of a cipher may appear to resemble that of a submissive. However, the submissive actively seeks a dominant personality, and works in a self-directed manner to please the superior individual. The cipher follows orders when motivated but feels no great attachment to any task, or sense of reward when he succeeds. He is an unformed blob of clay, waiting to be pulled into shape.

Because they are heavily suggestible, ciphers are often employed by Esoterrorists as hosts for demonic possession. What little personality they exhibit is easily overridden even by minor Outer Dark entities.

Verbal triggers: Ciphers respond with apparent eagerness toward nearly any verbal approach. Unfortunately, their answers may be influenced by unconscious cues given by the interrogator. The cipher tells you what he thinks you want to hear. A well-honed bullshit detector is required to separate truth from imitative behavior.

Sadist

The sadist gratifies himself by inflicting emotional or physical suffering on helpless others. This gratification is usually sexual in nature but may be sublimated beyond recognition. The sadist may be unable to achieve arousal by conventional means.

He serves Esoterror in order to gain access to a steady supply of fresh victims. The sadist may be a group leader, or act as a torturer, assassin, or guard. The sadist shares impulses with the beings of the Outer Dark and heavily identifies with them. He may believe, possibly correctly, that a catastrophic membrane event will transform him into an immortal entity of unremitting horror, able to torture innocent victims for all eternity.

Verbal triggers: A sadist may be tricked into revealing his true nature by a display of feigned weakness, using flirting or reassurance techniques. Displays of strength or dominance (intimidation, cop talk) cause him to retreat into his shell.

Exofetishist

The exofetishist is an individual of exotic sexual tastes whose physical desires can only be gratified through contact with Outer Dark entities. He is often recruited directly by these malign otherworldy beings. This contact may occur through dreams or via physical manifestation. The exofetishist is then introduced into an existing cell or instructed to build one from the ground up. In the latter instance he is likely to be operational leader of the cell. His controller entity performs the duties of a desk officer in a conventional intelligence agency, directing his efforts to weaken the membrane. After an initial, addictive exposure, the exofetishist's sexual access to his controller is sharply rationed, ensuring obedience. When congress does occur, it may biologically alter the subject, investing him with demonic traits. Captured exofetishists whose DNA has been mutated in this fashion can be identified on an intensive physical inspection. Look for new and unnatural orifices.

Exofetishists revel in a paradoxical sense of shame regarding their demonic copulation. The forbidden nature of their sexual activities heightens their obsession with it.

Approximately 45% of exofetishists are exposed during early puberty to extreme pornographic images of human-demon sexual contact. They may be recruited by older exofetishists or stumble across the material accidentally. As an OV investigator, you may called upon to roll up Esoterror porn rings, seeking to disseminate this material to impressionable persons as part of a recruiting process.

Verbal triggers: Biologically altered exofetishists fear exposure and imprisonment and respond positively to interrogation and intimidation. Non-alien sexual overtures leave them cold, rendering flirting useless. Consumed by self-loathing, they likewise reject flattery.

Hedonist

The hedonist seeks physical pleasure and the outward trappings of success. He follows the Esoterrorists in exchange for promises of wealth, intoxicants, and an endless parade of supple sexual partners. Hedonists tend to gravitate to the entertainment industry and are used by Esoterror to inject harmful cultural memes into the public consciousness. A hedonist may be a knowing agent of supernatural horror, or may reject talk of occult rituals and demons as so much nonsense. Only the former group, naturally, attains leadership status in any cell. Others are used as cultural tools and discarded when they lose their hold over the public.

Knowing conspirators, like dominants, may pursue the apocalypse lackadaisically, hoping that the end comes long after they depart this mortal coil. They like the world as it is, so long as they're squeezing all the juice out of it.

Dominants often have a hedonistic streak, but pure hedonists are interested in power only as a means to luxury and debauchery.

Verbal triggers: Hedonists fear a life of pain and wretchedness, and can be cowed by intimidation or streetwise threats. Accustomed to separating the players from the posers, they can spot insincere flirting and flattery a mile away.

Attention-Seeker

Driven by profound insecurity, the attention seeker pursues fame or notoriety. He signs on with Esoterror as a means of securing it. Like the hedonist, he may be drawn in by the conspiracy's connections in the entertainment and media industries.

When denied positive attention, he revels in destruction. He is all too happy to commit spectacular crimes that terrify the populace and weaken the membrane. A supreme narcissist, he fits the profile of the serial killer who sends a steady stream of taunts to the police. The attention-seeker might just as easily attempt the inexplicable assassination of someone who possesses the fame he seeks.

Attention-seekers are most often employed as cat's-paws, acting as apparent lone wolves. Scratch the surface of their solitude and you will often find a web of well-concealed Esoterror connections.

Verbal triggers: The attention-seeker yearns to tell you his story, provided you prime the pump with flattery or negotiation. Attempts to belittle him cause him to clam up, so avoid intimidation or cop talk.

Avenger

Believing himself to have been wronged by all around him, this personality type pursues a membrane tear out of unquenchable anger. He may direct his sense of grievance toward society, or even reality itself. He already lives in a world of constant suffering, and wants all others around him to feel the same. The avenger seeks out other misfits and haters, either joining an existing Esoterror cell or fashioning one from the ground up. He may be used as a pawn, taking on the missions of suicide bomber or lone gunman.

More often he spearheads operations of appalling violence, intending to fight until the end of days.

Avengers are sometimes victims of unrelenting childhood abuse. Others turn to cosmic vengeance after wrenching setbacks, such as the senseless accidental deaths of multiple loved ones.

Verbal triggers: The avenger rejects attempts to contradict his nihilistic world view, but secretly craves the agreement of others. Open him up through reassurance, by pretending to sympathize with him. Don't try to negotiate; he'll string you along and enjoy your suffering.

Quisling

The quisling's conscience and sense of identity have been irrevocably distorted by contact with the Outer Dark. Convinced that the end of days is nigh, he has thrown his lot in with the servants of unremitting horror. He betrays mankind in the hope that he and his loved ones will be spared the worst ravages of the coming apocalypse. His brush with the other realm may have been accidental but is often part of a targeted recruiting operation. The quisling is often a sleeper agent in a position of influence or authority who is kept in place for years until he is needed for the execution of a sinister plan. His controlling Esoterror cell has probably convinced him—possibly accurately— that the safety of his friends and family depends on his commitment to operational secrecy.

Verbal triggers: If Esoterror is threatening a quisling's loved ones, you must first reassure him that they will be protected. Attempts to intimidate him fall flat; he is far more afraid of Outer Dark entities than he is of you.

Recruitment

Esoterrorists and their otherworldly allies maintain a constant alert for new disposable pawns. We have identified the following primary means of induction into the Esoterror complex:

In-Cell

The leader of a current cell sets out to find new dupes or knowing accomplices. This scenario offers our best chance for infiltration. Unfortunately, the adversary knows this and screens candidates carefully. Individuals seeking the above psych profiles are preferred—whether is through conscious design has yet to be determined.

Cross-Membrane

An Outer Dark entity, either incarnate in this reality or communicating telepathically through the membrane, contacts a leadership prospect. Over time the subject is tested for suitability as the leader of a new cell. (Occasionally the entity conducts an in-cell recruitment for an existing cell it controls.) Esoterror techniques are psychically inculcated in the subject, perhaps through a blood ritual. The subject then sets about recruiting subordinates, either under the entity's direct guidance, or in a self-directed manner based on occult indoctrination.

Cell Fissioning

A subordinate within an existing cell is identified as a leadership prospect for a new cell. This may occur by mutual consent or as the result of an unresolved power struggle between leader and follower. The follower goes off to recruit a new cell. Cell fissioning offers our best chance of using information gained on one swept-up cell to find another. These leads rarely take us to more than one additional cell.

Daughter Cell

An existing cell recruits and assembles and entire new cell. Recruitment occurs via cut-outs and go-betweens, keeping identities of all or most members of originating cell hidden from the daughter cell.

Daughter cells are often formed to perform particular operations. If they succeed, they then continue on their own, developing agendas distinct from the parent cell.

Remnant Survival

Cell members escape an OV sweep, go on the lam and, after reaching a safe location, start up a new offshoot there. Members of the prior cell must keep an ongoing low profile. The new cell becomes an easy target for us if we pick up their trail. Because

we make an effort to catch the leaders of any cell we roll up, remnants tend to be underlings. Some rise to the occasion. Others are eventually usurped by more motivated recruits, returning to minion status.

Esoteric Awakening

An individual, usually a seeker of occult power, stumbles upon the existence of the Outer Dark. Using information gathered from forbidden books or suppressed Internet sites, he conducts a summoning ritual and is contacted by an unremitting horror entity. If judged worthy, the self-recruiting Esoterrorist is tutored in magic and tradecraft. The order monitors pseudo-occult groups to intercept attempts at self-initiation.

Our operations to deter esoteric awakenings include the subtle alteration of rituals. Would-be ritualists using sabotaged grimoires offend the contacted entities, prompting them not to recruit the seeker, but to consume him.

COMMUNICATIONS

Communications techniques within cells are well documented. Many a cell has been put to rest after agents discovered its messaging protocols. How cells exchange information, and in fact the extent to which they do so at all, remains a matter of high controversy.

Intra-Cell

Individual cells display a concern for communications security commensurate with their overall sophistication. Your archetypal family of inbred hill people relies entirely on verbal communication, leaving no electronic footprint. A conspiracy of well-heeled media moguls can afford to hire top security specialists to ensure maximally encrypted hi-speed communications through network autonomous parallel structures.

Between these two extremes sit the vast majority of cells. They are forced to make do with civilian-level telecom and Internet protocols. They protect themselves by using IP anonymizers, disposable cell phones, and simple word codes. The latter cloak mission-critical orders in the innocuous language of everyday life. This technique will be familiar to anyone who has ever listened to a wiretap of an organized crime figure.

For example, the neutralized cell leader Monte Gilbert of Bloomington, IN, used the following keywords while communicating with his crack-addicted juvenile minions:

Human sacrifices were referred to as ham (adult males), chicken (underage males), tuna (adult females) or sardines (underage females.) The six-backed forest entity to whom they were fed was code-named "the dumpster." Weapons were referred to as chopsticks (.22 pistol), rice cookers (Tec-9 automated pistols) or woks (long guns, including assault rifles.) Civilians Gilbert wrongly suspected of being OV operatives were dubbed roosters, hens, or ducklings, according to their perceived threat level.

Cross-Cell

Debate rages within our data sifting department as to the nature of communications between active Esoterror cells. This goes to the higher question of whether the enemy exhibits a high degree of coordination, or merely seems to do so, because its various autonomous units all strive toward a common goal.

Clearly there are completely autonomous cells who never exhibit any awareness of a wider conspiracy. The Rudersdal auto-erotic asphyxiation cult serves as a recent example of this. When debriefed, members of such cells display a low understanding of the overall Outer Dark agenda and cosmology.

Other cells do cross paths, share data, exchange personnel, and occasionally work together toward common ends. These are mostly the cosmopolitan cells whose members possess global influence independent of their Esoterror ties. This is where the controversy comes in.

One school of thought, currently propounded by analyst ADJURER HONCHO, has it that cells arise spontaneously but naturally come into contact with one another in the course of their activities. For example, cells might cross paths while searching for the same rare tome of forbidden ritual magic. On several occasions cells have attacked one another, each apparently assuming that the other was an Ordo Veritatis team sent to destroy them. (See case abstract R3489, OPERATION DRAINAGE PUSH, for an operation in which a single-handed station agent manipulated the Chilean cells of Santiago and Maipu into a war that resulted in the dissolution of both.) A cell leader who double-checks before attacking learns to distinguish between foe and previously unknown friend. The cells must then make contact to negotiate territory and ensure that neither trains friendly fire on the other. In what is probably a violation of operational protocols, contacts between cells may then continue after the point of original contact has been forgotten. Leaders treat their means of contact with allied cells as top secrets. This stands to reason—blowing the cover of a group of highly capable violent lunatics is not he safest mistake one could make. For this reason, in the aftermath of a sweep op against a given cell, we are rarely able to find contact information for others. This remains true even when we know that the target cell has enjoyed past cooperation from counterpart units.

The second school of thought is put forth by data sifting analysts led by codename TIDY TWILL. It theorizes that the conspiracy's most effective and elusive cells are in strong communication with one another, but not through any earthly messaging protocol. Instead, instructions are relayed through the membrane, by the inhuman entities that dwell there. Such a communications network would be, for obvious reasons, impossible for us to penetrate. This hypothesis folds into the larger question of whether all or most Esoterror cells are directed by a coherent leadership (see below.)

However, one can posit the existence of a supernatural communications network without also assuming a single command structure. It may be that a comparatively low-ranking or unwilled entity serves as the messenger between cells. The fragmentary Bacharach Manuscript, seized during OPERATION SINUS GATHER, alludes to a creature known as the harsher. This parasitic Outer Dark entity feeds on the dreams of the living. The unknown author of the Bacharach Manuscript partially outlines a method of enslaving a harsher and forcing it to implant information in the dreams of a willing, distant ally. (He alludes to lucid dreaming techniques that permit the harsher to eat only the unneeded detritus of the unconscious mind, but these seem to be detailed in the document's missing pages.)

Several debriefed and deprogrammed low-level Esoterror operatives reported situations in which they received or acted upon information apparently implanted in their unconscious minds.

Steven Keenan of Belfast, apprehended during OPERATION LATHE COAT, claims to have been instructed in a dream. A being he described as resembling a cross between a giant dragonfly and a sheep carcass told him to plant a hoax anthrax bomb in Windsor Park stadium.

Alexander Wayne Sandston, a.k.a. the Virginia Milk Crate Killer, reported visitations from a similar entity impelling him to his murder spree. It allegedly introduced him to the still-at-large accomplices who aided his improbable flight from arrest throughout the summer of 2004.

ESOTERROR LEADERSHIP: AN OXYMORON?

The debate over communication coordination between Esoterror cells raises a larger question: do the cells act at the behest of a coherent hierarchy or leadership, or do they all work in parallel toward a similar goal?

A recent poll of one hundred and thirty-eight past and present analytical and operational personnel found 63% in favor of the autonomous network theory, 24% leaning toward a coherent hierarchy, with the remaining remaining undecided.

A second split appears within the minority who believe that the network is run by a hidden leadership.

Some believe that the leadership is a council of human Esoterrorists, made up of the heads of prominent cells. When we bust one major cell, they recruit a new leader from an rising cell to take his place. Analysts who reject this hypothesis argue that we would have found some evidence for it by now. Esoterror operatives are smart, but not omnipotent. For such an entity to do business, it would have to leave a paper and money trail that we simply have not found.

Others proposing the existence of coherent leadership explain the absence of evidence with a terrifying and unprovable supposition—that the leadership is inhuman and resident in the Outer Dark. Over the past few months support for this theory has come in the form of confessions from multiple captured Esoterror operatives. Zavenda Jessup (OPERATION MAZE CONNECT, Telegraph, TX), Aung Htet (OPERATION DUNE POSSESSION, Dagon, Burma) and Essop Mashele (OPERATION PROMPT FIRE, Johannesberg, South Africa) all claimed to have been directed in their actions by an amorphous entity called the Overmouth. They variously described this being as the King of the Outer Dark and the Pain Emperor. Jessup indicated that the Overmouth was the supreme leader of the Outer Dark (which she called the Far Hell.) Aung painted this being as the head of a demonic junta. This may be a case of observer projection, as Jessup is a radical monotheist and Aung a resident of a nation ruled by a close-knit cadre of military dictators.

After these three confessions, signals traffic picked up messages indicative of a multi-cell disinformation blitz aimed at us. Skeptics at the analysis desk regard the Overmouth as the result of that effort. We are meant, they argue, to descend into paranoia at the thought of this all-powerful entity, who is in fact nonexistent.

Needless to say, we are anxious to receive any and all intelligence from investigative teams to definitively lay to rest the factual basis of the Overmouth in particular, and the nature of Esoterror leadership in general.

SUSPECTED CELLS

The following classified dossier contains information gathered to date on prominent suspected cells. If they are not the subject of an aggressive ongoing investigative operation, they soon will be. Your team may be called upon to conduct it. Even if you are not assigned to tangle with these well-defended adversaries, you will find it instructive to examine the structure, personnel make-up, and tactical profile of these emblematic Esoterror organizations.

5C Associates

Billing itself as an international security consulting firm, 5C Associates is in fact a torture-for-hire operation that reeks of unremitting horror. Each of its five principal officers is a refugee from an Eastern European Esoterror cell broken up by the order after the end of the cold war. This is not all they have in common: each was a highly skilled torturer and interrogator employed by an internal security service. After several lean years, the five gradually found each other. They formed 5C Associates in 1994 but achieved little success until the heightened security environment of the post 9/11 years. Since then have acted as interrogators or consultants in such global hotspots as Pakistan, Iraq, Sudan, and the Bangsamoro provinces of the Philippines. At present they appear to use Esoterror techniques to amass wealth and influence. Their supernatural objectives, if any, warrant additional investigation.

Operations against 5C Associates must proceed with caution, as our counterparts in several conventional western intelligence agencies regard their expertise as indispensable to the war on terror. Whether this misjudgment derives from innocent monomania or is the result of supernatural corruption has yet to be established. When and if we act against 5C, it must be with utmost discretion. Their past transgressions will not be enough to bring them to heel. Indisputable evidence of continued Outer Dark activities will be required.

Bulgarian Nenand Bonchev, 59, is the group's CEO and apparent operational commander. Gruffly charismatic, he is the only founding member ever to grant a media interview. (Granted to a journalist for a Sofia newspaper, it consisted only of bland public relations-speak.) His personal charm has allowed him to forge positive and profitable relationships with many western intelligence officers, who should know better. A fan of the Beach Boys and 1960s American surf music, Bonchev is known to sing while he tortures.

Veteran of Romania's Securitate, Ion Potocean, 61, is a gaunt, bespectacled vegetarian who collects exotic birds. Generally tight-lipped, he can be drawn out on the subject of animal rights, which he passionately advocates. This position has never prevented him from inflicting irreparable suffering on human subjects. Psych profiling pegs him as a sadist with dominant tendencies.

His fellow Securitate alumnus and former lover Mihaela Iosifescu, 56, recently dedicated herself to a life of celibacy. She can be identified by her severe haircut and fondness for electrical torture. Iosifescu manages the corporation's financial arrangements. She has amassed its impressive investment portfolio, tilted toward military contractors and arms manufacturers.

Ex-KGB interrogator Oleg Zharkov supervised the construction of several black prisons for the United States government, located in the former Soviet republic of Belarus. His name appeared in the Rolodex of Theodore "Rusty" Mistaugh, a key figure in OPERATION SLAUGHTERHOUSE. He may have been an undisclosed conspirator in that scheme. Zharkov carries a locked metal box with him wherever he goes. He killed a man in Instanbul for trying to steal it.

Pyotr Pavlovich, 38, is the group's youngest member. A protégé of Zharkov's born in Belarus, he takes special pleasure in interrogating women. They invariably emerge from his care disfigured, their mouths cut open into horrible smiles. Our psych profilers believe that he is an avenger, acting out his rage over his childhood abandonment by his mother, a prostitute. His appearance in various cities of Eastern Europe and the Middle East coincide with a series of similarly executed prostitute murders. Proof that Pavlovich has used his security clearances and relationship to

5C Associates to commit a string of serial killings could be used as the necessary wedge to separate the corporation from its patrons in the intelligence establishment.

Analyst TIDY TWILL, compiler of the full 5C Associates dossier, speculates that the 5C in some way harness the psychic energy released by their torture sessions and send it as tribute to their Outer Dark patrons. One or more of them may be infected with gut wrenchers, parasitic entities who reward their hosts with inhuman strength and cerebral energy, provided that they continue their torturing ways.

The Black Bullet

Already plagued by Taliban insurgents, the road between the Afghan city of Kandahar and the Pakistani center of Quetta now faces a new and stranger threat. Over the past six months, a small but growing Taliban offshoot organization has staged a series of brutal raids against local villagers and nomads. Calling itself the Black Bullet, it postures as a guerrilla army mixing Islamic radicalism with Pashto tribal nationalism. Its actions belie its dedication to either cause. The group strikes Pashto villagers and Taliban encampments with equal ferocity. Until recently the Black Bullet has avoided attacks against well-armed NATO forces. A pair of rocket attacks last month against Canadian patrol units suggests an increase in their confidence, ambition, and capability.

The Black Bullet claims to grant its insurgents supernatural powers. For every enemy a warrior kills with a specially blessed, hand-lathed AK-47, he allegedly improves his vision, determination, endurance, and strength. The group's leader, known only as Khepeska ("the Goblin") is reputed to have killed hundreds since he began his career as an anti-Soviet mujahideen. Legend has it that he can see through mountains, overturn a Humvee with his bare hands, and has not had to eat or drink since 1998.

For seven months last year one of our double agents went through a Black Bullet recruitment process, until group members abruptly broke contact. During this time he was presented with several levels of propaganda. Eventually, as they grew to trust him further, his trainers hinted that the Black Bullet served Allah through an intermediary spirit called the Death Of Deaths. They described it as a whispering beast with nine hundred mouths, who lived beneath the sands of Kandahar province. Invocations to the Death Of Deaths included keywords typical of Esoterror summoning rituals.

Our contact also photographed a foreign arms dealer in distant colloquy with Black Bullet trainers on the camp perimeter. Facial recognition analysis matches this image to Daniel Owen Bradley, Jr., 46, of Port Mars, Florida. Bradley is a gun runner tied to a long list of suspected Esoterror operatives.

By some lights the Black Bullet might appear to be a run-of-the-mill hinterland death cult. However, their proximity to the strategic flashpoint that is the Afghanistan/Pakistan border grants them the potential for wide-ranging geopolitical destabilization. Rapid deployment of an SSF team expert in central Asian languages and folkways is strongly advised.

The Caillet Family

At the top of a forlorn hill near Larzac in a rural area of southwestern France dwells the Caillet family, a close-knit band of incestuous farmers who we suspect of systematic serial murder in the name of Esoterror. After a series of standoffs over their refusal to obey municipal ordinances, local law enforcement refuses to venture onto their property. People in the nearby communities of La Barde and Ratebout openly refer to them as cannibals, and attribute their legal impunity to a pact with the devil.

In fact, police suspect them in a series of disappearances going back to the 1950s but have never gained sufficient evidence to permit a search of the property. None of the disappeared have been found. Not a drop of blood has been left behind.

The number of disappearances linked to the Caillets may be as high as seventy. Their victims are always strangers to the area, traveling alone or in small groups. They are never observed with the Caillets, but are often last seen near their property.

The Caillet property is known to be heavily booby-trapped. Tunnels purportedly run throughout their hilly domain, allowing them to move it about with the facility of Viet Cong guerrilla fighters.

The family patriarch, Eugene, fought in Indochina first for the French and then for Ho Chi Minh's revolutionaries, and may have built or expanded the tunnel network.

The villagers claim that the tunnels are also trapped to the nines—but if no one who enters them comes out alive, it is hard to see how this has become common knowledge.

Other rumors suggest that the Caillets are just the obvious spearhead of a much larger cult, one implicating many respectable members of the local community.

The family's Esoterror connection is traceable to 1954, when one of the three brothers who then ran the farm, Julien, briefly left for Paris. There he entered a life of petty crime and drug abuse, until he fell into the orbit of café owner Marguerite Bechard. Bechard made her establishment a center of the city's avant garde art scene. Acting as a heroin-dispensing muse, she inspired writers and painters to include Esoterror-friendly themes and images in their works. The origin of her Outer Dark allegiance has yet to be established.

Bechard employed Julien Caillet as debt collector and all-around muscle. Marguerite was found eviscerated in her bathtub in 1956, after which point Julien went back home. Paris police ignored Caillet to focus on Bechard's Algerian former lover, who was convicted and guillotined for the crime.

Unless one counts a pair of shaky incidents from 1949 and 1951, the disappearances began in earnest in the fall of 1956, after Julien's prodigal return. The first likely victim was amateur painter Bernadette Laforet, who was last seen a mile from the Caillet homestead. The most recent disappearance occurred just six months ago. Parcel messenger Farid Bencherif went missing two and a half kilometers from the Chaillets, his truck still idling outside an abandoned farmhouse.

The Caillets appear to interbreed, rendering exact family relationships muddy at best. Sometimes unknown individuals are seen on the property for a while, and then disappear. They might be living literally underground on the estate, or heading off to join other enemy groups. One Frenchman bearing the distinctive slope-browed look of the Caillets was found dead after a raid on an Esoterror compound in Guatemala in 1993.

By order of approximate age, the names of known Caillets are: Eugene (in his 80s), Jean-Pierre (50s), Emilie (50s), Bernadette (50s), Bernadette-Louise (40s), Patrice (40s), Claude (40s), Julien (30s), Estelle (30s), Jacques (30s), Jerome (30s), Pilate (30s), Gorgon (30s; may be a nickname), Camion (20s), Botte (20s), Fosse (20s), Chiffon (20s), Larve (late teens), Britney (early teens), Lindsay (early teens), Eugene-Julien (early teens), and an indeterminate number of minor children.

The Circle

In 2003, amid the widespread looting that followed the fall of Baghdad to American-led coalition forces, a group of military and civilian intelligence officials went briefly off the grid to explore the basement of a mysterious facility in the heart of Anbar province.

At the time, conventional intelligence analysts believed that the small cinderblock structure located there was a receptacle for documents cataloging Saddam Hussein's WMD program. They gave it the codename WHITEBOX.

We knew the truth, or part of it—WHITEBOX was a long-standing source of anomalous phenomena, sealed shut after the first Gulf War by Saddam's secret team of Sufi exorcists. Sources agree that the structure covered the entryway into a subterranean complex, but differ on its nature and contents. A former high-ranking Baathist (informant codename BOGGLE) claims that it was a natural cave network, and that it contained a series of scrolls written in reverse Arabic script, which he called the anti-Koran. Our inside man in the Sufi exorcism team (informant codename BIPED) says that was a ruin dating from the Early Dynastic period of Sumerian civilization (approx 2900 – 2300 B.C.) and that it was home to an ancient demonic entity known to humankind as Ereshkigal, queen of the underworld.

How the cell calling itself the Circle discovered the facility remains unknown. Confirmed facts are as follows:

On April 11, 2003, marine sergeant Neal Gingerich, army lieutenant James Rice, army communications specialist Ruby Kumar, CIA arms control operative Elizabeth Mitchell, Navy SEAL Bradford Lower and NSA cryptanalyst Joanne Waller joined together to breach the structure's defenses. They encountered and overcame stiff resistance from local tribal forces seeking to prevent their entry into the structure. In the course of the firefight much of the modern upper building was destroyed by surface-to-surface missile fire. The six rogue actors penetrated into the underground structure below, remaining there until April 13. On that date a National Guard unit appeared on the scene under orders to secure the facility. They

were ambushed by the surviving Circle members. Video footage taken by the guard unit shows one of the women—most likely Joanne Waller—rising phoenix-like from the structure. If the tape is to be accepted as real, she then reduces the guardsmen to ash with a sweep of her arms.

On April 14, we arranged for the underground complex to be bombarded with bunker buster bombs, bringing about what we hope is its permanent destruction. Later forensic exploration found the twisted remnants of a bloodied ritual dagger. The blood provided a DNA match to Sgt. Neal Gingerich, who has not been observed alive since. Although it is tempting to speculate that his erstwhile allies sacrificed him to "Ereshkigal", we cannot prove that the bloodletting was fatal.

International secret warrants sworn out for the six yielded no results. A special forces unit operating in the Iraq's Kurdish hinterland spotted persons matching the descriptions of Lower and Rice fighting alongside a group of guerrilla "foreign fighters" in the fall of 2003. This group conducted

supply raids on mountain villages throughout the fall and winter. Captured members of the group proved not to be foreign jihadis, but outcast Kurds. They claimed to have forsworn Islam to worship an incarnate goddess they called the Night Queen.

A top-priority raid on the group's encampment mopped up nearly a hundred local cultists but yielded no sign of Wallace, Rice, or the others. An operational post-mortem confirmed our fears—someone within the conventional intelligence complex send a coded warning to their location hours before the raid. The Circle still has allies within the US intel community. A counterespionage operation to root them out has so far been unsuccessful.

In the years following, members of the Circle have been spotted or briefly detained in Glasgow, Scotland; Palm Beach, Florida; Hokkaido, Japan; Overjissel, Netherlands; and Bryne, Norway. Meanwhile, violent guerrilla cults propitiating a deity known in local languages as the Night Queen have sprouted up in the backwoods of Peru, Romania, Bhutan, Tajikistan, Angola, and Burma. Interrogation of captured members reveal similar doctrinal keywords indicating a common origin for all of these cults. The speed of their growth, and their ability to turn previously ordinary and rational individuals into slack-jawed fanatics suggests a psycho-viral component to the cult's ideology which cannot be entirely mundane in nature.

In each case cult members are instructed to engage in brutal and apparently motiveless acts of rapacity against small population centers. They occasionally take supplies or kidnap young potential recruits. Their primary objective appears to be psychological destabilization. As such they fit the Esoterror modus operandi of weakening the membrane. Aside from these tactical similarities, we have yet to find evidence of contact with other cells. For that matter, the Circle may be unaware that their scheme serves the cause of the Outer Dark. Whatever Ereshkigal really is, we must assume that it is an extremely powerful being of unremitting horror. Its capacity to use a small group of humans to promote its worship worldwide indicates an enemy of fearsome calculation and intellect.

Colombo Cell

Law enforcement and intelligence sources have identified the existence of a large Esoterror cell, highly integrated into local society, crisscrossing with paramilitary and underworld elements, operating in Colombo, the capital city of the island nation of Sri Lanka, located off the coast of India.

The unifying core of the Colombo Cell is an interest in pedophilia. Cell appears to have been founded by expat European sex tourists seeking protection for their illicit proclivities. They seek transformative supernatural calamity in the belief that their sexual predation will be granted free reign in a post-apocalyptic environment. In the meantime their Esoterror cell has become a lucrative underground business operation in its own right, serving the desires of a larger ring of like-minded pedophiles who remain unaware of the group's conspiratorial or sorcerous agenda.

Leader of cell appears to be octogenarian American expatriate cartoonist Nelson Shiles, famed for his creation *The Schmoops*. This comic strip, featuring the droll antics of a protoplasmic family living in an imaginary town called Schmoop Valley, began in 1956 but reached the heights of its popularity in the 1960s and 70s. Although it has become less culturally ubiquitous since Shiles turned it over to ghost cartoonists in 1987, its central characters still generate millions of dollars in annual merchandising fees, especially from the Japanese and Korean markets. Current estimates of Shiles' net worth place it at around the billion dollar mark. Shiles remains a beloved figure in the United States and is revered in Sri Lanka for his multi-million dollar donations to children's charities and the works of other NGOs. He has been exceptionally discreet in his illicit activities, both sexual and supernatural, requiring any investigation into the Colombo Cell to proceed with extreme caution. Shiles' wealth (not to mention Esoterror connections) have purchased the loyalties of many key figures in the local government and military. The organization is unable to extend its usual protections to agents running afoul of him.

Shiles first visited Colombo in 1984, wintering there until his retirement, at which point he moved there full-time. It was during these early visits that he first became involved in sex tourism. The local government turned a blind eye to pedophilic sex tourism until 1995. As it announced its subsequent crackdown, Shiles was forced to take his proclivities underground. It is at this time that he linked up with a coterie of fellow pedophiles. Although Shiles prefers boys, other associates frequent underage female prostitutes. Known associates of Shiles, and presumed fellow Esoterrorist initiates, include:

Philipp Polenz, 48, Austrian citizen, minor heir to a pharmaceutical fortune, briefly imprisoned in Germany for pandering and possession of child pornography. Both Polenz and his now deceased father, Florian, have longstanding ties to Esoterror and are thought to have been participants at the deadly Europa ritual near Bruges, 1991. Polenz is presumed to be the cell's chief ritualist.

Julian Ho, 32, joint British and Malaysian citizenship. Funds group operations by creating and distributing child pornography. Believed responsible for the murders of up to four recalcitrant subjects of his video projects. Ho can be recognized via his penchant for white suits, panama hats, and his habit of fidgeting with a gold, diamond-encrusted cigarette lighter. He should be considered armed and dangerous.

Keith Hegarty, 29, Irish citizen, former member Irish Defense Forces, ex-employee of various mercenary companies. Tours of duty for latter include Afghanistan and Iraq. Hegarty serves as the group's anti-surveillance and tradecraft expert, as well as its enforcer. Draws on pool of thuggish contacts from Colombo underworld. Sources refer to a gift for mimicry as well as a native talent for languages. Known to passably speak local languages of Sinhala and Tamil, in addition to English, Manx Gaelic, Arabic, and Pashto. Social services files from his hometown of Mallow, Ireland, reveal Hegarty's background as the victim of child sexual abuse from multiple adults in his household. Following classic abuse pattern, Hegarty violently repeats cycle with child prostitutes under his control. Carries multiple weapons; treat as extremely dangerous.

Anura, surname and age unknown, Sri Lankan

national. Former underage prostitute turned pimp runs the day-to-day operations of the cell's prostitution ring. Well connected to local underworld. Commonly found cruising the hotel beaches of the Sri Lankan capital. Identifying features: shoulder-length hair, leather baseball cap, gold-framed aviator sunglasses, 16 cm scar across left pectoral muscle (acquired in a knife-fight.)

An unidentified, high-ranking military official assists in the cell's secondary mission, the provocation of violence between rebels and government forces in the nation's ongoing civil war. Although a ceasefire supposedly pertains, both the government and the LTTE (Liberation Tigers Of Tamil Eelam) rebels continue fitful hostilities. The Colombo Esoterrorists periodically stoke the war, to create the local sense of unease and panic which weakens the membrane and makes ritual magic easier to perform. They also enjoy the operating freedom granted them by Sri Lanka's continuing political instability.

The Colombo ring also either influences, or counts as a direct member, an unidentified high-ranking LTTE leader, who provides similar services in ensuring that the protracted contract between majority and minority ethnic groups is never peacefully resolved.

Enertia Funding Partners

Venture capital firm Enertia Funding Partners, headquartered in Silicon Valley, bridges the worlds of financial wizardry and cutting-edge software innovation. It is also, if keyword-based data sifting analysis is correct, a hotbed of Esoterror activity.

Enertia Funding was formally incorporated on October 31st, 1980. In intercepted electronic traffic, its founder, Curtis Lansberry, repeatedly remarks on the significance of this date. It was the Hallowe'en immediately preceding IBM's decision to hire the nascent Microsoft Corporation to develop a disk operating system. Whether this indicates a literal link between the Seattle-based software giant and Esoterror, or is merely an

instance of magickal correspondence, remains unclear.

In the twenty-eight years of its operation, the privately-held Enertia has been instrumental in funding countless tech start-ups, many of which now comprise the biggest names in the computer industry. Its current board reads like a who's who of the financial and tech sectors.

There is Lansberry himself: 80 years old, partial heir to the Andrews Brothers packaged goods fortune. Magnified his inheritance fourfold with daring stock market speculations between 1963 and 1980. His first massive payoff occurred when he shorted major blue chip stocks the day before the Kennedy assassination, then bought back in before their recovery a few days later. Diagnosed with inoperable lung cancer in 1998; pronounced himself cancer-free due to experimental treatment the next year. Stock in Pharmatrex, the company supposedly responsible for this cure, quadrupled over the next year. Lansberry was its major shareholder from its founding to the stock run-up, after which he divested. During electronically monitored conversations Lansberry refers to "the Pharmatrex" as if it is a person or entity of the female gender.

Other current partners:
Allen McClain (b. 1955): founder and ex-CEO of database giant Freshtext. Noted philanthropist and owner of NBA, NHL and MLB sports franchises.

Forest Rawley (b. 1953): inventor of .WEX sound compression format, co-founder of tech firms LoHal and Seedlot. Famed for his participation in Futurecamp, a protégé program to promote the tech visionaries of tomorrow.

Ernest Long (b. 1944): early equity partner of tech titans Kernelwerx, Larrup Systems, and Decimax. NASDAQ board member during its switch from phone to computer ordering in the aftermath of the '87 stock crash. As CEO of Decimax, oversaw its takeover of the computer voting machine market. Prominent donor to the US Republican party and unofficial technology advisor to Presidents Bush Sr. and Jr.

Kevin McDonagh (b. 1940) Real estate mogul and

developer whose family owned huge swathes of industrial-zoned property in Santa Clara, CA before it became the epicenter of the tech sector. Gave prominent tech companies favorable lease arrangements in exchange for equity in their companies. His first wife and mother-in-law were slain in 1969 in a still-unsolved Manson copycat murder.

Together Enertia Funding is responsible for jump-starting a complex web of software firms whose products globally fuel business and Internet communications. Its board members routinely benefit from catastrophes around the world. Their investment patterns suggest advance knowledge of destabilizing occurrences.

Intercepted conversations of the partners repeatedly refers to PROJECT REPROGRAM, an massive, multi-generational effort carried out by the various firms in which they collectively hold a controlling interest. For years our analysts believed that this was an attempt to use Y2K fears as a pretext for a collapse of the global economy, possibly by engineering a worldwide computer crash on January 1, 2000. When that date passed without incident, a new team of data sifters was assigned to determine PROJECT REPOGRAM's true intent.

We have concluded that it is nothing less than an attempt to reconfigure human consciousness. The user interfaces pioneered by Enertia-related firms may subtly train our motor memories to perform tasks in certain predetermined ways. Over several generations, these ingrained actions will alter the neurological structure of users' minds. This may render them more susceptible to Outer Dark control. In other words, thanks to decades of effort by Enertia, we are not programming computers. Computers are programming us.

This conclusion is supported by thought experiments but lacks hard evidence. The troubling user interface protocols pioneered by Enertia software are now so deeply embedded in everyday computer use that rolling them back seems inconceivable. It would require a restart of the entire software industry, causing a level of economic disruption greater than was feared at the height of the Y2K scare.

ECSC (Eternal conclave of secret chiefs)

As a rule of thumb, the Ordo Veritatis investigator can safely assume that any person or group openly purporting to practice ritual magic is not affiliated with the enemy. Nor are self-styled occultists able to perform any objectively efficacious ritual. Any benefits he gains from his workings can be explained by wishful thinking, placebo power, or other psychosocial phenomena. Conversely, enemy cells carefully hide their occult affinities from us.

The exception that proves the rule is the London-centered occult society Eternal Conclave of Secret Chiefs. Adherents and critics alike tend to refer to it by its acronym, E.C.S.C. (In keeping with its backward-looking affectations, the letters of the acronym are always separated, in old-fashioned style, with periods.)

Outwardly, the E.C.S.C. gives every indication of being a group of eccentric cranks. Nearly all of its members are well beyond retirement age. They publish a mimeographed newsletter consisting of cranky screeds directed at its perceived rivals. Its Internet presence consists of a single page of HTML that hasn't been updated since 1998. Like nearly every self-styled magickal association, the E.C.S.C.'s official history lays claim to direct descent from the original Hermetic Order of the Golden Dawn. As you will no doubt recall, the rituals and structure of that iconic Victorian ritual magic lodge were supposedly derived from German adepts known as the Secret Chiefs. The E.C.S.C. makes the surely spurious claim that its founder, Ashley Blackwell, was contacted directly by these covert arch-magi. They supposedly gave him the true, full rituals which had heretofore been forbidden to the leaders of the Golden Dawn. This, they claim, occurred during the 1901 revolt around the newcomer Aleister Crowley's induction into the order, which led to its fatal splintering.

Note how this report carefully skirts the Ordo Veritatis' own origin as a Golden Dawn offshoot.

As far as our historical research department can ascertain, neither Ashley Blackwell (1853-1925) or his son and successor Conrad Blackwell (1876-1946) were involved with Esoterror or possessed genuine supernatural powers. For most of his long life, the same seems to have been true of Blackwell's grandson, the current E.C.S.C. grandmaster, Bram Blackwell (b. 1918.) Until 1995, Blackwell's conclave of geriatric occultists behaved more like a weekly tea party than an Esoterror cell.

Then Blackwell received a new package from the Secret Chiefs, containing revised rituals and the alleged secret of immortality. Since this time, no E.C.S.C. member, no matter how elderly, has died. According to one informant, none of them now looks a day over seventy.

Infused with fresh energy, the E.C.S.C. now says it's seeking new blood. However, none of the younger members stay around for long. At least seven applicants went missing shortly after contact with the group, and have yet to be found.

Blackwell has become a fixture on British television and radio as an expert on the occult. His subtly unnerving books on the subject increase in sales every year.

The ultimate role of the group in the grander Esoterror scheme is at present unclear. It may serve as covert support for younger operatives in the UK. Or its members may be gathering strength for some dramatic strike against decent society.

Key aides to Blackwell include:
Phyllis Parsons (b. 1920): widow of the African explorer, bon vivant and British officer Wilfred Parsons. Silent partner in the publishing firm Tallon & Nesbit, which publishes Blackwell's books.

Percy Monkman (b. 1921): decadent poet and painter, friend to Kim Philby and Anthony Blunt; suspected peripheral figure in the "Cambridge Five" spy ring.

Cyril Longden (b. 1930): former Anglican vicar, editor of sixteen books of crossword puzzles.

Hubert de Ruelle (b. 1927): retired theater producer.

Sarah Paton (b. 1933): the sex siren of the group; for many years maintained an uncomfortable *menage a trois* with Blackwell and de Ruelle. Married to cinematographer and pioneering Western Buddhist Arthur Coleman from 1957-1963.

K-School

In the throes of a real estate boom that at times becomes literally explosive, the city of Mumbai, India has seen a resurgence in its once-infamous organized crime scene. Its notorious gangsters of the 1990s were chased offshore after wars within its formerly secular criminal subculture turned into a bloody conflict between Hindus and Muslims. The old dons ruled from abroad for years, until the new economy attracted a younger school of sharks. This new generation of gangster vies for money, prestige, and control of the city's lucrative land development and moviemaking industries.

A newcomer to the chaotic gang scene is a little-documented outfit dubbed K-School, after its putative leader, Raaghav Kongara. Unlike his peers, the short-statured and shorter-tempered Kongara is not a slum kid on the rise but a sociopathic outcast from a fast-rising family. Accounts differ as to whether he has been truly disowned by his tycoon father, Anand Kongara, or is simply furthering the family business by alternate means. Kongara is famed for putting his lieutenants through his own version of business school, and for the sudden violence with which he strikes his enemies.

In May of 2005 Kongara was shot in the head outside a disco near the fashionable Coloba Causeway district. Whisked away by supporters, he disappeared and was assumed dead. He resurfaced in the fall, now adopting a reclusive approach to personal security. In the ensuing months, six members of two rival gangs were found brutally slain in Mumbai, Hyderabad, and faraway Dubai City. Due to successful veil-outs in otherwise fruitless investigations, our teams were able to conceal from the public the true tenor of these killings. In four of the cases the victims's bodies had literally turned themselves inside out.

The fifth victims' brain had been substantially eaten by semi-transparent worms of no known phylum. The sixth was found cut into precise two-inch cubes, freeze-dried, and stacked into a new shape in the midst of a sculpture garden.

Needless to say, the means of these killings strongly suggest that someone within K-School is able to draw upon the services of unremitting horror entities. A moderately credible rumor indicates that Raaghav Kongara, while convalescing from his 2005 head wound, was visited by a "mountain holy man" whose name translates as Ocean Musician. If this is a reference to the ocean game, Kongara's guru could be a Mystery Man. What advantage such an entity perceives in an involvement with Mumbai gang warfare is a matter for high-priority investigation.

Partei-Verein

The Partei-Verein is the name of both an underground sex club in Dresden, Germany, and the co-operative of individuals who have run the club since the fall of the Berlin Wall.

The club began life in the 1970s as a secret society of sexual adventurers enjoying heavy connections to the Stasi, the much-feared East German internal security agency. Although we have known of it since its beginnings, the strange sexual side of the Stasi has only recently come to wide public attention. During this period the Partei-Verein involved itself in prostitution, creation of high-budget pornographic epics, and the rape of political prisoners.

Connections between covert Communist thrill-seekers and Esoterror date back to the first years of the organization. The first generation of Partei-Verein leaders has succumbed to attrition or been neutralized (in operations PROMPT ISTHMUS, 1979, and PERISCOPE TOGGLE, 1986) by Ordo Veritatis forces. PROMPT ISTHMUS quashed an attempt to infect Western tourists and diplomats with a sexually transmitted disease of supernatural ferocity. PERISCOPE TOGGLE busted an experimental surgery ring bent on the development of a sickening new pleasure organ.

The current group is avowedly apolitical and denies any connection to the Stasi cadre that once shared its name. On closer examination, familial ties connect key members of the present group to the original conspirators.

Now the Partei-Verein recruits operatives, usually as unknowing dupes, by drawing them into a world of extreme S&M practice. Well-sourced rumors state that cell leaders have synthesized a drug to rapidly regrow torn flesh and pulverized bone. Thus extreme pain aficionados can be subjected to tortures that would otherwise permanently disfigure or even kill them, only to be subsequently healed. It does not take a high-level desk analyst to surmise that the source of this drug lies on the other side of the membrane. Whether it is actually a pharmaceutically active substance or (more likely) a cover for the actions of one or more ODEs, is a subject warranting further investigation.

Warning: if it is a drug, resist the temptation to use it to heal your own wounds. Side-effects of such a thing would surely prove monstrous.

Club meetings are held on a floating basis at a variety of venues. Events are private and applicants carefully screened. Most are permitted to attend only gatherings which would be deemed innocuous by experienced denizens of the underground sex scene. (Agents unused to this subculture may be shocked even by this level of debauchery, so be prepared to act as if nothing untoward is going on.)

Only attendees who attend frequently, get to know the ringleaders, and exhibit telltale signs of disruptive perversity, are invited into the inner circle. There they are exposed to the healing rituals. Several have since gone on to commit unspeakable sexual crimes. The publicity surrounding these has weakened the membrane throughout Germany. Others are used by the leaders as personal slaves.

The group's apparent leader is Marquard Fuchs, 42, both of whose parents were high-ranking Stasi officials and founders of the Cold War Partei-Verein. In his daytime life he owns and operaties a chain of high-end furniture stores. Sources suggest that his original sexual organ is unresponsive, even with the aid of erectile dysfunction medication. His second penis, magically installed on his sacrum, more than compensates for this deficiency. While many other members of the cell display classic hedonist traits, Fuchs seems to be a cold-hearted dominant type.

Nicknamed "the Slug," Ulli Scheydt, 39, serves as the group's operations manager, securing facilities and maintaining counter-surveillance. A classic submissive, he delights in the abuse, verbal and otherwise, of his co-conspirators. His skin glistens unhealthily. In his civilian life he heads a computer security consulting firm.

Former model and current model agency manager Monica Raab, 29, attracts a devoted circle of would-be club members desperate to be trampled under her six-inch stiletto heels. Last year she recovered mysteriously from early-onset lung cancer. She can allegedly open a wound in her throat, causing it to sing a hypnotic siren song.

Her protégé, up-and-coming model Marcella di Luigi, 17, has recently been seen under an assumed name at inner-circle Partei-Verein events. Rumor has it that she possesses a portfolio of compromising photos featuring her underage self and a selection of Europe's most prominent politicians and business leaders. This may explain the legal impunity under which the club continues to operate.

One of these men is assistant to the German prime minister, Rudolf Schroeter, 62, who has recently begun to block necessary Ordo Veritatis liaison with Dresden-area law enforcement. His wife of 23 years recently died in her shower, of supposedly natural causes. A police officer NNA on the scene reports that the inside of Frau Schroeter's shower door displayed a series of strange scratch marks.

The Politburo Connection

From 2002 to 2007, the Ordo embarked on a long-hoped for initiative to establish an official beachhead within the Chinese government. Dubbed DRAGONBRIDGE, this political-diplomatic outreach program proved initially successful, forging relationships with several key second-tier officials within the PRC. Through their interventions, OV teams were able to conduct successful operations, complete with veil-outs, in Beijing, Shanghai, and in the rural areas around the Yellow Mountains. In 2006 these friendly elements were able to arrange for the first fully Chinese Ordo investigative teams to take the field. Three groups were made operational, racking up solid successes in operations ELECTRON PEARL, FALSE DECEIT, and PEONY LURE.

In September 2006, members of all three teams were swept up by a internal security forces. Two investigators escaped to Hong Kong, and from there to safe houses in undisclosed locations. Their high-level sponsors were not so lucky—all were abducted, interrogated, and executed. Their deaths were announced to us with the arrival of certain of their internal organs, packaged as if for medical transplants, to OV stations in Sao Paulo and Singapore.

As DRAGONBRIDGE was a trial effort, OV operational details were tightly siloed from our Chinese partners. Any information to which they were privy must be treated as blown. Any assets they were in a position to reveal have been dismantled or disguised.

Only one conclusion can be drawn from this incident—that as high as we reached into the echelons of Chinese power, an enemy cell preceded us. Although the task is exceedingly difficult and fraught with hazard, we must make the penetration and destruction of the Politburo Connection a matter of highest priority. We cannot afford to have an emerging power of such magnitude to be covertly influenced by the Outer Dark.

SUSPECTED OPERATIVES

The following profiles detail the activities of various apparent Esoterrorists, who are either independent operatives, or are tied to more than one known enemy cell. Each subject poses operational challenges. Some are targeted for immediate apprehension. Others are of such influence that we must amass further evidence before taking action. One must also entertain the possibility that some of them are innocent of the charges laid out against them, and that they have come to our attention as the result of enemy disinformation campaigns.

Sebastian Avruj

Cult Leader

Born Feb 13, 1975, Santiago del Estero, Argentina. Orphaned at age 3 after death of mother and father in bus accident. Resident of Prado Verde Children's Home until the age of 4, when he is adopted by Venezuelan nationals Dimas and Elba Maniquis. Dimas Maniquis is oil executive; his wife, a socialite. Raised in Buenos Aires, Argentina until age of 13, when adoptive parents move him to their home in Caracas. Background interviews paint a portrait of a sensitive, well-behaved boy who begins to act out after being uprooted to a country he has only visited. Teen years a blur of drug use and brushes with gang activity. Is briefly kidnapped for ransom at age 17 by gangsters from the favelas (Caracas' notorious maze-like slums.) Soon after his release aids his former captors in kidnapping several schoolmates. Disowned by adoptive father, serves brief prison sentence before winning amnesty from corrections official Rodolfo Landa. (Local intel suggests Landa is Esoterror recruiting operative, searching Argentina's crowded prison system for promising talent.)

Upon release in 1996, attends seminary in Caracas. Reports on reasons for departure murky: may have been expelled for moral turpitude, may have resigned. At this point informally reverts to birth surname, Avruj, though is still legally known as Sebastian Maniquis.

Resurfaces in 1999 as leader of the Flores de Santa Bernadita, a pseudo-Catholic cult resident in the favelas. His following grows as he gains a reputation as a faith healer. Leverages his adopted class background to serve as intercessor between community and local officials. In 2000 the order's Caracas station agent, following Bram Blackwell (p. 75) from airport, trails him to Avruj's favela compound. In following months Avruj is documented meeting with Oleg Zharkov (p. 68) and Rahul Kalkarni, a Mumbai lawyer on exclusive retainer with K-School (p. 75.)

Supports Argentinian president Hugo Chavez's 2000 reelection campaign, but denounces him in 2006 election. Also urges followers to vote against the removal of presidential term limits in the 2007 constitutional referendum. Reason for break with Chavez's Bolivarian party remains unclear, as are Esoterror's general interests in Venezuelan politics.

Avruj is believed to maintain a covert relationship with corrupt police officers. A member of his cult runs an unlicensed crematorium in the favelas. Avruj arranges for disposal of inconvenient corpses there. If his activities include murder, he doubtless makes use of it himself.

Caracas station has yet to pin down the nature and extent of Avruj's Esoterror activities. Overt ideology of his teachings shows few keywords consistent with social or psychological destabilization. Rather they blend a charismatic Catholic recipe of miracles and divine intercession with an emphasis on a personal relationship with God borrowed from evangelical Protestantism. However his claims to exercise supernatural healing and blessing power are cause for concern: if he is wielding these powers, he weakens the membrane, even if their short term results bring needed aid to desperately poor people.

The ranks of his cult swell in 2005 when Avruj announces the ability to suppress the HIV virus with a laying on of hands.

In 2006 a rash of unexplained animal maulings occurs in the favela, near Avruj's makeshift church. Tabloid press accounts jokingly refer to this as a chupacabra manifestation.

In 2007 an informant reports to have seen a third eye open up on the back of Avruj's neck. Reliability of informant unfortunately questionable: is a long-time IV drug addict with financial reasons to exaggerate his reports. Informant vanished after promising to supply cell phone photo of manifestation.

Avruj is a thin, malnourished-looking man who with unkempt hair and beard and fondness for ragged robes cultivates a Christ-like persona. Is wary, intelligent, paranoid, and a compelling speaker.

Marco Berdila
Minor Celebrity

Born January 5, 1978, Los Angeles, CA. Son of award-winning cinematographer Eldon Berdila (*The Nothing Lovers, Mother Park, Scattered Angels*) and screenwriter Charlotte Crean (*Call Me Anything, Pretender Reef, Sad Sacks*) Lead singer for band Wrongnight 2002-2004; albums: *No*

Strong Convictions; Faking It. Appears in secondary role on reality TV show *Band Makers* 2003-2004. Becomes tabloid fixture after brief relationships with series of party-scene starlets and pop singers: Joly Fuentes, DJ VJ (Amy Kalobritis), Pam Teetle. Appears in Internet-circulated sex tape featuring Teetle in 2005. This infamy results in coinage of a new slang term, as a sex act seen on tape is quickly dubbed "a berdila." Stars in reality show, *Doing A Berdila*, 2006. Arrest record: DUIs, 1996, 1998, 2004; possession of a controlled substance 2000, 2004, 2005; misdemeanor assault 2003, uttering a criminal or terrorist threat 2006. Convictions indicated in boldface. Last case still pending, though observers expect charges to be dropped.

Famous more for his rap sheet and list of ex-paramours than any creative achievements, Hollywood party boy Marco Berdila has come to typify the era's spirit of talent-free celebrity. A frequent object of blogger derision, Berdila has demonstrated a mastery of tabloid manipulation, building name recognition through an ever-escalating series of rakish excesses. With an upcoming role in a sure summer blockbuster and the full marketing efforts of a major label behind his upcoming solo record, it appears that his omnipresence will only increase in the years to come.

Berdila came to our attention as a result of MTA, in which appearances of Esoterror keywords are correlated with proper names. Although his direct involvement in Esoterror cannot be proven, further profiling yielded the following red flags:

- Berdila's most recent reality show is produced by Morten Gislason's American subsidiary. (See p. 85.)

- A glowing appreciation of the show's "pervasive emptiness" appeared in the latest Journal Of Post-Critical Studies, penned by Annette Foss-Havergal (p. 83.)

- He was featured in the "Losers Are Winners" print campaign for Zzzyyxx body spray, produced by Julian Landau (p. 87.)

- In a rare foray into commissioned

commercial art, the cover to his upcoming CD is a monstrous bondage tableau illustrated by Asumi Yanagi (p. 94.)

- Wrongnight played a 2004 corporate gig for Enertia employees, vendors and stockholders (p. 73.)

- Berdila suffered minor cuts and bruises in the February 11, 2005 Aptos, California forest bombing, as presumably committed by Esoterror bomber Fabrizio Rulli (p. 91.) Berdila refused medical treatment after being hit by wood splinters and other flying debris.

Two months ago we dispatched an investigator to assume the role of a journalist writing a puff piece on Berdila. Over the course of a two-hour interview, our asset used numerous Esoterror keywords in an attempt to provoke a telltale reaction. She described his reaction as either supremely skillful subliminal deception, or genuine obliviousness.

We cannot discount the former possibility, which would indicate that Berdila is a highly-placed and knowing enemy agent. After continued surveillance, the assignment desk has instead come to the provisional conclusion that Berdila is an Esoterror dupe being groomed for a role in a critical future operation. Speculation on the forms this may take are given below.

- Berdila's mere presence on the media landscape is a persistent emotional irritant which makes the world seem more surreal and thereby weakens the membrane. He is in effect a walking, talking psychological warfare operation.

- High-ranking Esoterror operatives are grooming him for stardom, and will then engineer his disturbing and violent demise.

- As above, but they induce him to commit murder, which will then make him the centerpiece of the latest circus-like Los Angeles homicide trial. If they run yet another iteration of this classic Esoterror operation, they will doubtless arrange for a jury acquittal of an obviously guilty defendant, further resigning the general population to the absence of cosmic justice.

- Berdila may himself be an Outer Dark entity known as a "fame eater." The traits of this entity (and in fact its entire existence) are at present unconfirmed. All we know of it is its name, discovered in a communications intercept from the shadowy Esoterror asset codenamed Toy Girl.

Our operative describes Berdila as a buff, self-centered young man effortlessly exuding lazy charm. He appeared at times disturbed not by the experience of fame—in which he took obvious delight—but by how easy it had been to acquire. "If I was an ordinary person, like some other guy, and I saw Marco Berdila on television and in the paparazzi pictures all the time," he laughed, "I'd fuckin' hate that guy, just like everybody else."

Djoko Borcsok (a.k.a. Uncle Joker)

Pornographer

Born February 22, 1966, Pomaz, Hungary. Emigrated to United States in 1992. From 1992 to 1994 worked as nightclub promoter, manager of phone sex firm and alleged pimp in southern Florida. In 1994 founds Hot Candies, an early amateur porn site on the Internet. By 1996 expands Internet pornography empire to three dozen interrelated sites, each with its own unique focus and branding. Early foothold in fast-growing market is secured by his connections in native Hungary, a burgeoning source of sex workers after fall of the Iron Curtain. Subject is unmarried with children from three former girlfriends, all of them past or present sex workers. Borcsok maintains sole custody of each: Mary, 6, Thad, 5, and Bertrand, also 5.

Mother of latter child, Ariana Beles, died of apparent drug overdose in 2006. Death was ruled accidental but independent analysis of autopsy results by OV forensic anthropologists suggest ingestion of barbiturates may have been involuntary. Evidence proving Borcsok's complicity in her murder might serve as leverage to end his Esoterror activities.

Many but not all of Borcsok's sites are branded under "Uncle Joker" banner: Uncle Joker's Gonzo Adventures, Uncle Joker's Youngest, and so on. These sites feature caricatures of Borcsok under his pseudonym "Uncle Joker."

Documented criminal connections include biker gangs, South Florida's Cuban narcotics dealers, and old-line Mafia. FBI sources indicate that he offers access to his models in exchange for protection, and also provides consultant services to clubs owned by organized crime.

Borcsok's Esoterror contacts are unknown but his media subversion activities strongly match enemy modus operandi. His sites offer video downloads in variety of pornography genres. Although many of his so-called extreme brands would evoke revulsion in viewers uninterested in the specialized interests they serve, none cross the line into snuff, heavy violence (simulated or otherwise), much less child pornography. Instead the spiritual destabilization he offers is subliminal. Borcsok's site managers monitor client credit card activity, identifying heavy users who show a long-term commitment to his services. Using credit card information, they evidently continue their psychological profiling by then performing background checks on high volume downloaders. Selection process remains unclear, but we theorize that Borcsok targets a) the psychologically unstable and b) persons of strategic import.

The files sent to targeted customers are identical to the pornography downloaded by ordinary visitors, with one exception—additional images are concealed within the digitized video frames, via a process similar to steganography. Although these fleeting images are invisible to the naked eye, experimentation at OV Research Facility Nocturne show that they exert a powerful emotional effect. Images recovered from the altered files by our data retrieval teams are those of horrifying Outer Dark creatures, many of them otherwise unidentified. Photographic analysis of reconstructed images suggests appalling prospect that Borcsok is somehow able to capture images of the Outer Dark itself.

Borcsok was identified as a person of interest after membership on his site was pinpointed as the common element between the cases of Raul Ramirez, Sandro Licotier, and Rick Koennes.

On March 26 of last year, Ramirez cut off and cooked his own left leg from the knee down, then called local media outlets in Memphis Tennessee to announce that he had done so to reduce the impact on the poor of the coming financial collapse.

On July 9, Licotier, a specialist aboard a US submarine, was caught in a hypnogogic state, having performed a supposedly impossible act of computer systems engineering which left him minutes away from launching a nuclear-armed warhead against Dubai City.

Rick Koennes of course is the infamous Schwenksville sniper, who gunned down seven people attending the Philadelphia Folk Festival.

All were found with files from the Uncle Joker's porn sites on their home computers; occult steganographic images were located on all of these files.

Like many in his line of business, Borcsok delights in the persona of sleazemeister. He favors colorful tropical themed shirts, which he typically leaves open to expose his belly and vast expanse of graying chest hair. Uncle Joker punctuates his sentences with jabbing waves of his cigar, which is most often kept unlit. He is also associated with old-style gold-rimmed aviator glasses, hip-hop jewelery, and a pink plush baseball cap.

Until two years ago, Borcsok was regular fixture at pornography industry conventions and gatherings. Since finding traces of an investigative team's surveillance equipment in his Las Vegas hotel room, he has shied away from public appearances. Instead he now deputes his second-in-command, wiry porn actor Adam Budd (real name: Erik Haddy) for public appearances. Since exposure to that failed operation, he has become increasingly reclusive, staying inside his Miami mansion.

Adil Chaudhary
Politician

Born October 14, 1958, Himachal Pradesh, India. Emigrated to Canada with his family in 1969, age 17. Employed as roofer 1970-1973 in Vancouver, B.C. B.A. Political Science Simon Fraser University. Law degree, University of British Columbia. Assistant Crown Attorney, province of British Columbia, 1980-1989. Crown Attorney 1989-1994. Recruited as Ordo Veritatis asset 1987. Serves in OV investigative team 1988-1989. Participates with distinction in nine operations, most notably MILKSOP, TYPEFACE, MOLESKIN and TUBER. Receives wound in OPERATION CURTSY (suppurating chest puncture from unknown entity). Diagnosed with PTSD in wake of OPERATION FRAIL. Reassigned to analytical detail 1989; serves in this capacity until 1992. Resigns to concentrate on civilian duties. Runs as Member of Parliament for riding of Port Haida-St. Wilson 1997 under Liberal Party banner. Elected; appointed to cabinet as Minister Of Veteran's Affairs 2000; promoted to Attorney General 2002. Remains in Parliament but loses cabinet post with 2006 change in governing party. First suspected Esoterror contact in July of that year (approximately six months after move to opposition benches.) Further suspected contacts March and October 2007.

Today Adil Chaudhary is a stout, gray-haired and balding man whose official website portrait projects a sense of bland distinction. Twenty years ago, when he served as an OV investigator, he was a muscular, nattily-attired operative who radiated indignation at the evils of Esoterror. Chaudhary came to the attention of recruiters after independently discovering that his brother-in-law's sudden lapse into drug addiction was attributable to an inconclusive online brush with a Sisterite (*Book Of Unremitting Horror*, p. 105.) His attempt to covertly marshal B.C. Law enforcement resources to track and destroy the demon was co-opted by the OV network. Chaudhary's recruitment report describes him as determined, self-assured, and aggressively persuasive. During operations he leveraged his uncompromising charisma to pump contacts for information, used his political savvy to bend bureaucracies to his will, and charged into danger with little concern for his own safety.

In contrast to the pattern typical of our operatives, Chaudhary maintained his civilian ambitions throughout his association with the order. He won the approval of his superiors in the B.C. justice ministry through his tirelessly prosecution of complex cases of white collar fraud and biker-based drug trafficking.

At the time of his discharge from active duty with us, his out-counseling officer described him as ill-adjusted to the transition. In denial regarding the severity of his PTSD symptoms, he insisted that he could recover his "stolen sense of identity" only through additional active case work. It appeared to us that his contributions as a consulting case analyst helped to reconcile him to his new role within the order. When he resigned shortly thereafter subsequent to a promotion in his civilian job, we considered his out-processing complete.

Chaudhary went on to successfully run for federal parliament and gain two cabinet posts, one of them prestigious. His dark turn appears to have occurred in the wake of the defeat of his party. Unaccustomed to the doldrums of the opposition MP, he drifted with surprising speed into prescription drug abuse and an affair with an underage prostitute. When the girl went missing in the spring of 2006, he reached out to us through his old drop point, claiming that she had been taken by an ovvashi. A team was dispatched and found her working the streets of Toronto. It determined the girl to be untouched by supernatural forces.

Although Chaudhary expressed vehement dissatisfaction with the team's decision to place the girl in a shelter rather than returning her to his custody, the matter seemed closed. Then communications intercepts caught Chaudhary offering his services to an Esoterror handler known to us only by the codename Acorn.

A tap was placed on Chaudhary's phone lines. In an electronic anomaly we have yet to account for, only his voice can be heard in his conversations with Acorn. In March he promised to use his influence on behalf of an individual codenamed Stamina. We believe that Chaudhary used old connections to bring about the parole of federal prisoner Andre Bilodeau, convicted of the 1987 slaying of a nun in northern Quebec. In October he is overheard reluctantly supplying Acorn with the descriptions and cover names of various Order contacts, including investigative team members and his out-processing counselor. We have alerted all surviving members of this list to exert additional security precautions. Should harm come to them, or should he again compromise OV operations, we will launch an operation to reel him in. Until then we keep him under discreet surveillance, hoping he will lead us to Acorn. His apparent remorse after giving up his former colleagues suggests the possibility of turning him back to the light side. We may be able to use him as a double agent to penetrate a previously undetected enemy network.

Despite his indiscretions, Chaudhary remains married to Neelam, his wife of thirty-five years. They have four grown children: John (age 34, corporate attorney), Sheela (32, marketing consultant), Ian (31, civil servant) and Anil (age 29, personal trainer.) Until his father's establishment of Esoterror connections, recruitment desk was considering an approach to John Chaudhary.

Annette Foss-Havergal
Academic

Born December 4, 1948, Plano, Texas. B.A. Camden College; M.A. University of Chicago; Ph.D. Stanford University. Professor Of Cultural Studies, Duke University 1992-Present. Married to mining engineer Bill "Bob" Stucas from 1968 to 1972 and to poet Evan Sandiford from 1973 to 1978. Mother to two children, Millie Stucas (homemaker and Ebay seller, Plano, TX) and Shea Sandiford (HMO claims investigator, Atlanta, GA; name legally changed in 1994 from Che Sandiford.)

Subject is author of numerous papers in academic journals as well as the books *Edith Wharton: Faultlines and Agonies* (1971), *Revolutionary Readings: Criticism As Subversion* (1974), *Reframing Discourse* (1990), *The Meaning Of Meaninglessness* (1993), *Reframing Madonna* (1996), *Reframing Reality* (2001) and *Flash Craft* (2004.) Foss-Havergal is a popular lecturer, occasional television interview subject, and the presenter for the Arts Channel documentary series *Culture Popped* (two series to date, 2003 and 2005, with a third series now in production.) She also writes an irregular column of arts and public affairs commentary for the online magazine *Spite*.

Foss-Havergal is the creator and chief advocate for an offshoot of deconstructionist cultural theory which she calls meta-frame theory and is popularly known as reframing. (This is not to be confused with relational frame theory, a psycholinguistic approach to language acquisition.) Like many threads of post-modern literary criticism, meta-frame theory emphasizes the essential subjectivity of all perception and communication. Most such theories use this perception to privilege the critic's circuitously written personal observations over authorial intent or aesthetic judgment. Reframing goes one step further. Foss-Havergal, liberally appropriating terms from quantum mechanics, hints that reality itself is malleable. She describes the codification of the humanities and sciences that has occurred since the Enlightenment as a trap meant to prevent true mental evolution. The Industrial Revolution's emphasis on the material and technological distracted the human mind from its true transformative potential. Now, however, a second revolution looms, ushered in by the Internet, which she calls a subjectivity engine, just as the printing press was an objectivity machine. It, she claims, will enable humanity to reframe its collective consensus reality, ushering in a new golden age.

In informal private tutorials for her graduate students her fusion of New Age and deconstructionist beliefs becomes clearer. She claims that hoaxes, pranks and misinformation are the alchemist's tools of the 21st century. Those who perpetrate them will be able to effect measurable physical changes in so-called reality until its underlying subjectivity is finally revealed. A harmonic convergence then ensues, completely upending the operation of all physical laws.

Foss-Havergal's undergraduate course in meta-framing makes little mention of its ritualistic elements. However, she does require her students to establish flash mobs, groups of people connected by the Internet who spontaneously converge to enact cryptic collaborative performance art pieces. Where other flash mob practitioners lean toward the whimsical, Foss-Havergal encourages more disturbing content. Actions instigated by her students include the lobbing of chicken carcasses into a garden party, nailing headless and mutilated dolls to the wooden fence of a day care center, and the announcement of a hoax First International Snuff Film Festival in Durham, North Carolina. The latter stunt included the creation of glossy handbills and one-sheet posters, which were used to surreptitiously poster the town, and a convincingly complex and detailed web site, complete with credit card ticketing. Investigators suspect that contact information phished from would-be customers attempting to purchase tickets was later used in Esoterror recruitment and blackmail operations. In almost all cases the flash mob activities were picked up by wire services and national media but explained as the activities of Satanists or vandals.

Attempts to remove Foss-Havergal from her position of authority at the university are ongoing but have yet to yield results. She carefully maintains plausible deniability for her students' more outré flash mob operations. Administrators attribute their inability to act against her to her tenured status and popularity as a lecturer and media figure. Without direct proof of criminal

culpability, her dismissal, given her celebrity in academic circles, would only lead to a bidding war for her services at a competing institution.

An Ordo Veritatis operative, who will here be referred to by the name of her cover identity, Loretta Muñoz, briefly secured a position as one of Foss-Havergal's graduate students. The intelligence given above regarding the revelations provided to subject's inner circle are taken from Muñoz's field reports at the time. In her final dispatch to us, Muñoz indicated that Foss-Havergal had selected her from all of the graduate students to take part in a great working. She believed that this would be a ritual involving top Esoterror practitioners from around the globe. Muñoz disappeared from the Durham, NC area shortly after filing the report. She was found seven months later in the bloodied backroom of a maquiladora along the US-Mexico border. Muñoz apparently burst into the factory, an assembler of handheld computing devices, armed with a long knife. She used the weapon to kill four workers, injuring seven others, before holing up in a storage area. After extraction by local Ordo assets, Muňoz was taken to Camp Fantasia for debriefing. There it was discovered that she suffered from delusional amnesia, in which she believed to be a child named Du-0-p born and raised on the surface of Neptune. Muňoz was pregnant when recovered but miscarried soon afterwards. The deformed fetus was found to bear several anomalous genetic markers.

Since Muňoz's disappearance, Foss-Havergal has won the coveted Wade-Pompano Prize for advances in cultural studies, and signed an agreement to produce multimedia lectures to be made available as free video podcasts on Itunes.

Morten Gislason
Reality TV Producer

Born August 18, 1951, Holbæk, Denmark, this bearish, snowy-haired television executive is lauded and decried as the father of modern reality television. His production company, Mortetat, spawned the original *Betrayal Hunt, Talent Shop,* and *Chain Of Love* shows. It now cranks out variations of these, and dozens of other programs, for over fifty markets throughout the world. Through an aggressive program of lawsuits, it has won license fees from imitators accounting for millions of additional dollars per year.

This report will not waste the reader's time by enumerating the corrosive effects of reality television on the membrane. The question with Morten Gislason is not what he is doing to bring on the Outer Dark; the question is, *what is there that he isn't doing*? What he is not attempting now he will surely be trying tomorrow.

Gislason is unique among Esoterror operatives in that he takes few pains to disguise his allegiances. He reckons, perhaps correctly, that he is so famous and controversial a figure that any action we might take against him would do great harm to the membrane. It is also possible that has become arrogantly reckless after exposure to one or more Outer Dark manifestations. Although he never admits to an interest in the supernatural or membership in an international cabal of would-be sorcerers, he routinely uses red flag words in the many interviews he grants to the press.

One expects a man who makes his living providing entertainment to maintain an ingratiating image, but Gislason is quite the opposite. He baits reporters and burnishes his reputation as a hardball negotiator by coolly explicating his contempt for the human race.

"People are not monkeys," he said in one interview, "they are insects, stimulated into frenzies of compulsive behavior by deeply ingrained chemical receptors. I make my program for bugs. Bugs and worms. *Betrayal Hunt* is the television equivalent of a pheromone. Our higher faculties see it and are repulsed, as if by carrion. Our insect selves see it and think, this is what I truly am. This is my programming as an organism. All my shows, in one way or another, are about feeding and fucking. And dominance. Which is how one gets to feed and fuck."

In another profile Gislason elaborates: "It is because the shows are hateful, that they reveal the true squalor of our hearts, that we cannot look away. We crave stupidity, humiliation, shame. Others would say, we must rise above this. Because I hate people, I give them what they want. The programming that will strip away the lies, and destroy their souls. To the audience I say, if you think I am wrong, then look away. You cannot do it. You cannot look away."

Gislason's misanthropic pronouncements have made him a target of opprobrium in the international press. Nowhere is he more hated than in his native Denmark, whose cozy communalism he eviscerates at every opportunity. He survived two amateurish assassination attempts (neither of them sponsored by us) in the spring of 2003. In 2004 he challenged equally controversial film director Stefan Rasmussen to a duel, blinding him in one eye and destroying his depth perception.

Interviews with former employees reveal him as a controlling and coldly abusive boss. When angry, he lowers his voice. His well-funded security arm compiles detailed dossiers on his underlings. Gislason supposedly prefers to hire people whose dark secrets allow him to blackmail them into lifelong compliance.

Openly homosexual, Gislason recently terminated

a two-year relationship with model Stoeps Lambiel. It is rumored that Gislaslon measures the wrinkles on his live-in lover's faces with a micrometer, dismissing them with a large cash settlement when they reach a certain threshold. Gislason's only close non-business relationship appears to be to his brother Lars, who suffers from cerebral palsy and works for a disability awareness organization in Copenhagen.

Singleton Kroes
Foreign Policy Analyst

Born September 8, 1967, Boston, MA. Graduate of Yale University and Harvard Law School. Author of *The American Millenium* (Paragon Press, 1999) and *Threat Count: Ten Emergent Dangers To American National Security and What You Can Do About Them* (Anvil Publishing, 2005.) Member of Special Advisory Board To the President On Geopolitical Affairs, 2002–2006. Senior Fellow, National Policy Studies Group, 1996-present. Married 1995–2004 to Elisabeth Langdell (daughter of former Maine Senator Victor Langdell); subject is childless but maintains close relationship to former stepson, Wilton Kroes, who took his name in 1997.

Subject is a high-profile member of Washington intellectual establishment who until 2006 enjoyed Ordinary Secret security clearance. A frequent fixture on the talking heads TV talk circuit, he is noted for his eloquent advocacy of hard-line foreign policy positions. Kroes is employed by prestigious, Republican-aligned think tank National Policy Studies Group. Prior to 9/11 was best known for arguing for in favor of new arms race with China. Afterwards became a staunch supporter of military action in Afghanistan and Iraq. In early years of Iraq conflict, worked to build ideological bridges from movement conservatism to so-called liberal hawks. His paper "New Boundaries: Reconsidering Interrogation Techniques in the Age Of Terror" was heavily cited by administration officials in the formulation of their policies on coercive information-gathering techniques.

During his stint on the Special Advisory Board To the President On Geopolitical Affairs, Kroes' awareness of geostrategic-level psychological destabilization operations brought him to the attention of Ordo Veritatis assets. Kroes' name was submitted for evaluation as a potential recruit. A routine background check performed prior to approach unearthed a number of red flags, which led to the transfer of Kroes' name from the recruit shortlist to the suspected operatives database. Level seven textual analysis performed on his post-9/11 writings, especially his best-selling 2005 book, showed the persistent use of Esoterrorist keywords. These were arranged so as to subliminally induce feelings of panic, loss of control, and desire for violent retribution. Kroes was found to be a member, while at Yale, of the secret society Meat and Taxes.

Ostensibly a gourmet club for networkers and restaurant-hoppers, Meat and Taxes was founded by Esoterrorist operative Elmer Howard Hogan (1954-2002; mastermind of Operation Savior and the Suriname Incident.) Other notorious Esoterror operatives and suspected operatives have been included on its rolls since its foundation, including recently-identified CIA officer Theodore "Dusty" Mistaugh (Operation Slaughterhouse.)

Surveillance of the New York underground club MK-7, known as a hub of Esoterror cross-cell activity, turned up a number of photographs (from 8/13/05, 9/18/05 and 4/10/06) which a facial recognition software scan gives a median 76% chance of belonging to subject Kroes. Scrutiny of travel records indicates that he was present in New York City on all three occasions. Interviews with ex-wife suggest a dramatic change in his behavior, possibly indicative of a psychotic break, in the spring of 2004. The author of this report speculates that this may have been engendered by a viewing of the Az Zubayr tape, a viral video from the Iraq conflict which caused widespread spiritual dislocation prior to our successful suppression of it in summer 2005.

These combined facts led to the suspension of Kroes' security clearance, as effectuated by Ordo Veritatis assets within the American executive branch. Despite pushback from his patrons within the administration, the OV has succeeded in maintaining this suspension. It is important to stress that Kroes' continuing popularity within certain quarters of the power structure cannot be interpreted as proof of wider Esoterror infiltration within the executive branch. As a longstanding and effective advocate of administration policy views (on which the OV takes no position), Kroes has established strong personal and professional ties to figures of high influence.

Further, concrete evidence of any direct involvement by Kroes in Esoterror operations, beyond the psy-ops overtones of his recent written output, remains elusive. Kroes is, if our suspicions prove accurate at all, most likely a "soft sleeper", an asset or cat's-paw who performs entirely licit ideological activities while waiting to advance himself to a high position. Only after he reaches such a position will he be activated to perform more specific duties for the conspiracy.

Subject remains under limited surveillance by OV cut-outs. Plans to entrap Kroes with a staged Esoterror recruitment remain in abeyance pending further investigation.

Julian Landau
Advertising Executive

Born London, England January 10, 1967. After an undistinguished secondary school career leapt directly into London's advertising industry by catching the eye of eccentric ad mogul Armon Binns, who saw in him a brash, unpolished version of his younger self. By age of 30 was creative director of Binns and Company's London branch. During this time he launched such iconic campaigns as the M&S cigarettes "slim as a knife" ads, the Blakestone Mints happy tiger, and the Hepworth Insurance grumbling oysters. At 35 he broke from Binns to form his own boutique shop, famously poaching many of his former clients. Since then he has cemented his role as the voluble bad boy of British advertising, a constant fixture in trade magazines. Three years ago he opened a New York branch. 2005 saw the launch of his reality show, *Ad Wars*, in which he barks and screams at a group of would-be creative directors as they compete to launch fake ad campaigns. A US version launches soon; both under the aegis of Morten Gislaslon's (p. 85) production company, Mortetat.

Landau's television persona matches the many trade magazine profiles written about him: he's a stork-thin man possessed of an almost childish energy. Even more than his round, colorfully-framed plastic glasses and spiky hairdo, his constant animation lends him the aspect of cartoon character come to life. From his television appearances, our psychographic analysts peg Landau as a high-functioning bipolar. Throughout the series, he rockets from delight to screaming abuse to disconsolate despair.

Landau appeared on our radar after the 2006 interrogation of captured Esoterror asset Graham Tjissen, mastermind of the Paris airport corpse shipping scheme. Tjissen claimed that his cell commander Rupert Henley (1966-2005; ; see closed case file HWP4A54) once boasted that Landau had done more to weaken the membrane than any other operative. It was then discovered that Landau hires associates of the K-School (p. 75) as bodyguards while traveling in India, and that Curtis Lansberry (p. 73) is a board member of his US subsidiary.

Henley supposedly told Tjissen that Esoterror financed Landau's agency and encouraged his split from Binns and Company. Subsequent comparison of ads produced by Landau at Binns to those created afterwards shows an intriguing difference. Aside from his most famous campaigns, many of the Binns ads are disturbing to a confrontational degree, featuring distressed models, bleak landscapes, and an atmosphere of violent oppression. His later ads, allegedly produced under Esoterror guidance, are outwardly softer, friendlier, more welcoming. However, when our researchers placed them in front of focus groups, they always evoked a sense of indefinable disquiet. After months of analysis, it was found that many of the images were subliminally off. Models were digitally airbrushed so that their proportions were subtly inhuman. Shots of buildings manifested ever-so-slightly distorted perspectives. Off-putting color values provoked involuntary biological reactions, including anxiety and nausea.

Our research showed that sales of the products associated with the campaigns always went somewhat down for many months, then dramatically up, as if viewers were meekly succumbing to the consumer equivalent of

Stockholm Syndrome. Beamed at millions of eyeballs a day, they foster both psychic disturbance and unconscious obedience.

Although an intelligence team has been detailed to Landau for many months now, we have yet to uncover the slightest indication of either illegal or supernatural conduct on his part. Our Wall Street contacts have managed to steer some potential clients away from him, but he is in such demand that he is still turning away companies himself. Without concrete proof of wrongdoing, we cannot move against him. Tjissen has at best proven to be a witness of questionable veracity, sending our teams on several wild goose chases. Yet the possibility that Julian Landau is indeed the enemy's leading warrior in its war against the membrane remains a source of grave unease.

The Mouse
Assassin For Hire

Among our top targets for neutralization is an unknown assassin known in organized crime circles as The Mouse. Although descriptions of this elusive operative vary, our profilers have compiled a composite list of her most likely traits.

Her name seems to derive not only from her effective, traceless infiltration technique, but to her physical appearance and demeanor. Witnesses describe her as "plain," "ordinary", "forgettable", "unremarkable", "downcast" and "slightly homely." She is a slim Caucasian woman between the ages of thirty-five and forty-five. Her hair is lank, poorly cut, and of a blond, ash-blond, or light brown hue. Her height is between 5'1" and 5'5". Claims of eye color are all over the map, although one witnesses described them, peculiarly, as "clear." She favors drab, cheap-looking clothing which reveals little of her weight or figure. The Mouse favors sunglasses and a scarf, but these are never stylish or attention-attracting. Rather, they evoke, like the rest of her wardrobe, a shabby discount-store aesthetic.

A woman matching her appearance has been implicated in the murders of American mob figures Paul "the Butcher" Citrinti (in 1999), Richard "the Kid" Romano (2000), "Fast" Daniel Perchetti (2001) , Lou Farber (2001), and Albert "Peaches" Romano (2002.) Rumors persist of her involvement in seven other mob killings, though most have been dismissed by our researchers. The Mouse has now passed into urban legend among the criminal underground. These days rumor credits her with nearly any carefully planned murder in which the killer makes an uncanny escape.

In 2002 The Mouse is thought to have killed her first member of the Ordo Veritatis, investigator and book dealer Mike Saturnino, in San Francisco. His team was looking into a series of still unsolved waterless drownings that occurred throughout the summer months in the Bay Area. Hotel security cameras caught a woman matching her description entering Saturnino's room minutes before he was found lying in his bathtub, the killer's garrote lying at his feet. By the time the tape reached custody in our west coast evidence facility, the video footage had been unaccountably erased.

In December of that year, assignment desk officer Laura Gaines was shot to death in a Washington, D.C. parking garage. The lot attendant provided the most complete description of The Mouse to date. This witness was found dead a month later, from botulism poisoning. No contaminated food items were located in her home.

Subject must also be considered a possible suspect in the murders of:

- Nathan Norwich, OV investigator and homicide detective, dead of artificially induced heart attack in an Austin, TX hospital. Norwich had been admitted after suffering gunshot wounds in a firefight with Esoterror-linked human traffickers. Several nurses reported seeing a woman in scrubs near his room prior to his demise.

- Gilberta Theug, investigator and military affairs analyst, found dead in a hotel elevator while looking into alien abduction reports in the suburbs of Brazil.

- Charmione Cuvilier, lab technician at west coast evidence facility. Died in her lab from exposure to unknown nerve toxin. Appears to have been administered through a time-release capsule. There is no reason

- No drugs were found in Nathan Norwich's system — as if he had been literally frightened to death.

- The metal walls of the elevator in which Gilberta Theug was killed were buckled, as if by extreme heat distortion. Yet the luxury hotel's sophisticated fire detection system never detected a spike in temperature, which would have triggered its sprinklers.

- Charmione Cuvilier's husband reported that his wife had recently experienced a recurring nightmare, in which a woman with strange clear eyes visited her and calmly warned her to settle her earthly affairs.

As the ritual magic capabilities of the enemy still do not extend to the acquisition of such abilities, we are forced to entertain the unpleasant possibility that The Mouse is either an Outer Dark entity, or acts as a human host for same.

Although we would by far prefer the capture and interrogation of The Mouse, the danger she poses to our operatives is so great that her death is vastly preferable to another escape. Moreover, if she shows up and tries to kill you in the midst of a case, your team must weigh the possible consequences of momentarily abandoning your previous objectives to make her apprehension your new number one priority. Unless your original investigation stands to forestall a major catastrophe, drop what you're doing to pursue The Mouse instead.

to believe that The Mouse infiltrated our facility.

Aside from the likely identity of the killer and the Esoterror nature of the cases our murdered personnel were working, no common threads unite the dead. We can therefore surmise that The Mouse is called in on a for-hire basis when Esoterror cell leaders require an assassin's assistance.

How they go about contacting her remains an urgent question. Captured Esoterror operatives are routinely questioned about her, but none claim specific knowledge.

For several years her direct involvement in the occult was a matter of debate at the assignment desk. Given her role in what still appear to be routine mob hits, it seemed that she might easily be a mere hireling of the Esoterrorists, with no knowledge of their agenda or techniques. This theory lost currency when she began to display what appeared to be supernatural powers:

Dario Pedroso
Pollster

Born August 18, 1962, Sao Paulo, Brazil. B.A. in History, University Of Sao Paulo. Graduate degree in political science, Oxford University. Doctorate in political science, Harvard. Advisor to political campaigns of Senators David Keddy (Virginia), Robert Cooper (California), and Scott Duke (Wisconsin) as well as Governors Denver Marion (Michigan), Patrick Scurissa (Massachusetts) and Sydnie Alan (Virginia.) Founder and chairman of polling and research firm Pedroso, Bash, and Cibulski. Co-author of books *Breakpoints* and *Opinion Shaping*

In an era where pollsters seek quasi-celebrity as television talking heads, the reclusive Dario Pedroso stands out as a reclusive anomaly. He rarely appears or speaks in public, preferring to impart his iconoclastic expertise in small meetings with clients. Rarely photographed, Pedroso is often confused with his extroverted business partner Joe Bash (b. October 28 1944, Chicago, IL.) Bash is stocky, voluble, and amusingly foul-mouthed. Informants describe Pedroso as boyishly skinny, awkwardly formal, priggish, and reluctant to make eye contact. Bash's private nickname for him, "the stick insect" is apt—and never used in his presence. Our psychographic research department speculates that Pedroso may suffer from a mild form of Asperger's syndrome, the autism disorder which limits subjects' ability to navigate social interactions. This may account for Pedroso's strength as a social scientist. He studies human decision-making with all of the disinterested detachment of a Martian, making intuitive connections that defy conventional wisdom.

Born in Brazil with educational connections in the UK, Pedroso sank deep roots among the American political establishment. He soon gained fame for engineering legendary turnarounds in uphill political campaigns, including those of the figures listed above. He claims to have done so through a technique he calls UOS, for Unrelated Opinion Shaping.

Like other high-paid political firms, Pedroso, Bash, and Cibulski is able to change public opinion in the apparent process of measuring it, through a technique known as push-polling. In a push poll, the supposedly neutral questioner in fact floats a number of highly tendentious questions meant to change the listener's voting behavior. To pose a crude example, one might ask, "How has the revelation that John Smith's son once hanged and decapitated a dog altered your comfort level with his candidacy?"

UOS performs in a lateral manner. Instead of asking crudely detectable questions about the candidates in a race, it poses a series of obscure queries on apparently unrelated subjects. These are designed through psychographic means as yet unknown (and impossible to divine from reading Pedroso's

dry and technical tomes on the subject) to elicit surprisingly potent shifts in broad outlook by the listener. The interviewer then concludes with a brief positive mention of the candidate, which appears to create an almost post-hypnotic bond between the politician's name and this alteration in worldview.

Our researchers have studied tape recordings of UOS interviews. They contain such queries as:

> "If you knew that you were about to die and had to select a last meal, how would the means of your impending death affect your choice of foods?"

> "Many people claim to dislike certain musical notes as created by electronic instruments. Why do you think they're being dishonest?"

> "What's worse—an assumption or a reassumption?"

> "On a scale of 1 to 5, with 1 being strong disapproval and 5 being strong approval, how do you respond to the word *collagen*?"

UOS polls, conducted in the days immediately prior to primary or general elections, swung the vote to Pedroso's clients by as much as 15%--or so he claims. More importantly, independent follow-up polling by our own social scientists have found that people in areas blanketed by his efforts change their self-descriptions in such matters as party affiliation, the acceptability of sexual practices, and even religious beliefs.

Pedroso's efforts do not appear to serve any consistent ideology so much as they induce volatility in respondents' sense of self. One UOS poll may move the target population toward fear, intolerance and rigidity, where the next shifts the same group toward optimism, adventurousness, and heterodoxy.

The benefit of Pedroso, Bash and Cibulski activities to the Esoterrorists appears to be in increasing the public's suggestibility and emotional malleability. We strongly suspect that his polls weaken the membrane. Whether the subtle effect they exert on behalf of his chosen candidates is in and of itself supernatural remains unclear.

However, they clearly ingratiate Pedroso to rising stars of the US political establishment. All of the above-mentioned legislators and executives have on multiple occasions acted to quietly block funding, laws, and operational support essential for the Order's smooth operations in US territory. In fact, Pedroso first came to our attention as the connecting fiber between this otherwise disparate collection of undistinguished officials, who cross party and demographic boundaries. It is our present belief that most if not all of them are mere Esoterror dupes, and not knowing assets of the conspiracy. The depth of Pedroso's political reach renders any operation against him a matter of intense sensitivity, one that, if ill-managed, could easily lift the veil on which our organization so completely depends.

Fabrizio Rulli
Bomber

Born June 14, 1963, Milan. Fabrizio Rulli was six years old when his father, Augusto Rulli, participated in an attempted post office bombing in Milan. The elder Rulli was a sympathizer and collaborator with the neofascist organization Ordine Nuovo. The post office operation was meant as a complement to an earlier bank bombing staged on December 2nd. Rulli's bombing was foiled when an alert citizen spotted a detonator in his pocket as he waited outside the post office. Security guards tackled him; he fled, and was shot down by police. Rulli's mother, Teresa, testified against her husband's collaborators in a subsequent trial.

During Fabrizio's eleventh birthday party in 1974, a sniper's bullet pierced the window of his apartment, passing through his mother's shoulder. No one was ever apprehended for the crime. Fabrizio became withdrawn and was entered into therapy by his worried parent. Symptoms described in his files from the time suggest post-traumatic stress disorder. Fabrizio began to fail his classes, showing an interest only in mechanical repair. He dropped out of school in his early teens to take informal training as an auto mechanic.

In the late 90s, he fell in with members of a new Brigate Rosso. Although these young terrorists were the ideological opposites of his father, Rulli showed them how to make bombs. He also allegedly provided them with escape vehicles. After the 1999 murder of cabinet minister Giacinto Pallavicino,, Rulli fled to Switzerland.

There he was recruited by rapist, counterfeiter and Esoterror asset Emanuel Waber (1968-2007; see closed case file WEW8P45.) Waber showed Rulli the weakness of all human ideological systems. He argued that Rulli's father would have served the cause of what he called "metaphysical nihilism" had he only been properly indoctrinated. Since then Rulli has traveled the globe conducting bombings designed to cause public confusion and dismay.

He never contacts the media to claim credit for his actions. His explosives always contain a signature trace element (pulverized tungsten), allowing us to identify his handiwork. In a strategy perhaps conceived to keep him on the back pages of international news sections, Rulli takes apparent care never to commit mass murder. After approximately a dozen bombings, the death toll from his attacks stands at six. Another seventeen victims have been badly injured or maimed, including several blindings.

Past targets include:

Date	Location	Bombing target
March 25, 2000	Brussels, Belgium	Parking garage
November 9, 2001	Lakeland, Florida	Strip club
November 22, 2001	Gainesville, Florida	Petting zoo
January 13, 2002	Balzfeld, Germany	Nunnery
September 5, 2003	Sao Paulo, Brasil	Boat rental shop
September 14, 2003	London, England	Convention center
January 21, 2004	Paris, France	Indoor circus
February 11, 2005	Aptos, California	Protected forest
May 29, 2005	Hsinchu, Taiwan	Archaeological site
July 5, 2006	Melbourne, Australia	High school gymnasium
November 1, 2006	La Defense, France	Church
May 9, 2007	Quezon City, Philippines	Office of anti-poverty activists

In seven of the above cases, possible sightings of Outer Dark creatures occurred within three months of the bombing. This indicates that Rulli lays the groundwork for a summoning or membrane penetration by staging a bombing, increasing the distress level of the local population. Whether the other instances did not result in successful summonings, or the ODE manifestations escaped our notice, cannot be conclusively established.

Despite a worldwide APB and his presence on all no-fly lists, Rulli has shown considerable success in concealing his identity as he moves around the world. He has never been caught on surveillance camera or, as far as we know, detained at an airport or security checkpoint. The last known photograph of him predates his meeting with Emanuel Waber by six months. It shows a thick-necked, sullen man who wears his sandy hair closely cropped to his wide skull. His eyes are brown; his frame, broad. The baby toe from his right foot may be missing.

In October of last year Rulli's estranged mother was rendered comatose after suffering a stroke in Milan. Several weeks later she died after her life support was mysteriously switched off. The obvious inference is that Rulli returned to his mother's bedside to facilitate her demise.

Rocki Streets
Motivational Speaker

Born July 3, 1957, Upper Hutt, New Zealand, as Georgina Allison Louise. Convicted as a juvenile of vandalism and assault. Suspected by child welfare authorities as victim of physical and sexual abuse by father. Reported abuse denied by mother.

At age 17, travels to California under student work abroad program. Remains in country illegally, adopting identity as Georgia Streets. According to her 1992 motivational tome, *Pull Yourself Up*, works series of waitressing and retail jobs, slowly gaining weight and suffering through a series of abusive relationships. Co-workers give her the nickname "Rocky", a reference to the constant state of her love life.

In 1986 takes advantage of immigration amnesty; becomes US citizen in 1988.

Shortly thereafter undergoes epiphany setting her on the path to success as a self-help author and motivational speaker. As detailed in *Pull Yourself Up*, she sees her 280 pound frame in a mirror, examines the bruises on her face, and resolves to never again allow her deflated sense of self-worth to determine her destiny. Loses half her body weight in one year. Meets literary agent Colin Gladden (1953-2004; Esoterror asset, see closed casefile GAW9K758) while working as fitness instructor in Burbank, CA. He scouts her as promising talent in the motivational/self-help category. Gladden brokers book deal for *Pull*

Yourself Up, published under name Rocki Streets. Successful series of follow-up books and lecture circuit career follow. Expands themes from weight loss and self-esteem to *Gaining Personal Power* (title of 1997 book) and *Expanding Personal Power* (2001.) Spreads her gospel of relentless self-actualization through heavily saturated infomercial campaign. This seemingly low-rent media strategy presents her message undiluted by input from syndication executives. It turns the format into a stealth medium, granting her mass media audience without correspondingly high public profile.

Streets' infomercials contain repeated and multiple uses of Esoterror keywords. They emphasize the ability to reshape one's consciousness, and from there the world around you. Her Personal Power program takes two forms. There is the public version appearing in the infomercials and mass market publications, and an esoteric advanced workshop available only by paying high fees. These pay for for special publications, audio materials, personal appearances, and intensive workshops.

The workshops are more explicitly mystical. What outwardly appear to be motivational and trust-building exercises are in fact rituals in which participants unknowingly grant their psychic energy to Esoterror summonings. Magical leakage sometimes allows participants to become possessed by Outer Dark Entities. (See closed case files for operations VAGUE, PORTER, and WATCHBAND.) This collateral effect is apparently unintended and has not been observed for several years. We hypothesize that Streets and her unnamed Esoterror confederates have taken measures to curtail them.

Last year major operation against Streets (OPERATION UNREEL) concludes with shoot-out near Research In Motion head office in Waterloo, ON. Streets and company flee; one agent killed, two wounded and one placed on psych disability after appearance of previously undocumented devouring cloud entity. Streets goes underground; recent sightings include Spokane, LA, Belleville, IL, and Leiden, Netherlands.

Attempts to force infomercials off the air are ongoing. Efforts to track Streets from book royalty payments unsuccessful. Her inability to stage personal appearances and workshops has hampered income to her empire but influence remains. Content of mail-order publications has changed since her disappearance, from group-oriented reinforcement to mystical exercises which can be performed alone. Mail intercept service has prevented 67% of these packages from reaching their intended recipients. In their place, ideologically harmless versions of the materials based on *Pull Yourself Up* are substituted. Agent in charge of compiling this adaptation is now on permanent leave after spontaneously developing Tourette's Syndrome while completing task.

During raids concurrent with OPERATION UNREEL, audio tapes were recovered in which Streets confesses to an unknown confederate the truth behind her mirror epiphany. Streets stood in front of the mirror, ready to slit her wrists, her agony summoning an otherwise undocumented being she called a monnorr. Appearing to her only as a reflection, it offered her power beyond her imaginings, in exchange for her cooperation in communicating its message to the people of earth. The monnorr, described only as a "radiating absence with serrated teeth" does not apparently manifest on this plane. It can issue instructions to Streets through any large mirror.

At another section of the transcript, Streets refers to "ovum saturation", and her unidentified interlocutor refers to "the eraser gum gambit."

Asumi Yanagi
Illustrator of Eldritch horror

Born June 7, 1974, Kyoto, Japan. First gallery show *Visions Of Hell*, 1999, Tokyo. 2000-2001, shows *Screams Of Hell* and *Blackened World* mounted in Tokyo. *Visions Of Hell* and *Screams Of a Blackened World* published by Jigoku Editions 2001. Shows in Kyoto, Yokohama, Sapporo through 2002. First international show Galerie Arsen, Berlin, 2003. First international publication *Visions Of a Screaming World*, Ablebenpresse, Berlin. Production designer: Verdi's *Macbeth*, Tokyo, 2004. Concept designer for films *Weeping Ghosts* (2005, dir. Aoi Saito) and its American remake (2006, dir. Rafi McFall.)

Asumi Yanagi's manga-inspired visions of shocking torment in a surreal landscape now fetch upwards of $500,00 for a large canvas. Working in acrylic, with a stylized, strongly graphic approach to representation, her horror art leaps genre boundaries. It appeals equally to otaku, fans of the macabre, and the high art set. Critics from the latter group applaud her sense of pop culture deconstruction, particularly her *Schmoops In Hell* series. (For more on the Esoterror connections of the popular Schmoops comic strip, see p. 72.) In these paintings the beloved comic strip characters are gruesomely and hyper-sexually dismembered by entities strongly reminiscent of the Outer Dark. Included among their tormentors are obvious representations of snuff golems, sleep hags, and members of the Practice.

Yanagi herself is a personable woman who affects the sweetly nonthreatening persona of the nerdy boy's dream girlfriend. She wears fashionable spectacles, dresses in jeans and message Ts , and favors kooky, crayon-colored hairstyles. In interviews she is assumes a persona of giggly modesty. Yanagi asserts that her disturbing images allow her to rid her mind of anxieties, and that they're all in good fun. Interviewers, especially for high-end art magazines, tend to imply that her peppy, unassuming presentation is a feigned extension of her art. As Malin Winters-Quiles wrote in the June 2006 issue of *ArtFORage*, " Yanagi's candy-coated personal affect exists in a disturbing discourse with the sado-masochistic despair of her figuration, forcing those who encounter her to envision her as the subject of violently pedophilic fantasy."

Although Yanagi works slowly, unveiling only half a dozen large-scale pieces a year, her works frequently come up for sale, as their owners experience sudden downturns in fortune. Along with a string of broken marriages and financial failures, at least six purchasers of Yanagi pieces have been murdered or gone missing under ominous circumstances. Forensic examinations of three victims (Nancy Portland, Burbank, CA; Hitomi Suwa; Tokyo; Luciana Stelovsky, Vilvoorde, Belgium) displayed telltale signs of injury by Outer Dark entities.

The Order has commenced a program of purchasing and destroying Yanagi's canvases, but the rapidly spiraling prices of her work have placed this operation under budgetary stress. Furthermore, her chief gallerist, Takako Daike, carefully screens prospective clients to ensure maximum exposure for her client's work. She has refused several attempts by OV assets to purchase Yanagi's works. This selectivity is a standard business practice of the art world, and may nor may not indicate Esoterror leanings on Daike's part. It does reduce us to covertly removing paintings from crime scenes we investigate. We are currently evaluating a proposal to preemptively steal her works from their current owners.

Widespread print and electronic reproduction of her images poses a further problem. So far it seems that the original paintings themselves pose a direct threat that their reproductions do not. We have seen no correlation between ODE appearances and ownership of her books or prints. That said, purchasers do seem to suffer from a higher rate of mental disorder, including depression, suicidal ideation, anxiety attacks, and low impulse control, than the population at large.

We have found that many low-level Esoterror assets own Yanagi prints and merchandise. Possession of these items likely serves as a receptivity signal to recruiters. Known Esoterror recruiters Menon Roco, Andrea Pieper, and Marius Beuran have all been observed at Yanagi art openings. This open activity may be curtailed after an OV extraction team used the occasion of a Yanagi opening in Bucharest to apprehend Beuran.

In August of last year, Yanagi was briefly taken hostage at Daike's offices by a fanatic admirer who claimed that she's stolen imagery from his dreams. A police standoff ended when the hostage-taker, after lengthy discussions with Yanagi, surrendered himself to Tokyo police. Shortly thereafter, he died in police custody. An autopsy revealed that his lower intestines had disintegrated.

Unaffiliated Operatives

Our work would be simpler if only we lived in a world of absolute moral certitude, with sharp lines delineating friend from foe. Unfortunately for the field agent's sense of investigative clarity, it is possible to be aware of the Outer Dark but to belong neither to our side, nor to Esoterror. Certain components of the supernatural underground use their knowledge for their own ends—some selfish, others allegedly altruistic. We refer to these unpredictable individuals as UOs—unaffiliated operatives.

Although it is the official position of the Order that all contact with arcane forces weakens the membrane, on occasion it becomes expedient to deal with these dwellers in the gray zone. Although they can often provide pivotal information and field support, investigators must carefully weigh the benefits of any relationship with them against the risks. Some are in contact with forces they cannot fully control. Also, one must always bear in mind that a UO who barters information *to* you will barter information *about* you.

The Anthropologist
Esoterror Defector

This profile is a conclusions precis from the Signals Intelligence Analysis branch. Work product available on a need-to-know basis. Except where otherwise noted, all code names in this document are OV-assigned, as per protocol DP11-A.

Three months ago, a routine communications intercept from a source putatively originating in Karlsbad, Sweden was identified by ETS as a voice call from Esoterror leader PRECEDENT to otherwise unknown Esoterror asset, hereby codenamed LIMNER. Relevant passage of intercept as follows:

```
PRECEDENT: It's confirmed. The
   Anthropologist has gone rogue.

LIMNER: To the pluggers³?
```

---

3 An Esoterror codename for Ordo Veritatis.

PRECEDENT: Don't think so. You'll have
    to neutralize him first.

LIMNER: He knows we know?

PRECEDENT: Likely. Not sure. Neutralize
    him.

Scouring the intercept database, we recovered another communication made two days later, between PRECEDENT and another unidentified Esoterror leader, codenamed CRATER.

PRECEDENT: Failure on the Anthropologist
    front.

CRATER: I told you to--

PRECEDENT: I put a top hitter on it, but
    Anthropologist was tipped. Laptop,
    toiletries, basic clothing were gone
    from his cottage. Another team is
    sitting on his city apartment but
    nothing so far.

CRATER: You should never have let him
    handle the cube.

PRECEDENT: At least now the epiphany
    effect is proven.

CRATER: Small consolation. He'll go
    plugger now for certain.

PRECEDENT: That's what I'm hoping.

CRATER: Elucidate.

PRECEDENT: If he goes to ground, we
    won't find him. Seeking out a plugger
    cell means sticking his neck out. When
    he does, we cap him. Bag a plugger
    team in the bargain.

CRATER: Where will he try the approach?

PRECEDENT: He might try Toronto. He met
    the blond there. Or New Delhi.

The reference to "the blond" in Toronto is perhaps to Janice Mitkowski (1981-2007), an OV investigator killed in the line of duty in Jakarta, Indonesia, during OPERATION UNMAKING. We have yet to pinpoint a mission on which she might have encountered the Anthropologist. Mitkowski's civilian home base was Toronto, so unauthorized contact may have occurred between missions. Investigation of Mitkowski's activities during 2006 and 2007 may lead to information on Anthropologist, or put team in position to make contact, if he is indeed hoping to defect.

We have yet to conclusively identify the Anthropologist. Our best possibility is Duncan Chang (b. May 5, 1965, Flint, Michigan) adjunct professor of Sociology at the University of Toledo in Ohio. Chang was reported as a missing person by his father, Kam-Yuen Chang, at about the same time as the communications intercepts above. He lived in a apartment in the city of Toledo and maintained a modest lake house in Dellroy, OH, about three hours away.

Chang keeps a low Internet profile. His brief biography on the University of Toledo site lists his specialties as Urban Studies, Economic Studies, and the Sociology of Deviance. His few published papers examine from different angles the connections between economic inequality and social deviance. His most salient paper was the last he published before a long dry period. It posited that one could increase the level of social deviance in a subculture by causing its members to believe themselves to be economically disadvantaged compared to society at large. This thesis may have attracted the attention of Esoterror recruiters. A statistics analysis team has determined that minor sexual offenses, including indecent exposure and public lewdness, have increased by 27% in the Toledo area since last year. This may be coincidence, or could be the result of an Esoterror psychosocial subversion operation spearheaded by Chang.

Another possible correlation: rise of an urban legend in disadvantaged Toledo neighborhoods about "the straph", a sexually transmissible disease which causes one to speak in tongues, see ghosts, and hear colors.

Suggest field interviews with friends, family and colleagues to develop new leads on Chang and his possible Esoterror connections.

If Chang has defected, we want to recruit him as a voluntary informant, removing to a secure facility. (Naturally precautions must be taken to prevent Chang from learning location of facility or identity of agents, should he prove to be a double. Full medical examination must be conducted to ensure that he does not carry exo-parasites or exhibit possession symptoms.) Mild coercive measures are authorized to persuade Chang to cooperate, as are promises of financial reward. Take maximum precautions to ensure that contact team is not under surveillance by Esoterror assassins. As alluded to above, they will seek deaths of both Chang (if he is in fact the Anthropologist) and the investigative team.

Gemma Courtland
Crusading Exorcist
Born July 24, 1983, Pembrokeshire, England. Father: Jonathan Courtland (1953-1994.) Mother: Jane Courtland (1954-1985.) Last known location: Zurich, Switzerland.

The glittering dark eyes of Gemma Courtland, coupled with her youthful figure and forceful personality, have proven too much for more than one young male investigator. Her twin chrome-plated pistols and supply of specially fortified sacred water have saved our operatives' lives on more than one embarrassing occasion. Ms. Courtland is an implacable foe of the Esoterrorists, and a scourge to the creatures of the Outer Dark. Yet her activities do nearly as much to threaten the integrity of the membrane as the beast she stalks. Despite the help she may be able to offer you in the prosecution of your cases, all field investigators who cross her path are urged in the strongest possible terms to apprehend her, once and for all.

A journal confiscated from Gemma's hotel room after a botched apprehension attempt sheds light on her peculiar history and methods.

Gemma's father Jonathan acted as a self-ordained priest in a tiny Catholic splinter group known as the True English Church. He and his fellow worshipers, who met in the back of his bicycle repair shop after hours, subscribed to numerous heresies. They denied the authority of the Vatican, refused vernacular mass, and eschewed priestly celibacy.

Gemma's mother suffered from what may have been undiagnosed post-partum depression. When she began to report encounters of ethereal, watchful entities, Jonathan dismissed these as hallucinations tied to her fragile mental state. When Gemma was two, Jane Courtland slit her wrists. Shortly after the funeral, Jonathan glimpsed one of the beings (an Outsider, perhaps?) and underwent a mental breakdown of his own. Teaching himself the rudiments of Catholic exorcism ceremony, he became a traveling demon-hunter, performing DIY bug hunts first in England and then throughout Europe. During this time he discovered the Esoterror conspiracy, adding it to his enemies list. Deeming Courtland too unstable for OV recruitment, a veil-out team attempted psychological reconditioning. This process failed to overcome his emotional barriers.

During the early years of his solitary crusade,

Courtland left Gemma in the care of his sister. When Esoterror assets bombed the sister's house, Jonathan plucked her from school and kept her at his side. From a young age he trained her in the techniques of exorcism and combat. At the same time he tutored her extensively in maths, science, literature, and the classics.

Jonathan died fifteen years ago, when Gemma was ten. Wounded after an bloody encounter with an organ grinder, he was packed into an ambulance—which then exploded en route to hospital.

Gemma, following a plan pre-established by her father, adopted a cover identity and went into hiding as an orphan heiress at a Swiss girl's school. When she reached the age of fourteen, she hit the road, systematically tracking and annihilating the Esoterror cell that killed her father.

The enemy of our enemy is not our friend. Gemma Courtland takes no precautions to keep her efforts out of the headlines. She doesn't apprehend or turn Esoterror assets—she murders them, often spectacularly. Worse, her pseudo-Catholic rituals exert genuine magical effects. Even though these are always used to impede or destroy supernatural entities, they render the membrane porous just as surely as the works of the monsters she seeks to destroy. Repeated attempts to explain this to her, to tame her and convert her into a good agent of the Order, have miserably failed.

There is no other recourse. If you see her, shoot to kill. And don't forget to remove all trace of her existence when you perform the veil-out.

And whatever you do, don't fall in love with her.

Luciano Gaudio
Occult Broker

Born March 4, 1956, Bagheria, Sicily. Arrests: vandalism, assault, pandering, extortion, theft, hijacking, suborning perjury, bribery, sexual inference, corruption of a juvenile, improper disposal of a corpse, indignity to a corpse. Convictions: none.

Luciano Gaudio, a.k.a, the Altar Boy, was born in Sicily to a father deeply enmeshed in the local Mafia. Through his adolescence and early adulthood, He followed in his papa's boot treads. Shortly after the discovery in 1976 of three executed former Mafioso in the hills outside his hometown, Gaudio decamped for Rome. He took over the territory of a rival pimp, then worked his way up from street panderer to enforcer for a high-end prostitution ring. This too, he took over. Among his clients was the self-styled sorcerer Carlo Gerini , the Count of Puntonello. Seeing another opportunity to diversify, Gaudio attached himself to Gerini as bodyguard, procurer, business manager, and all-purpose thug. Gerini flirted with Esoterror involvement throughout the 1980s but kept his distance, preferring to invoke magic of dubious efficacy to enhance his sexual and pharmaceutical adventures. By the time of Gerini's fatal and apparently auto-erotic hanging in 1991, Gaudio had established a worldwide contact list of occultists, deviants, parapsychologists, and the middlemen who serve them.

Advertising his services as a broker and consultant, he has since operated as a high-priced vendor of discreet services to the occult underground of Europe and beyond. His nickname, "the altar boy", derives from his favorite catch phrase, in which he charmingly disclaims all knowledge and responsibility of whatever his clients are about to do with the information, equipment, or other contraband he has just supplied them with. "What do I know? I am only an altar boy."

Gaudio is aware of both the Ordo and the Esoterror conspiracy without being a member of either. He refuses to disclose the identities of his clients or nature of his transactions, but it is clear that Esoterror forces number among them. The Ordo has never acted against him, despite his unsavory character and mercenary attitude, because he has on occasion proven an invaluable paid (*highly* paid) asset to us.

The Altar Boy dresses in sensual high style, favoring men's fashions with a couture edge. He often affects a long red silk scarf, which he wears in the manner of a priestly stole. Gnarled gold rings dot his fingers. Gaudio is long-faced, balding, and thin-lipped. Unless they have done something to make him fear them, he flirts insinuatingly with young interlocutors of either sex. His perverse demeanor belies his impotence; a 1989 encounter with an incubus has left him with a case of erectile dysfunction no drug will remedy.

Gaudio can be contacted by via SMS messaging to an untraceable phone number. Through means unknown he is able to completely elude electronic surveillance. After contact is established, he will make arrangements to meet in person with a trusted client at a café either in Rome or Milan.

By strict policy, he will not sell information regarding clients in good standing. This courtesy extends only to individuals, not organizations. We speculate that a large portion of his annual proceeds come from clients who do not really require his services, but wish merely to purchase his silence.

Gaudio's intelligence is reliable but expensive. As his fees for information begin in the high five figures, Ordo operatives may only use Gaudio as an informant with prior budgetary authorization from their Mr. Verity. Instead we urge investigators to pound the pavement and do their own, infinitely more affordable, legwork. On occasion Gaudio may approach an investigative team to offer an exchange of data. As long as the information you're trading does not relate to the Ordo or compromise operations, these arrangements are acceptable to the organization.

The Ordo prefers to use Gaudio for non-informational transactions, when it is necessary to purchase artifacts, tomes, charms, and specimens on the black market. As with his intelligence, it is best not to question his sources and methods. Most recently Gaudio was able to secure for us the mummified appendage of a death tapper, which proved essential in developing a serum to reverse a case of churning rot suffered by agent SAGO ESPRIT.

Recent events suggest a temporary cash flow problem for the Altar Boy. He has taken to contacting us with valuable leads into possible membrane-weakening phenomena. Gaudio is likely using us as an instrument for the punishment of delinquent clients. Even so, his tips always lead to something of interest.

He has refused repeated lucrative offers to share his evasion techniques with us. We have offered him more than enough money to retire on. His reply is always the same: without the game, he wouldn't know what to do with himself.

Paul Genestoux
Research scientist

Born December 31, 1950, Rennes, Bretagne, France. Holder of twin masters degrees in Physics and Mathematics from the University of Paris. Doctorate in Biochemistry, also from University of Paris. Married to boyhood sweetheart Emilie Seuzerat 1972-1998, and to former research assistant Fermine Ronchin 2000-2005. Four children from first marriage: Gerard (b. 1973; lab technician), Jerome (1975-1998; died of leukemia), Claire (b. 1976, technical writer), Yves (b. 1990, music student.)

The website for French biotech firm CYCADE lists the gray and unassuming scientist Paul Genestoux only as its head of research. In truth Genestoux is, along with his gregarious brother-in-law Maurice Freiss, a company founder. (Freiss is married to Paul's younger sister Marie-Claire, an interior designer.) Where the walrus-like Genestoux cultivates a dull, almost sleepy demeanor, the broad-shouldered Freiss is a never-ending well of compliments, guffaws, and witty banter.

CYCADE, located in a sleekly modernistic industrial park on the outskirts of Paris, makes its money as a service bureau for other researchers. Academics pay them to perform DNA sequencing, dipping into their research budgets to farm out time-consuming genetic grunt work to an efficient and fully accredited outside agency.

Maurice Freiss uses his income from CYCADE to furnish his home in the country and keep himself in new sports cars. Genestoux funnels it toward a stranger hobby: performing genetic sequencing on mutants, aliens, and demons. We know for certain that Genestoux has attempted to use his technology to map out the biological blueprints of supernatural entities including torture dogs, skitches, and torture larvae. His capacious storage tanks doubtless harbor the remains of untold other horrors.

Genestoux, though not a member of the Ordo Veritatis, is aware of our organization and our general mission. It is permissible to contact him for analysis of biological samples which may be of non-terrestrial origin. He has shown the repeated ability to to identify supernatural organisms which baffle our own forensic researchers. However, Genestoux will insist on payment in kind, receiving samples of alien/demonic organisms, and as much information you can provide him about their behavior in the wild. While general discussion of supernatural threats is authorized when the potential benefits warrant, you are under no circumstances to provide him with details of OV operations or personnel. Genestoux is as willing to acquire samples from Esoterror assets as he is from us. It is all too easy to imagine him revealing information about your investigation in exchange for a particularly interesting creature sample.

It is our current opinion that Genestoux is a pure researcher, interested only in the scientific truths that can be wrung from a comparison of human DNA to those of supernatural beings. At the same time, we fear that Freiss could pressure him to apply what he learns to marketable therapeutic techniques or pharmaceutical compounds. The thought of widespread human exposure to monstrous DNA conjures the worst fears of science gone amok.

Two years ago we were able to place an undercover operative in CYCADE's offices. From her we learned that Genestoux kept at least one living specimen—a glutinous, ropy, two-headed beast reminiscent of Hugh Lofting's pull-me-push-you, which he called a hishyoho—in the lab's sub-basement. Merely allowing others to see a captive creature would surely pose a threat to the membrane. The thought of a YouTube video is truly chilling. The consequences of an escape would be even worse.

Our undercover asset was dismissed when found in an unauthorized area. Since then Genestoux and Freiss have been kept under light physical and electronic surveillance. It is our hope that Genestoux will remain a somewhat untrustworthy contact, and that an operation against him will not become necessary.

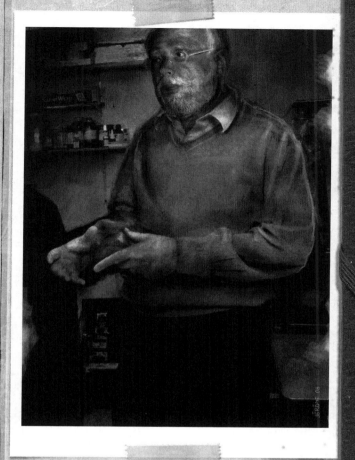

"Jimmy Wayne James"
Serial Killer

Date of birth unknown. Known murders: Nicole Nakamura, age 23, April 2, 1999, Salt Lake City, UT. Alexis Son, age 27, December 15, 1999, Coalville, UT. Lisa and Stanley Garner, March 9, 2000, ages 25 and 58, Heber City, Utah. Stephen Soenarto (a.k.a. "Annette Foxx"), age 19, September 7, 2000, Bloomington, IN. Juliana Smocot, age 29, July 3, 2001, Bloomington, IN. Stephanie Grass, age 26, November 22, 2001, Orland, CA. Anita Wohlers, age 16, April 30, 2002, Harper Woods, ID. Claire Keller, age 32, December 28, 2002, Austin, TX. Angel Muradian, September 24, 2003, age 36, Brentwood, CA. Nathan Hornby, age 46, July 23, 2004, Argentine Township, ID. Kristyna Timkova, age 22, July 21, 2005, Rochester, NY. Camila Giessel, age 23, May 4, 2006, St. Pete Beach, FL.

The unknown serial killer who identifies himself to police in taunting letters as Jimmy Wayne James sent his first missive to Salt Lake City homicide detective Sam Reid six months after the death of his first known victim, college student Nicole

99

Nakamura. Since then he has left a trail of bodies across North America, following them up with letters to media outlets and law enforcement officials which only serve to increase his grim legend.

James originally stuck to a tight modus operandi: he preyed on attractive young women, sexually assaulted them post-mortem, and dismembered them, burying the body parts and leaving the head by the side of a rarely frequented roadway. Victims were slain with a single bullet to the back of the head. His first variance from the pattern came when he killed Stanley Garner, father of victim Lisa Garner, who apparently interrupted his kidnap attempt. Stanley Garner was left where he was shot.

As of the killing of Anita Wohlers, evidence of sexual assault vanishes, though James leaves one of his readily identifiable letters on the corpse to prove his identity. In 2003 he makes another surprising shift, killing a male who is also a minor celebrity: the golf pro and part time actor Angel Muradian. Muradian rose to tabloid fame ten years before, as a peripheral figure in the circus-like murder trial of disgraced golfing great Lambert Abdel. Acquitted killer Abdel was briefly suspected in the Muradian killing until James' letter, sent to cable network CNN, prompted detectives to look for his increasingly subtle signature on the body.

James now seemed to be seeking increased fame, and public dismay, by targeting celebrated individuals. He continued this trend with the 2004 murder of controversial documentarian Nathan Hornby. This time his missive to the media included a harrowing tape recording of the victim's frantic pleas for his life.

The name James is assumed to be a pseudonym, an attempt to sound like a serial killer. He has never been described by a witness, much less caught on security camera. His DNA was found on his first five victims (save for Stanley Garner, who was shot from a distance), but has never turned up in any database.

Each message is printed on an old-fashioned dot matrix printer. They are mailed from locations throughout the country, suggesting a high-mobility occupation, such as long haul truck driver. In some messages James alludes to a personal fortune, but this is likely a deception.

Several hoax letters and videos purporting to be from James have been ruled out by document analysts. In March, April and May of 2003 a drifter named Christopher Scott Dunkley committed a series of five copycat killings before being apprehended in Salem, OR. Messages to the media were only crude matches for his style. Dunkley claimed to have met the real Jimmy Wayne James at a truck stop, saying that he had granted him a "franchise." The truck stop described by Dunkley does not apparently exist.

Although his communications include no Esoterror keywords, they do include frequent references to the occult. He is often referred to in news accounts as a Satanic killer. Our analysts have instead determined that James is likely not an occult practitioner, displaying no knowledge of the subject that couldn't have been gleaned from obvious pop culture sources. We believe that his references to the devil, demons, and the black crow who caws in his ear are all meant as a scare tactic, and perhaps to lay the groundwork for an insanity plea, should he ever be caught. That said, supernatural manifestations spike throughout the world whenever a new body is discovered or an authenticated letter revealed to the press. The forces of Esoterror are surely content with James' activities as they are and have no wish to deter him by making contact.

James' negative impact on the membrane is such that an OV team has been detailed to assist police whenever a new body turns up. The existing detail, having met the same brick walls that confound police, have asked to be relieved. Should another killing occur, the case will be reassigned to a fresh team.

Faye Kerns
Freelance Reporter

Born Faye Lucille French, December 17, 1966, Jacksonville, FL. Married Ted Kerns, 1986. Son Edward David Kerns born 1987, died 1997 of apparent cerebral hemorrhage. Divorced Ted Kerns 1998. Journalism degree from Jupiter Career

College 1999-2005. Staff writer *Jupiter Weekly Shopper*, 2005. Fired after inserting unvetted article into paper claiming Florida as a hot spot of demon infestation. Freelancer 2006-present for magazines including *Spectral*, *Ghost Tracker*, *New Beliefs*.

According to files retrieved from her hard drive, Faye Kerns witnessed a spectral manifestation when her son died before her eyes during a school basketball practice in Indiantown, Florida. Kerns believes that the horrifying, malign entity she saw that day killed her son. After an attempt to distract herself by seeking a new life as a reporter, she has embarked on a mission to use her newly acquired journalism skills to expose the appalling reality of the supernatural hidden behind the veil of everyday life.

Kerns has made herself into a complicating factor in a number of important investigations, including OPERATIONS CALORIE, LAKEBIRD and CAUSALITY. Through a combination of luck and hard work, she has shown an alarming propensity to sniff out supernatural activities throughout the US east and south. Signal intelligence targets her communications; her movements have on occasion tipped us to cases in need of investigation.

Kerns wears thickly-applied makeup, out-of-fashion eyeglasses, and aggressively colorful pantsuits. Her bleached blond hair is usually combed into a chaotic rat's nest. She smokes (but claims to be quitting) and speaks in a rattling machinegun rhythm.

Do not be fooled by her homey, soccer mom persona and propensity for mispronouncing big words. Kerns is a wily and determined adversary, and a threat to any veil-out procedure. She appears to suspect the existence of the order, although she seems to believe that we represent a "black agency" of the US government. Kerns repeatedly pitches her editors stories promising to uncover this agency. So far our contacts at the magazines she works for have managed to forestall her.

Kerns cooperates with efforts to apprehend human abettors of the occult, and to destroy supernatural beings. Her ultimate goal, however, is inimical to ours: she seeks to familiarize the public with these horrors. Of course, widespread acceptance of their existence would weaken the membrane and advance the cause of Esoterror. Our assets have on numerous occasions attempted to explain this dynamic to her, but have failed to persuade. PPU speculates that on an unconscious level she fears the paralyzing delayed grief that might follow the abandonment of her crusade.

The reporter's emotional volatility, suspicion of authority and unwillingness to work with others render her an unsuitable candidate for recruitment. As vexing as she is, she is still an innocent and as such deserves the full protection of investigative teams. Should she insert herself into your case, you are to protect her from threats, even those she stumbles into of her own accord. Our wish to remove her as an obstacle should not be regarded as permission to allow her to be murdered by enemy agents or devoured by Outer Dark entities.

Willa Robison
Cult Leader

Born September 9, 1936, Gabbs, NV, as Willa Northcross Callahan. Married radio repairman Elbert Robison, 1954. Moved to Mammoth Lakes, CA, 1956.

In 1957, Elbert Robison experiences a life-changing vision of a UFO visitation, in which he is taken aboard an alien craft and introduced to an entity called Coadun. Elbert reports the encounter in a mail order pamphlet, advertised in back pages of paranormal and science fiction magazines. Through 1960 Robison continues to expand his oeuvre, based on psychic communications from Coadun and several other entities from his home planet, Lumen. In 1961, establishes the Coadunite Center, a quasi-religious compound at Mammoth Lakes. Elbert and Willa preside over a communal household of misfits, seekers and worshipers. In May of 1962, Willa makes her first claim of mental contact with a Lumen entity, a spiritual guide she calls Ingusar. Community grows steadily, exploding in numbers during the hippie era. Additional Coadunite centers established in Taos, New Mexico; British Columbia, Canada; Sao Paolo, Brazil; and Hokkaido, Japan. Membership reaches 10,000 paying donors, only a tiny fraction of whom live in Coadunite compounds. (The

group's own figures overestimate membership by a factor of 10.) Movement contracts after murder-suicide at Taos commune in 1975, in which its young priest shoots his ex-girlfriend and turns the gun on himself. Continues to shrink after 1987 death of Elbert Robison (coronary embolism.) Willa takes on role of high priestess, now claiming direct communication from Coadun himself.

Current estimated number of followers is 1,000. Of the satellite compounds, now only British Columbia and Sao Paulo still extant. Average attendance at weekly meditation meetings at main compound now approximately 100.

In May of 2002 Willa is hospitalized after a debilitating stroke. This leaves her paralyzed from the neck down and unable to communicate. Her protégé, 56-year old former used bookstore owner Bruce Spurgeon, adopts the mantle and staff of leadership. By June Willa undergoes an inexplicable and complete recovery, resuming cult leadership. Spurgeon breaks with the cult, establishing a splinter group in nearby Bishop,

CA. Willa revises the cult doctrines, reporting a new and more complete communion with Coadun during her period of "regeneration." In the wake of this announcement, membership creeps up again, attracting a new generation of UFO mystics. A new Coadunite website goes online, with a hit rate eventually settling at 8,000 unique visitors per week. Cult receives sporadic press interest, invariably spotlighted as a charmingly kooky human interest story. Coverage spikes during UFO flaps.

The Coadunite cult has always preached a message of universal love and brotherhood. It emphasizes inner transformation through meditation, discussion, and positive thinking. Worship services conclude with parades around the compound, in which Willa waves maternally to followers, perched atop her sparkly 1968 Cadillac convertible. She wears her everyday garb, consisting of flowing chiffon gowns covered in shiny appliqués. Other followers promenade behind her, also colorfully costumed, bearing banners and papier maché representations of spaceships, heavenly bodies, and alien beings.

Order analysts consider Robison and her Coadunites nothing more than a harmless and not particularly fringe group until March 2005. At this time an investigative team scours the mid-mountain region of California in search of a rampaging residue daemon. Contact with the entity leaves two agents seriously maimed and on the brink of death, far from emergency medical assistance. Willa Robison appears on the scene, bearing a "crystal staff", which consists of an old wooden yardstick with a lump of clear quartz glued to one end. She undertakes a "soul reading", drops into a meditative trance, and performs a faith healing. Both agents not only recover but return to full strength within days. To his later dismay, Robison's procedure also reverses one agent's vasectomy.

Robison performs a remote viewing, enabling the group to locate and destroy the residue daemon. She describes it as a Null-Unprime, an entity composed of negative thoughts sent from Crepus, the enemy planet to Lumen. Invasions from Crepus have increased in recent years, Robison explains. Her stroke, she alleges, was the result of a Crepusian attack. However, the forces of light had turned it against them, granting her healing powers, which she had used many times since her recovery.

How Robison acquired the abilities to conduct healings and remote-locate Outer Dark entities remains unknown. She also claims to have taught the technique to disciples dispersed throughout the Americas. What seems to be clear is that her use of these powers has weakened the membrane around Mammoth Lakes. Although the use of Coadunite powers may survive a cost-benefit analysis during casework, we are left with the challenge of discouraging or preventing their use overall. Robison and her followers are pleasant, friendly people, who will not be shaken in their naïve beliefs. Recruitment to the order has proven impossible, as the metaphysical prism through which they perceive these paranormal events is incompatible with the truth as we know it. Our next step in this delicate matter is, as of this writing, undetermined.

Somerset Panther
Alien Big Cat

Legends of alien big cats, or ABCs, comprise a standard element of Fortean lore. Throughout the world people report the existence of animals which should not exist in a given habitat. In southern England's Somerset National Park, the reigning ABC is a large black panther local papers have nicknamed "Mr. Somers." Officially regarded as an urban legend, the creature has been spotted over the course of several generations, starting in the 1970s. ABC hysteria reached its peak in 1984, when nearly a hundred sheep belonging to several nearby farmers were found with their throats torn out by an unknown animal. Naturalists attributed the deaths to a pack of wild dogs, which conservation authorities discreetly exterminated over the next few months. Yet sightings of the panther continue to this day. In 2004, hikers made casts of well-preserved big cat tracks. Traces of black fur found in the bark of a fallen log the next summer were tested and shown to be consistent with the *panthera onca*, or jaguar, an animal native to South and Central America.

No supernatural intervention would be required to let a wild animal loose in the vast Somerset park. It is rather harder to explain away the long history of sightings, which extends past the jaguar's 12-15 year lifespan. As actual physical evidence of genuine animals mounts, naturalists have been forced to conclude that a breeding population exists in the park.

News accounts of panther sightings increase supernatural activity throughout the British Isles as they occur. It is possible, though in no way proven, that an Esoterror faction stocks the park with jaguars for precisely this reason. However, if a breeding population were found, the uncanny aspect of the story would be dispelled, strengthening the membrane.

Vicky Yau
Culture Jammer

Born March 19, 1985, San Francisco, CA. Media Studies undergraduate, University Of San Francisco, 2006-present. Parents: Vincent Yau (b.1966, Carmel, CA; structural engineer), Mae Yau (b. 1968, Taipei, Taiwan.) No siblings. Personal blog *Vicky's Variances*, 2002-2003. Culture jamming blog *The Messedness*, 2005-present. Briefly engaged to Martin Warshawsky, MBA student.

On first glance, the effervescent activist and aspiring artist Vicky Yau scarcely looks like a threat to the membrane. On her website the manifesto of her tiny movement, Dissonography, names as its goals the opening of "human consciousness, questioning of media authority and hot fun." Dissonography is a cuter stepchild of the situationist movement, which attempted to use art techniques such as collage, manifesto and spontaneous performance to engender Marxist awareness. Dissonography uses the Internet, streaming media and pranks to freak out the middle class and middle aged. Yau vaguely argues that her "guerrilla love interventions" encourage their subjects to reconsider their place in a confusing world. Her critics call her a self-promoter profiting from ad placements on her site.

At first, Yau and her collaborators performed her interventions in San Francisco, but its lingering vibe of counter-cultural acceptance led to a disappointing scarcity of raised eyebrows. She then embarked on a series of road trips into the heart of middle America, choosing counties and towns that voted heavily Republican in the 2004 election cycle.

The typical intervention is highly visual, exposing bystanders to a peculiar or inexplicable sight or activity. These are then videotaped and uploaded to streaming media sites. Sometimes webcams record reactions to her pranks in real-time.

Her most famous "love interventions" include:

- The Truck Of Disappointment, in which an ice cream truck trawls through a suburban neighborhood, attracting children with its siren tinkling bell. When the kids arrive, Yau and friends serve them free mushy vegetables, causing dismay and crying. Surprisingly angry confrontations with parents ensue.

- Trash Rejection: members of Yau's team rifle through household trash bags, recovering spoiled or embarrassing items. Posing as government inspectors, in full hazmat gear, they return the trash items to the people who discarded them, claiming that they contravene various absurdly worded new ordnances.

- Street Buttering: in which teams of scantily clad clowns cover sections of street or sidewalk with butter and margarine.

- Drive-Through Intercepts: team members hijack the audio of a fast food drive-through window and try to talk customers into eating healthy and "less spiritually degrading" foods.

Nothing about Yau's writings or interventions suggest a familiarity with, or interest in, the occult. Nevertheless, reports of hauntings, possessions, and demonic manifestations increase anywhere from 12-40% in the places where she conducts them. The more culturally conservative the location, and more heated the response to her activities, the greater the spike in supernatural occurrences. Yau is unknowingly replicating the Esoterror methodology, making the world seem more surreal to its inhabitants.

Though her writings portray her as cocky and amusingly self-righteous, in person Yau is almost painfully withdrawn, preferring to have her frequent collaborator, half-Samoan ex-quarterback Oscar Parliament, act as her spokesman.

We recommend the dispatch of an investigative team to conclusively establish whether Yau is connected to Esoterror. If she is not, shutting her down and veiling her out without violating her civil rights will prove exceptionally challenging.

Dread Locations

Homo sapiens has always believed in haunted places—bewitched locales where the wise man dares not tread. As a member of the Ordo Veritatis, you know these as as Low Membrane Strength Locations (LMSLs), places where the barrier between this world and the Outer Dark have become perilously weak.

MEMBRANE PERMEABILITY

The integrity of the membrane cannot be measured using current technology. (Attempts in the 1930s to detect membrane strength through limited sorcerous means led to the infamous Menlo Park disaster, and the reinstatement of total restrictions against ritual usage by Ordo members that remains in place to this day.) However, the relative strength of the membrane within a general area can be indirectly inferred through observation of secondary effects, most notably:

- reports of hauntings and unexplained phenomena

- rates of murder and violent crime

- rates of mental disease, substance addiction, cancer, and heart disease

- incidence of extreme or anomalous weather patterns (known as the pathetic fallacy effect)

- incidence of electronic equipment failure, including glitches in satellite photography and audio recording devices. Anomalously high (or low) failure rates of batteries and computer hard drives is also indicative of low membrane strength.

In populated areas, polling data is also useful in measuring fluctuations in membrane strength. Our demographic research unit (DRU) conducts polls throughout the developed world. Masked as ordinary consumer or political surveys, they are devised to elicit subliminal responses to certain keywords.

Rate Of Decay

The membrane is now approximately 39% thinner than it was in 1900. Rate of decay varies in accordance with the general level of global distress. It accelerates during periods of crisis and flattens or even decreases during times of prosperity and confidence. The past century's first severe dip occurred in 1925, as the spiritual malaise brought on by WWI reached its height. A second bottoming out is seen in 1946, as the enormity of the Holocaust sank into public consciousness and an era of cold war paranoia beckoned.

Decay rates are relative to consensus perception and do not reflect an objective metric of global quality of life. Even as the worldwide incidence of war, famine, crime and poverty has decreased through the final decades of the 20th century and the first of the 21st, media perceptions drive collective anxieties to all-time highs. This correlates with an ever more rapid rate of membrane decay.

The chart below marks the ebb and flow of membrane permeability from 1900 onward. Note how the bulk of the decline in overall membrane thickness has occurred since the mid-1990s.

A very severe dip follows the December 6, 1969 killing at the Rolling Stones concert at the Altamont Speedway. It seems to mark the death of hope and optimism in the youth movement of the 1960s.

The confluence of the O.J. Simpson murder trial and the Clinton-Lewinsky scandal, with their accompanying sense that the news had become surreal, did more to degrade the membrane than World Wars One and Two combined. The attendant horrors of the latter events engendered relative dismay by the standards of their time. Nonetheless, they lacked the frisson of the bizarre that allowed comparatively minor stories of the 1990s to eat away at the membrane.

LSMLs, which are more compromised than the

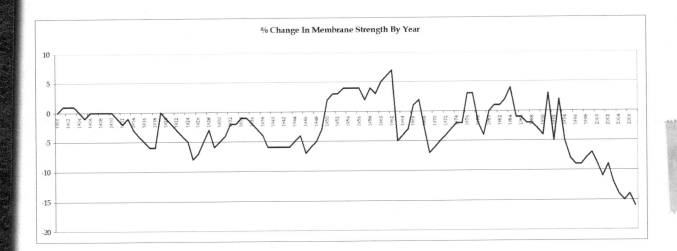

% Change In Membrane Strength By Year

membrane as a whole, serve as the vanguard of a changing membrane. They are to our consensus reality what the seasonal polar ozone holes are to our atmospheric integrity. When the overall membrane drops in strength, the ability of unremitting horror creatures to act through LSMLs increases commensurately. In fact, there is some reason to believe that the barrier at an LSML degrades even faster than the surrounding membrane when the global sense of reality sustains a palpable hit.

Effects

Although the harm done by increased rates of violent crime, mental and physical disease, and catastrophic weather patterns are not to be dismissed, the chief ill effects of membrane permeability are supernatural in nature. The thinner the membrane in a given area, the easier it becomes to perform summoning rituals. Outer Dark entities find it easier to use their innate powers, whether for their own purposes or through enemy intermediaries. Thus LSMLs draw the enemy to them. This dynamic carries both benefit and drawback: the enemy is easier to find in such places, but is more powerful when encountered. In any contact with the enemy at an LSML, tactical advantage can be gained by somehow luring the unremitting horror entities away from the zone of maximum membrane permeability.

If and when the enemy stages a physical invasion

of this world from the Outer Dark, this will surely take place through the world's various LSMLs. Every time you repair an LSML (see below), you make it more difficult for the adversary to commence its inevitable endgame.

Origin Of Damage

While the membrane is thinning worldwide, localized psychosocial conditions can reinforce or weaken it in comparison with its average thickness. Damage to the membrane leads to the formation of an LSML. Damage occurs when an area becomes associated by the local populace with violence, brutality, unreason, or strangeness. Urban legends surrounding an LSML reinforce it over time. Supernatural activities permitted by an area of thin membrane become part of accumulated body of negative lore. Thus does a negative feedback loop come into being.

An LSML may remain potent even when the incident sparking the original damage has been long forgotten.

Repair

Just as the entire membrane regains thickness over time in the face of positive psychosocial conditions, LSMLs can be repaired through activities that reduce its psychic footprint among local populations. A successful veil-out can not only provide a logical explanation for the supernatural activities of the enemy, but can also debunk the LSML as a place of special terror. The human mind craves mundane explanations for unlikely events. Useful cover stories to veil out an LSML include:

- hoaxes by college students and other pranksters

- supposed publicity stunts conducted by horror movie producers

- attempts by real estate developers to buy up land cheaply

- "marsh gas" and other pseudoscientific explanations for anomalous phenomena

- Known LMSLs

This section provides precis reports on LSMLs of current interest to the organization. It has been chosen to indicate a range of LSML types, varying by quality of intelligence, type of location, and degree of immediate menace.

Camp Pata

Location: Bong Mountain Range, Liberia, Africa.

Physical Description: An unprepossessing, disused timber camp in the mountain highlands of Liberia, recently refortified by its Esoterror-sponsored guards.

Security Status: Guarded by heavily armed and well-paid, if poorly trained, mercenary soldiers. Soldiers are dispossessed veterans of 1999–2003 Liberian civil war who have not been successfully reintegrated into that nation's still-struggling civil society.

Origin of Membrane Damage: Timber camp was the site of two separate atrocities. During Liberia's 1989-1996 civil war, forces loyal to then-rebel leader Charles Taylor displaced local population, causing them to occupy timber camp as ad hoc refugee housing. Rebel forces attacked timber camp in 1993, killing hundreds or even thousands of displaced individuals. During subsequent 2000-

2003 civil war, forces hostile to then-President Charles Taylor used Camp Pata as facility for imprisonment, torture and execution of perceived enemies. Death tolls from either the 1993 massacre or ongoing 2000–2003 atrocities are impossible to accurately estimate but may approach 10,000.

All human atrocities give aid and comfort to the forces of Esoterror, and weaken the membrane by bringing Outer Dark creatures to the borderlands between realities to feed on the fear and misery they generate. Events in Liberia, and especially at Camp Pata, reached a level of depraved madness, including killings of, and by, child soldiers, paralleling the worst modern war crimes.

Operational Status: Camp Pata is occupied by enemy forces, consisting of a Esoterror cell of unknown size and composition. Fragmentary intelligence suggests that the cell consists of both local and foreign enemy operatives.

Camp does not appear to be actively protected by the current Liberian regime, which seeks to rebuild the nation through a truth and reconciliation commission. Rather, its remoteness, compounded by lack of means on the part of local authorities, allow Esoterrorists to operate there with impunity. (Unreconciled soldiers continue to pose a serious general obstacle to the new regime's pacification efforts.)

Esoterror operatives at Camp Pata are assumed to be engaged in ritual magic. Outdated informant reports suggest that their main objective was something other than summoning, although unknown entities have been attracted to the site as an unexpected by-product of ritual activities.

Symptoms of supernatural activity include night time choruses of unearthly screams, detonation of phantom land mines, sightings of dead relatives, and aforementioned bogey sightings. Items constructed with timber culled in nearby region may resonate with malign supernatural energy. (Unsupported speculation: are Esoterrorist occupiers fashioning ritual implements out of this wood and importing it to other groups, in hopes of fortifying their magic?)

Action Recommendation: Our governmental

sponsors are unable to authorize large-scale military or paramilitary attack on Camp Pata, as a resumption of violence in Liberia could easily destabilize its fragile pro-Western, pro-civil rights regime. Recommend further monitoring for evidence of escalating manifestations. Should manifestation level increase, dispatch of investigative team, authorized to conduct small-scale covert op depending on conclusions of their recon efforts, may be indicated.

Special Circumstances: An Ordo Veritatis contact is in place near the Camp Pata site. This person's identity is available on a strict need-to-know basis. This individual is not infiltrated into the encampment itself (thus the sketchy information on its personnel) but is periodically permitted limited contact with it.

A prior informant has ceased contact and is presumed dead. Action teams will be required to exercise extreme tactical discretion in protecting the life of the brave and selfless civilian who has stepped in to fill his or her shoes.

The Caperton 1233

Location: Multi-level suburban homes built according to the Caperton 1233 plan can be found throughout the United States and Canada, especially in housing developments constructed between 1982 and 1994.

Physical Description: The Caperton 1233 was a widely available set of home plans for a multi-level home in the "country transitional" style. The comfortably familiar design includes a balcony, two-story foyer, built-in fireplace, decorative columns, three spacious bedrooms, a two-car garage and a side deck with kitchen access.

Security Status: Caperton 1233 homes are so numerous as to be impossible to monitor or patrol. Locations of up to 86% of such homes in the continental United States are tracked in our central database. When indications of Esoterror activity are found in a community, the assignment desk performs a check to see if any Caperton 1233s are proximate. If so, agents assigned to the scene are made aware of its presence and tasked to perform basic recon to determine if it has become a locus of supernatural phenomena.

Origin of Membrane Damage: In 1990 an urban legend developed around the hit 1987 motion picture *My New Dad*, starring Eddie Murphy and Michael J. Fox, by then already past its prime as a video catalogue title.

The movie itself is a family comedy with a mildly rebellious streak typical of its era. The plot turns around a DNA test revealing that the true father of a fast-rising young advertising executive (Fox) is a gruff African-American janitor (Murphy, in old-age makeup.) Many of the scenes are set in a pleasant, upscale suburban home belonging to Fox's mother (Blythe Danner.)

During the spring of 1990, a rumor spread that the movie captured a ghost on film. During the famous food fight sequence, several shots show what seems to be the blurry silhouette of a young girl near the fireplace. A explanatory legend sprang up, claiming that a young girl had been raped and murdered in the house where the scene was shot. Video rentals for the old title increased nationwide as amateur ghost-hunters freeze-framed the scene of the supposed manifestation.

Eventually the film's producer commented on the urban legend, explaining that the scene had been shot on a soundstage. No murdered girl was ever linked to any location used in *My New Dad*. Nor did the set resemble the actual interior of a Caperton 1233 home.

Nonetheless, rumors took hold in the Vancouver, Canada suburb where exteriors for the film were shot. Poltergeist activity, bobbing lights, and eerie temperature changes were soon reported around the home in question. On January 12, 1991, neighbors responded to a series of flashes and shrieks coming from inside the house. Its residents of the home were found inside, partially eaten.

That home was demolished and a veil-out staged, but the legend soon metastasized. Residents of suburban communities throughout North America came to believe that *My New Dad* had been shot near their homes. Ghost houses, all conforming to the Caperton 1233 plan seen in the movie, were identified in Hartford, CT, Bellevue,

WA, Plainsboro, NJ, and Nashport, OH. Minor paranormal phenomena were reported around the first two; events at the second two led to deaths by apparent entity attack. In the years since, another sixteen Caperton 1233 homes have lit up as hotspots for hauntings and gruesome demises.

Operational Status: An estimated 16,000 homes nationwide match the Caperton 1233 plan. This number is too large to permit a systematic demolition effort. Also, there is no indication that the legend would not then migrate to other very similar home designs, as appears to have already happened in Vista, CA (2005) and Acton, MA (2008.)

This is unfortunate, as Esoterror assets have begun purchasing and occupying existing homes built from the Caperton 1233. They do so in the belief that the negative psychic energy surrounding them increase the success rate of summoning rites.

Although we succeeded in having the plan withdrawn from the market in 1998, we cannot prevent enemies from having new ones built using blueprints copied from the original. As the design is now considered somewhat dated, new starts using the plans are highly likely to be motivated by Esoterror objectives.

The Dark Church

Location: 438 Norton Avenue, Boyle Heights, Los Angeles

Physical Description: A modest two-story church in Spanish/Colonial, with bell tower (condemned) sits at the corner of Norton Avenue and 6th Street, in a mixed residential/commercial neighborhood.

Security Status: Guarded under our auspices by employees of Strick McFadden, a local security firm. Shifts are overseen by a retired investigator now working for Strick McFadden. Guards are equipped with sidearms and can make immediate radio contact with the home office, which is then relayed through a double-redundant messaging system to the Los Angeles OV station. An SSF squad can be dispatched to 6th and Norton within 27 minutes.

Origin of Membrane Damage: The Norton United Methodist church was founded in 1937 and prospered until the mid-1960s. At this time, dwindling attendance brought about by demographic shifts led to the building's sale to a primarily Hispanic evangelical church in 1965. It was briefly occupied by Korean Baptists before being deconsecrated in 1971. Later that year, during its attempted sale to a fourth congregation, it was taken over by apolitical squatters. They were in turn pushed out by members of the radical organization Collective Action Vanguard (CAV). This Esoterror front recruited campus radicals and used them to commit destabilizing acts of political violence. Led by glassy-eyed enemy operatives Minerva Neal and Bryce Cannon, the group staged acts of vandalism and petty protest throughout 1972. Then, in 1973, it staged the simultaneous kidnappings of celebrity offspring Catalina Clark (19, daughter of actress Zina Clark), Jamie Boston (18, son of star baseball player Ron Boston) and Lesley Constant (17, daughter of news anchorman Cornell Constant.) None of the victims was ever found.

Neal and Cannon were killed two years later in a shootout with an OV extraction team in southern Mexico. CAV dupes Charles and Janie Hardie, apprehended in a station wagon with a bloody shirt belonging to Clark, claimed that the bodies had been hidden somewhere in the church.

Despite an exhaustive search of the church premises, no trace of the bodies was ever found. The church has become the property of the city of Los Angeles. Efforts to demolish it have been stymied by injunctions. The Clark and Constant families have intervened to preserve the site on the grounds that it may contain their relatives' bodies.

In the meantime, the church has withstood numerous episodes of vandalism, including a strange 1998 incident in which it was painted black overnight. Although located in a densely populated neighborhood, no one saw or heard the vandals at work.

Exactly one year later, an OV asset videotaped four suspects slipping into the poorly secured church. Subsequent examination of the tape identified two of them as known enemy operatives Johnny "Potatohead" Mull and Anna Garrick, until then thought to be marginal figures in the Esoterror conspiracy. Before aid could be dispatched to the scene, the intruders performed a ritual unleashing a creature later designated as the Norton Street Entity. The entity burst from the church basement and into the neighborhood. Visible only in the infrared spectrum, the creature fatally mauled seven citizens over a three-day period. An SSF team trapped and slew it on the Golden State Freeway on August 13, 1999.

Since then we have interrupted as many as three possible break-in attempts by enemy agents. Esoterrorists succeeded in accessing the property again in September of 2003, summoning Winged Entity Seven. This creature, modeled on the mothman of longstanding urban legend, maimed two agents and a civilian before flying off for parts unknown.

Action Recommendation: Maintain present security protocols at site. Continue legal efforts, working through assets in Los Angeles municipal government, to overturn injunctions on demolition of property. Launch renewed effort to persuade Clark and Constant to drop them voluntarily.

Garrison, TX
Location: West Texas

Physical Description: Garrison is a town of approximately 2200 people located on a flat, arid plain. Its picturesque town square dates back to its founding in the 1860s as a railroad watering stop. The town's proximity to Big Bear National Park and the Davis Mountains attracts a modest but steady tourist trade.

Thanks to pieces of conceptual art installed on its outskirts by the late sculptor Ervan Primus, this tiny town serves as an improbable locus of cultural activity,. Twin foundations preserve and display his works and those of his contemporaries. A new amphitheater hosts a modern dance extravaganza in the late spring and an outdoor film festival in August.

Security Status: Guarded. A single OV station agent is always assigned to deep cover duty at Garrison. At present this job is performed by retired sheriff and former OV investigator Preston Eves, who now writes a column for the local weekly newspaper, the Garrison Highlight.

Origin of Membrane Damage: Garrison poses a curious case to the student of LSMLs and their related activity. No single triggering event seems to explain its history of paranormal events. Further, these occurrences depart from the dripping horror that characterize most points of connection to the Outer Dark. Here paranormal events tend more toward the peculiar than the terrifying. No particular history of violence attaches itself to Garrison. If people here are prone to madness, it is more in the form of endearing eccentricity than dangerous psychosis. However, Garrison does match the LSML profile in other ways, including strange weather patterns, troubling DRU responses, and electronic instability. This has led former analyst PLURAL CASHMERE to theorize that Garrison intersects with a trans-dimensional reality other than the Outer Dark—one comparatively benign in nature.

Garrison is the subject of a notable urban legend, a variant of the Roswell New Mexico UFO crash mythology. According to local lore, the decommissioned army base outside town once served as the ultimate repository of alien bodies recovered from the Roswell crash. Garrison residents who believe the tale invariably nod knowingly at the mention of Area 51. They describe it as a cover story to hide the real alien graveyard. The officer who led the convoy to Garrison is always named as a Captain William Valero, who is said to have retired here. No records of exist of either a Garrison taxpayer or American military officer matching the name William Valero.

Some residents further insist that three years after the Roswell Incident, in July 1950, an earthquake shook the army base. Small humanoid figures, covered in a green glow, were that night seen prowling the town. The standard story implies but never quite states that the supposed bodies had been in a state of suspended animation and escaped from the base after regaining consciousness. In some tellings, the aliens vanish in a cloud of green vapor after the Garrison thrum (see below) begins to sound. This in effect becomes an origin tale for the otherwise inexplicable thrum.

Nature of Phenomena: Three major recurring paranormal events are associated with Garrison:

The Garrison Thrum: The town is periodically subject to seismic vibrations accompanied by a nearly inaudible rhythmic thrumming sound. The vibrations are strong enough to rattle dishes. A person standing on the open ground can feel them in the soles of the feet and as a rumble in the chest, as one might expect with a much louder bass sound. Thrums occur in a mathematically unpredictable, non-musical pattern, and last for periods as brief as thirty seconds and as long as thirty minutes. The thrum occurs most frequently between March and September, with virtually no occurrences in December or January. The jolts originate from no consistent epicenter. Theories to explain the thrum range from the mass movement of migrating subterranean insects to the operation of equipment below the supposedly abandoned military base outside town. None satisfactorily explain the phenomenon. The idea that the thrum is a vestigial effect of the technology that rescued the Roswell aliens raises more questions than it answers.

The Bollard Glow: Perhaps the most iconic of Ervan Primus' Garrison sculptures is *Rimrock Bollard,* an earthwork constructed from flat stones, arranged around a rusted metal post. Located two miles outside town, it is a frequent tourist destination for the culturally inclined. On extremely clear nights with rising barometric pressure, the stones and post of the sculpture are said to glow a faint green color. None of Primus' writings suggest that he was responsible for this effect. His daughter and executor, Dinah Primus, says that he would have been aesthetically dismayed by the glow, and by the circus atmosphere it provokes.

The Toll Clicks: For two decades radio host John Toll has hosted *Tolling the Hours,* a talk show devoted to primarily to conspiracy theory and the paranormal. From March of 1997 to May of 1999, Garrison resident Jeremy Brown detected a strange audio anomaly on recordings he made of Toll's show. At least once a week, always while discussing paranormal or UFO-related topics, Toll's voice was overridden by a series of ominous rhythmic clicks. Brown eventually contacted Toll to discuss the audio mystery and became a regular on his show. Others were able to replicate the effect, but only while taping *Tolling the Hours* in the Garrison area. Recordings made from the same station but in other towns never included the clicks. Shelby McEwen, an amateur sound analyst from Byron, Georgia, identified the clicks as the amplified working of insect mandibles. This comparison was later confirmed by our own audio technicians.

At the height of the phenomena, Toll went to Garrison, amid great fanfare, to broadcast his show. The clicks became louder and more insistent on recordings made of the broadcast from other locations in town. During his stay both the Garrison thrum and Bollard glow manifested themselves. Three days before the scheduled end of his run, Toll abruptly left town, claiming to have been confronted and threatened by an "agent of influence." (Although we have periodically run veil-out operations on Toll, including episodes of mild intimidation, the Order was not responsible for this confrontation, if it happened at all.)

Toll's departure occurred in April 1999; the clicks rapidly trailed off after that, ending completely a few months later. The radio host later accused Brown of hoaxing the entire event. Brown left Garrison the following year, pursuing construction jobs throughout the southwest. On August 8, 2005, he was found dead in a gas station restroom outside El Paso, TX. His death was ruled an amphetamine overdose. Toll continues to broadcast, abruptly changing the subject whenever his callers quiz him about the clicks. After Brown's death was announced, he took a two-week leave of absence from the show, but never acknowledged it on air.

Operational Status: Known Esoterror operatives occasionally show up in Garrison, often staying until they can view the Bollard lights and experience the thrum. Perhaps due to the conspicuous surveillance of station agent Eves and his old buddies in the sheriff's office, they rarely stay for long. If any of them have staged aggressive operations in Garrison, or have used information gleaned her to launch them elsewhere, we have seen no evidence of it.

Action Recommendation: Retain the services of Preston Eves as long as he is willing and able. At present the grant committee is considering a proposal from occult science analyst COOPER COMPARE to study the characteristics of the Garrison phenomena to determine if a membrane to a benign alternate reality in fact exists here.

The Guardham Line
Location: County of Herefordshire, England

Physical Description: An allegedly ancient ley line running roughly parallel to the A440, near the Welsh border. The line passes through the hamlets of Dulham, Shaffer's Mill, Bridgeford, Guston, and Hardy Carr.

Security Status: Hostile territory.

Origin of Membrane Damage: The Guardham line is mentioned as one of the many ancient pathways through Britain identified by armchair archaeologist Bernard Creel in his 1921 book *Many Walkways*. Though dismissed by professional archaeologists, Creel's works were, to his surprise, soon taken up by occultists, including the writer Fiona Blackater and dowser Henry Forsyth. They ascribed mystical significance to the lines, treating them as geometric patterns between England's various henges and megaliths. In her 1936 novel *The Horned God's Cry*, Blackater names the Guardham as the most sinister of England's ley lines, connecting it to a degenerate tradition of Pictish human sacrifice. (That the Picts lived in Scotland did not trouble Blackater's sense of historical accuracy.)

As the neopagan and New Age movements took nascent root in the 1960s, the worst fringe of the occult scene migrated to the hamlets near the Guardham line. Spearheaded by accused rapist Colin Kilforth, the new arrivals formed a loose sect of nature worshippers. Police raids in 1968 and 1969, at the height of the hippie movement, reinforced the line's reputation as a center of dark occult activity. A spate of church burnings in the wake of Kilforth's 1972 arrest on child endangerment charges caused many long-time residents to leave their communities for nearby towns.

By the mid-70s, pamphlets and articles in occult magazines routinely referred to the Guardham line as a place of madness and murder. They added lurid new details to the Kilforth story and construed ordinary incidents of accidental death as the outcomes of supernatural curses.

Sloppy reportage became self-fulfilling prophecy. The membrane weakened. Meanwhile, Esoterror operatives migrated to the Guardham line. They replaced Kilforth's hangers-on by attrition. More old time community members moved off in response to the growing mood of hostility and lawlessness in the five hamlets.

Operational Status: The Guardham line represents the densest cluster of known enemy assets and sympathizers in the civilized world. It has become essentially a retirement community for elderly, disabled or sedentary Esoterror assets. Community elders stash international fugitives in its decaying barns and sheds. Ritual fires light up the night sky between planting and harvest. Backpackers and sightseers passing through the five hamlets disappear on a regular basis. Visual surveillance via telescopic cameras suggests that one or more nonhuman entities freely mingle with Guardham residents. At least two beings of distinct morphological types (one a snake-like beast with a human head, another a humanoid constructed of what looks to be wicker) have been sighted. They most often appear around the farmhouses of former Kilforth associates Donald Cowper (b. 1939, Croydon) and Myra Eccles (b. 1960, Gloucester.)

Action Recommendation: The sheer magnitude of the Esoterror presence at the Guardham line poses a knotty psychomythic challenge. Any large-scale sweep effort will attract widespread attention, reinforcing the line's now significant Outer Dark resonance. The short term benefits of such a preemptive action must therefore be measured against the long-term costs of an operation that will itself weaken the membrane. The wisest course of action is as follows:

- continue to monitor activities at the Guardham line

- develop multiple sources of human intelligence within the target area, by inserting undercover operatives and/or recruiting current residents as moles

- plan and prepare for a massive raid which can be launched on short notice, should evidence of apocalyptic activity become unmistakable

Ice Station Onyx

Location: Hughes Ice Shelf, Nyby Bay, northeast Weddell Sea, Antarctica

Physical Description: Ice Station Onyx is comprised of a pair of connected metal tubes which are almost entirely submerged beneath drifts of snow. Three observation towers, bristling with satellite dishes and radio antennae, protrude above the drifts.

Their state of tilting disrepair reveals the station's state of abandonment. Entrances to the station appear in the southernmost and easternmost of the three towers. Vertical tubes, lined with inset ladder rungs, lead down to the main body of the complex. Steel plates, covered in polymerized carpeting, square off the bottoms of the thirty-foot diameter tubes, creating a level floor surface. The tubes are divided into a series of chambers, arranged in sequence, as per a railroad apartment. Living quarters are arranged at the four tubes, to minimize the necessity of moving through others' quasi-personal spaces. Other chambers are given over to laboratories (ozone measurement/meteorology, chemistry, life sciences, atmospherics, materials engineering), power generation, lavatories, kitchen, mess, recreational facility/library, snow melting (for water supply), a medic bay, and a radio operator's room.

Security Status: Unguarded; facility is considered too dangerous and punishingly remote to justify permanent stationing of OV personnel.

Origin of Membrane Damage: Established in 1968, Ice Station Onyx began its career as an American covert signals monitoring outpost used to track Soviet submarine movements. Its first year-long duty rotation passed without incident. In early 1970, half of its team was prematurely recalled and replaced after suffering mental breakdowns attributable to extreme isolation. In 1972 the base was closed in the wake of a second wave of mental health crises, culminating in the murder and mutilation of the base commander by mutinous crewmen.

Initial damage to the membrane on the Hughes ice shelf appears to have occurred at this time. Originating factors most likely included the sense of isolation experienced by base personnel and cold war paranoia. The creation of an amateur radio play by base personnel based on H. P. Lovecraft's Antarctic-set horror novella *At the Mountains Of Madness* may have also served as a catalytic factor.

Operational Status: In 1992, Ice Station Onyx was refurbished and put into service as a research station under the auspices of Georgetown University. Persistent rumors that the new Onyx served a

covert intelligence agenda have been investigated and disproved (to the extent that one can refute a negative) by OV team HELSINKI COZEN. (Case file abstract available on request.) In 1995, Onyx was abandoned again. Interviews with the thirty-six researchers who spent time at Onyx during the Georgetown years include reports of phenomena including:

- ghost manifestations

- feeling of being observed by unseen eyes

- auditory hallucinations

- strange voices heard on radio transmissions

- sabotage to vital equipment performed while all hands were accounted for

- repeated sightings of biologically improbable creatures on the ice sheet. Nicknamed "glacier cats," these animals

were semi-translucent, and, unlike all known earth vertebrates, were not radially symmetrical. Blurry video footage, taken on two occasions, shows something moving out on the ice, though anatomical details are unclear.

The 1995 mission culminated in the still-unsolved murders of three station researchers and one member of OV investigative team HELSINKI COZEN. The veil-out attributed this latest abandonment to funding shortfalls.

In 2002 the station reopened under the control of a research team affiliated with the Rosencrantz Foundation, a deep-pocketed but previously unknown funder of environmental science and advocacy. Attempts by OV assets to dissuade the researchers from their mission met with stonewalling. Background checks on the team leader, meteorologist Pauline Williams, revealed tenuous connections to the Esoterror-inspired serial killer William Rod Taylor and renegade occultist Daniela Del Pego.

In 2004 the Rosencrantz Foundation covertly funded the viral release of an Internet video entitled "A Crack In the World." Ostensibly an expose of the very real threat represented by the polar ozone holes, the documentary further posits that global warning threatens to open a hole to a monstrous other world. It ties its pseudoscientific theories to old Hollow Earth stories. The documentary includes video footage of the so-called "glacier cats." This includes both new footage, and clips somehow acquired from the 1995 Georgetown crew. (We believed these successfully contained by the HELSINKI COZEN veil-out.)

Action Recommendation: With the release of their viral video, the Rosencrantz Foundation clearly signals its use of the Esoterror modus operandi. Its covert publicity campaign yokes legitimate fears concerning environmental degradation with the supernatural and Outer Dark. We must embark on a two-front sweep operation to shut them down. A team well steeped in forensic accounting must follow the money to the true controllers of the foundation. Meanwhile, an action team equipped for the rigors of the polar environment must head to Ice Station Onyx to learn what Williams and company are doing there, and to take steps to apprehend them and ensure the permanent destruction of the station facility.

Ka'atka

Location: Bong near Belize, near Guatemalan border; exact coordinates available on need-to-know basis

Physical Description: Beneath a strangling mass of jungle vines looms a pyramidal structure composed of limestone-heavy bricks. By manipulating certain of the bricks in a particular order, it is possible to open a secret entrance into the structure. This leads to a partially collapsed catacomb complex bearing the tombs of the ancient Yultala kings.

Security Status: Control of the Ka'atka complex seesaws between rival gangs of jungle mercenaries, mostly of Mexican or Guatemalan origin. One group, the Gallo Rojo, accept Ordo Veritatis stipends to keep outsiders away from the complex. (They believe they are paid by the National Geographic Society to protect a precious archaeological site.) A second gang, the Morenistas, has been known to scatter the Gallo Rojo in order to usher enemy assets to the site.

Origin of Membrane Damage: The ancient Yultala civilization is found in no legitimate textbook. Due to our continued veil-out efforts within the anthropological community, this surviving offshoot of the Olmecs is treated as a ridiculous fiction of historical revisionists. Only in the ancient astronauts section of your local New Age bookstore will you find them mentioned.

The Yultala did exist, subjecting Mesoamerica to a reign of terror between 400 BC and roughly 200 AD. Like any major Pre-Columbian Central American culture, the Yultala practiced blood sacrifice. Their dark fertility rituals took the practice to heights which would chill the blood of any Mayan or Incan priest. Multi-week festivals of torture and self-flagellation climaxed with the arrival of otherworldly beings, who feasted on fields of flayed human flesh.

Even though the few inhabitants of this sparsely populated jungle region know nothing of Ka'atka, they recognize their last surviving tomb complex as a very bad place. This belief may be enough to keep the membrane stretched tight here. It is just as likely, however, that Ka'atka has always been a natural bridging point between this world and the Outer Dark. The Yultala did not make this a permanent LSML; they came here because it was already so. If this is the case, the means of closing it may elude our grasp. However, we must continue to keep the existence of the Yultala a secret from humanity, lest the Ka'atka membrane breach widen even further.

Operational Status: The site's mercenary bands maintain their sanity by keeping a safe distance from the ruins. They patrol a perimeter around them but enter Ka'atka proper only when fighting off their rivals.

Attempts by either us or the enemy to establish a permanent base at Ka'atka have always failed. In 1953, 1965 and again in 1976, we attempted to set up a station manned not by proxies but by a dedicated SSF team.

Anyone trying to occupy the ruins for more than a few days at a time becomes susceptible to complete psychotic breakdown. Survivor reports indicate that the membrane spontaneously opens here, allowing one to peer directly into the Outer Dark. Worse, its inhabitants are able to reach through these gaps to perform gruesome acts of predation. In 1953 most of our twelve-man team went screaming off into the jungle, never to be found again. In 1965, after a pair of suicides and an unsolved murder, the remainder of the team turned its guns on one another. The 1976 team led a fatal assault on a Belizean military patrol, apparently believing them to be demons.

We have documented at least six attempts by the adversary to establish permanent camps at Ka'atka, as early as 1933 and as recently as 2000. The failure of this missions proves that even the most hardened Esoterrorists break down under sustained exposure to the Outer Dark. A few survivors of the last mission languish in private psychiatric facilities. Unless constantly restrained, they lunge for the nearest sharp object in an attempt to carve off and swallow chunks of their own skin.

Nonetheless the idea of "cracking the Ka'atka code" remains an obsession of top Esoterror theorists. Communications intercepts crackle with speculation regarding the exact ritual preparations required to survive its corrosive psychic environment. Tending as they do toward megalomania, many believe that they will succeed where their foolish predecessors have failed. Adding to this temptation is the obvious fact that the Yultala ruling class managed to live cheek by jowl with the Outer Dark for centuries.

Recently the battle for Ka'atka has shifted to other archaeological sites throughout the region. Enemy anthropologists, led by Professor Sabrina Sun of the University of British Columbia, have commenced a systematic effort to find Yultala artifacts in the excavated settlements of later Meso-American cultures. There is a certain logic to her quest: these cultures did sometimes preserve artifacts of predecessor civilizations as trade items. Sun has found a number of copper implements, including a sacrificial bowl and a headdress, which she believes form the regalia of a Yultalan high priestess. If she does succeed in finding what she accepts as a complete set of ritual pieces, she will doubtless travel to Ka'atka in an attempt to achieve *raka'a*, the Yultalan state of monarchical oneness with the outer gods.

Action Recommendation: Although our own anthropological experts are divided on the reliability of Sun's surmises, caution requires us to interfere with her scheme. It may also become necessary to remove her current collection of alleged Yultalan artifacts from her possession. These are secured in a high-tech vault beneath a disused fish cannery at Longview, B.C.

Proposals to bomb or otherwise raze Ka'atka have been deemed unwise at this time. Ka'atka was once a much larger complex of brick pyramids. Our '53 and '65 missions substantially dismantled it. However, attempts to destroy the catacomb pyramid have yielded only temporary success. The bricks can be pulled down, only to leave a spectral copy of the structure that appears during the next full moon. This phantom version of the pyramid eventually hardens into a solid replica indistinguishable from the original, right down to signs of aging and erosion.

Perhakstka

Location: 650 km miles due north of the Siberian town of Bozeva-Svirirsk.

Physical Description: A starved and twisted boreal forest struggles for life across the face of an enormous impact crater more than one hundred kilometers in diameter. The region surrounding the Perhakstka crater is one of trackless wilderness, home to a nascent hunting industry. This tourist trade supports approximately five hundred Russians and about twice as many aboriginal peoples of the Dmitsal tribe.

Security Status: Monitoring the crater area on a part-time basis is a single-blind OV agent, Konstantin Fadushin. A hunter and pilot, Fadushin periodically surveys the crater area from a helicopter. He issues written reports of all unusual activity, including the presence of strangers, in the vicinity. Fadushin is not a knowing agent of our cause. He believes himself to serve the Green Initiative, an international NGO that works to preserve old growth forests. It is essential to maintain this cover in the course of any dealings with him.

Fadushin's last communique to us is now nine weeks overdue. Although he submits reports with less than perfect punctuality, he has never been this late.

Perhakstka is also subject of regular satellite surveillance. The most recent photos show what may be the remains of his chopper in the northeastern boundary of the crater.

Origin of Membrane Damage: In 1906, the remote region became ground zero for an unprecedented impact. According to the veil-out, Perhakstka was struck by the backwash from a comet or asteroid passing through the earth's upper atmosphere. The impact flattened trees and instantly killed hundreds of Dmitsal tribesmen. The area was not explored until 1926, when an expedition by Soviet geologist Vasili Batalov photographed a still-devastated landscape.

In truth, Perhakstka marks the remains of the worst intersection between our world and the Outer Dark ever recorded. Credit for the disaster belongs to half-Russian, half-native Leonid Iura. Born in the region, he migrated to France in the late 1890s, where he fell in with crypto- Esoterrorists Serge Nitzer and Fabrice Boutté. Iura blossomed under their occult tutelage, quickly surpassing their own capacity to contact beings of unremitting horror. According to Boutté's journals, now in our possession, Iura advanced by applying the framework of his shamanic upbringing to their western-style rituals.

After fatally poisoning Nitzer and impregnating Boutté, Iura returned to his native Siberia. There he surrounded himself with a cult of Dmitsal outcasts and halfbreeds. Promising them power undreamt-of, he enlisted them in a mass ritual to bring the industrial revolution to a devastating end. Iura and his celebrants performed the ritual, only to be annihilated as a gate to the Outer Dark opened cataclysmically in the heart of their ancestral homeland. Fortunately, the order's top investigative team had been delayed en route to Iura's encampment and were not present to be caught in the enveloping disaster. Leading a troop of Czarist forces, they arrived in time to drive a pack of slavering creatures back into the gateway. All but one of our agents, and nearly all of the Russian soldiers, were killed in the firefight.

Operational Status: The extreme remoteness of the crater has enabled us to suppress its true nature from the civilian public. The Perhakstka Incident, in its guise as a near-miss from a celestial body, is now known only to astronomers and enthusiasts of Fortean phenomena. The deaths of Iura and his entire cult prevented the truth from reaching his fellow Esoterrorists or other members of the occult underground. For nearly a century, we have successfully kept the Esoterror movement ignorant of the planet's largest and most vulnerable LSML.

We now fear that the integrity of this veil-out has reached its end. Three months before his disappearance, Konstantin Fadushin's name appeared in multiple electronic intercepts. These were not traceable to identifiable sources but included numerous Esoterror keywords.

Further, the Russian oil conglomerate Osmokol, controlled by oligarch Daniil Merkuryev, has announced plans to explore the Perhakstka region.

Geologists express confusion over the decision, as the area does not match the geologic profile of Siberia's oil fields. Further, Merkuryev's ties to the Russian mafia place him within two degrees of separation to several known Esoterror figures.

Action Recommendation: A team must be prepared for operations within Russian and dispatched to ascertain the fate of K. Fadushin. Also determine extent of possible Osmokol involvement in exploitation of Perhakstka membrane weakness.

Special Circumstances: With the original incident scarcely registering in the public consciousness, it is thought that the localized membrane has been steadily healing since 1908. Although it is only 4.93% as thin as it was in 1926, this still holds out the potential for serious supernatural interference. It may be possible for human ritualists to work considerable non-summoning magic without the aid of ODEs in and around the Perhakstka crater.

The Red Bison Triangle

Location: An area forming a triangle between the settlements of Red Bison, Cameron, and Sifton, in northern Alberta, Canada.

Physical Description: The triangle consists mostly of aspen parkland, a transitional geographic region between prairie and northern muskeg. The top points of the triangle jut into a region of boreal forest. The area is a remotely settled wilderness. The easternmost point of the triangle sits to the north of the Athabaskan oil sands and the booming city of Fort McMurray. It lies to the south of Wood Buffalo National Park.

Security Status: The area is too large and remote to effectively patrol or monitor.

Origin of Membrane Damage: Unknown. This area has little apparent psychomythic significance. File clippings reveal no more than the expected number of UFO sightings for a remote region of its size. The most notable of these is a slimly reported 1967 incident in which camp cook Verda Case (1921-1987) briefly claimed to have been abducted by a UFO but soon recanted her testimony. The region actually has fewer recorded Sasquatch sightings than neighboring areas. Its murder rate is slightly elevated for its demo-geographic profile. None of its violent incidents over the years have received national press attention or passed into local legend.

Though the origin of its membrane weakness remains a mystery, other metrics clearly show the telltale correspondences: weather anomalies, atmospheric disturbances, and frequent appearances of Esoterror keyword combinations in polling responses and local media.

Operational Status: The Red Bison triangle is also unusual for an LSML in that reports of Esoterror activity in the area are all but nonexistent. A map depicting hotspots of membrane vulnerability captured in Den Haag in 1965 includes the triangle. Marcel Chubb, leader of the notoriously violent Madison cell, committed suicide in a pickup truck on the outskirts of Sifton in 1978. However we have yet to document any instance of an actual enemy operation or ritual taking place within its boundaries.

As far as unexplained phenomena are concerned, the triangle's is most notable as a place of inexplicable vehicle disappearances. Since 1934 more than a hundred people have vanished without a trace within its boundaries. All were last seen in a car, truck, airplane, or boat. (The triangle encompasses several rivers, including portions of the Peace, Birch, and Wabasca.) Recent disappearances include:

- the Wolf family (parents Adrian, Patricia, and children Caden, Jason, Ginifer) in a recreational vehicle, March 21, 1995. A week later, Adrian Wolf's mother, Andrea, of New York, reports a voice message on her answering machine in her son's voice, repeating the word "croatoan" several times. Once analyzed by our audio experts, the recording is revealed to have been artificially produced by an unknown process.

- White water rafting coach Nancy Baisch, and her pilot Lorne Bowerman, May 30, 1998, in his twin-engine Cessna.

- Sport fisherman and retired sanitation

facility manager Gordon Carnine, February 18, 2008, while driving to the Pine Grove lodge in his Dodge Ram pickup truck

- Pauline Fornier (48) and her niece Sue Ketcham (19), while driving to Cameron to run errands, February 26, 1994

- orthopedic surgeon Dr. Edward Wingrove, August 30, 2000. Wingrove had just bagged a moose with a party of fellow doctors and left the group to move their rented truck to a road near the kill site. When his friends arrived with the moose, neither Wingrove nor the truck were anywhere in evidence.

It is perhaps unusual that this record of disappearances, well known to our organization, has gained no traction whatsoever in the body of Fortean and paranormal literature. The Red Bison is responsible for more bona fide vanishings than its famous marine cousin, the Bermuda or Devil's Triangle. In an intriguing theory, data analyst SUFFER IROQUOIS suggests that a veil-out is in ongoing process here—arranged by some other organization or being. To support this speculation, he points to a marking on the Den Haag map, which refers to northern Alberta as a "forbidden place" and includes a symbol perhaps meant to evoke a horned, inhuman face.

Action Recommendation: Unless disappearances escalate or more overt supernatural activity is detected, situation warrants further study only.

Road To Nowhere

Location: Usually central Nebraska; sometimes found in Wyoming, South Dakota or northern Kansas.

Physical Description: The Road To Nowhere is a straight, flat highway stretching into the horizon across the American plains. Accurate-seeming road signs label it as US Route 182, a nonexistent highway.

Security Status: Access unpredictable. See operational status, below.

Origin of Membrane Damage: During his notorious 1959 killing spree, in which he killed eleven victims during a long drive through Nebraska and Wyoming, 21-year old delinquent Tony Poorhill described himself as riding a nonexistent highway called US Route 182. Poorhill was gunned down by police while in pursuit of his twelfth victim. His references to Route 182 come from the testimony of his young girlfriend, Lorena Ridell. Ridell's statements made it clear that Poorhill saw Route 182 as a metaphor for his mental state. There is no reason to believe that he believed in its physical reality or hallucinated its existence.

In 1963, an article entitled "Hell Ride On 182" by freelance journalist Hal Meaney appeared in the sensationalist magazine *Destiny*. It retold the Poorhill story from a fanciful angle, asserting that he and Ridell briefly found themselves on a ghost road that dipped into hell. According to the Meaney story, it was this detour into a supernatural realm that drove Poorhill mad and inspired his kill spree. Meany further supplied a wholly fabricated history of encounters with the ghost road, dating back to the 1860 influx of homesteaders into the

region. Happily flouting basic geography, Meany intimated that the Donner Party became lost on this hell trail.

The issue of *Destiny* in which the article appeared hit newsstands a week after the Kennedy assassination. Perhaps due to the ensuing period of high membrane permeability, its contents quickly seized the imaginations of Midwest residents. By 1967, stories about Route 182 had achieved urban legend status in the Nebraska area. Teenagers told the story to one another as if true, unaware of its source in a recent magazine article. Meany's historical fabrications mutated in the telling, granting the imaginary road a more credible provenance.

The earliest known verifiable indication of membrane damage is found in 1970, when traveling claims adjuster Gary Thomas Holderman arrives home from a long road trip to murder his ex-wife and three young children. Under interrogation by local police, he claimed no memory of the killings. The last thing he remembered was getting lost on the road after making an accidental turn onto Route 182. Our data analysts, finding Esoterror keywords in his confession to police, dispatched a PPU team to evaluate him. They concluded that his brush with the supernatural was authentic and not an attempt to lay the groundwork for an insanity plea. (Naturally, in the interests of a veil-out, we did not disabuse prosecutors of their opinion that Holderman's delusions were feigned.) Holderman died in prison in 1988.

Operational Status: The road reveals itself only to drivers meeting certain conditions, including but not necessarily restricted to the following:

- driver is alone in vehicle

- driver is in a state of altered consciousness, for example substance intoxication or sleep deprivation

- driver has some degree of emotional investment in his vehicle, or in driving: may be professional driver, an auto hobbyist or have experienced a previous traumatic event connected to vehicle (collision, vandalism, hit and run)

- driver has experienced setbacks in attainment of life goals or considers himself to have victimized by society

Until recently our only known experiencers of the Road To Nowhere were white males between the ages of twenty and sixty from middle class or upper working class backgrounds. In addition to Poorhill and Holderman, other murders connected to Route 182 include those committed by:

- gas station attendant Gerald Liss, 27, who shot three black or Hispanic patrons in 1974.

- long haul trucker Nathaniel Lafond, 49, convicted in the 1979 stranglings of roadside prostitutes Karen Keith and Kathern Veazey; strongly suspected of three other similar killings.

- Nicole Eaves, 26, who drove through a rest stop picnic area in 2006, killing one and seriously injuring three.

However, not all of those who swerve onto Route 182 go on to commit crimes. It is likely that many remain secretive about their encounters, due to the stigma associated with the road's most notorious travelers. OV case files include testimony from six drivers who have found themselves on the road between 1974 and the present day. They can only represent the tip of the reportorial iceberg.

In a communications intercept picked up in 2007, enemy agent Jon Jacob Post (b. 1933, Coffeyville, Kansas, see adversary profile PJ493-33) discussed the Road To Nowhere with an unidentified male co-conspirator. Post instructed him to drive randomly through Nebraska until he strayed onto the road, at which time he could "make eye contact with the Red Ones" and gain "the cleansing blessing." The unidentified male may have been Freedy Pawlak (b. 1987, Stopover, Kentucky; see adversary profile PF076-87), who two months later killed three fast food employees in Louisville, KY and was last seen in Zurich, Switzerland, staying in a flat rented to private security consultant and suspected Esoterror sympathizer Urs Schmid (b. 1951, Kloten, Switzerland.)

Action Recommendation: Activities of Post, Pawlak, and Schmid warrant an investigation to discover their operational intent.

The Road itself, like many loci of urban legendry, seems extremely difficult to veil out. Debunking reports in friendly journals such as *The Rational Inquirer* and *Skepticism* merely serve to reinforce the myth in believers' minds. Submit suggestions for new approaches to the Psychomythic Adjustment Committee; promising approaches will result in research grants.

Serizawa Building
Location: 6-11-21 Ueno District, Taito Ward, Tokyo

Physical Description: An glum and unprepossessing apartment block, the Serizawa Building displays a defiant concrete drabness emblematic of the worst of 1970s utilitarianism. Its six floors wrap around a forlorn garden/courtyard. Floors two through six contain twelve apartment units apiece, most of them spacious by Tokyo standards. The ground level includes nine apartment units, a meeting room, a superintendent's station, and janitorial/storage facilities.

Security Status: Building security is lax; a sleepy superintendent keeps watch through antiquated security equipment during daylight hours. A member of our Tokyo station pays surreptitious visits to the building on a bi-weekly basis and monitors media reports for signs of new trouble at this address.

Origin of Membrane Damage: Neighborhood lore attributes the high turnover rate of the Serizawa's unappealing but bargain-priced apartments to its status as a haunted building. Allegedly a young mother drowned her two toddlers in a bathtub during the building's first year of operation over thirty years ago. Although no records of such an incident can be found, sightings of a ghostly faceless woman or pair of dripping, drowned children have been reported here since 1982.

The real cause of the membrane damage appears to be a series of unauthorized electrical repairs conducted by the building's young superintendent, Ryota Namiki, in the spring of that year. Namiki, a student of electrical engineering, was later diagnosed as a paranoid schizophrenic. He reconfigured the building's wiring according to a pattern that came to him during a vivid hallucination. His writings at the time suggest that he was attempting to create a wifi Internet network decades before the technology would become feasible.

The wires appear to have allowed Namiki to unconsciously transmit his delusional fears and anxieties throughout the complex. The resulting localized spike of distressed psychic energy weakened the membrane, turning the Serizawa into an LSML. Since then the building has been the site of just under a dozen murders and over thirty inexplicable accidents resulting in death or serious injury. Although each has been subjected to our ongoing veil-out, stories have inevitably traveled along the neighborhood grapevine.

Operational Status: From 1994 to late 1998 Esoterror ran a successful operation under the noses of our Tokyo station. Over that period as many as thirty-nine enemy assets were placed as tenants in the building. Through consciousness-altering techniques including fasting, meditation, and consumption of hallucinogens, they were able to break through the membrane to mentally contact unremitting horror entities. Imbued with extra-human capabilities, they went on to stage Esoterror operations throughout the Pacific Rim. In 1998 this training ring was discovered and broken up. At this time Namiki's wiring system was discovered and dismantled.

In 1999, after another murder-suicide in the building, Ordo investigators performing a frequency analysis discovered that Namiki's wiring, even though destroyed, was still transmitting. It was a ghost of a machine.

In 2001 and 2004 Esoterror operatives circumvented our screening attempts to briefly lodge in the Serizawa. Given its reliable access to the Outer Dark, we expect more attempts in the years to come.

Manifestations experienced by our operatives at Serizawa over the years include:

- visual field distortions

- screaming faces seen on walls

- floor tiles sweating blood

- visions of parasitic infestation

- sightings of ghostly children, drowned women, or a tortured, translucent Ryota Namiki

Action Recommendation: Since 1998 we have been attempting to bring about the building's demolition. Frustratingly, the building's fate has become mired in the slow-moving Japanese court system. True ownership of the Serizawa has been in doubt since an incident in 1993 in which one of the owners killed the other and then himself.

According to a white paper written by occult science analyst PLANT VESPER (available on need-to-know basis), it is a distinct possibility that any new structure would continue to be haunted even after the demolition of the current structure.

At present the Tokyo station keeps tabs on the Serizawa in a manner commensurate with available resources. Inspection duties must be performed by junior operatives. Agents with prior exposure to Outer Dark manifestations elsewhere seem additionally vulnerable to the building's influence.

GM Guidance

The following chapter consists of advice for *The Esoterrorists* GMs, written in out-of-character voice. It contains no secrets, so players are free to read it, if they want. Although geared specifically to this game, you'll find much of the following advice adaptable to any iteration of GUMSHOE.

CONSTRUCTING SCENARIOS

Many story-focused GMs are accustomed to games in which they establish an environment and a cast of characters, and then allow the PCs' interaction with these to determine the shape of your narrative. These games have the advantage of being easy to run once you get them rolling. After perhaps establishing an initial plot line, you can allow new stories to organically develop out of old ones. When stuck for material, you can look at a relationship diagram between major GMCs and quickly spin a new conflict out of them that builds on previous installments. Once the characters have an ongoing stake in the world, you can sit back and allow them to pursue their own agendas. You can react to what they do, without much prep work on your part. Scenario generation starts to take care of itself.

This is a perfectly enjoyable mode of play. In "Station Duty," p. 32, we show you how to construct such a series using the *Esoterrorists* setting. In addition to being easy on GMs, this series mode appeals strongly to self-motivated players eager to pursue their own agendas. Storyteller and character actor players prefer the freedom it gives them to explore tailored plot threads and the immersive world of their characters' psychology, respectively.

Like any style of play, the interactive environment mode brings drawbacks along with its strengths. As the threats to the PCs escalate, the cast of supporting characters steadily increases and the plots gain complexity through sheer accumulated detail, players often come to feel overwhelmed. The very narrative richness that allows for the easy creation of spontaneous storylines begins to feel oppressive, especially in the horror genre. An unfortunate plot turn or resolution result can send the entire series in an unwanted direction that's hard to credibly extricate yourself from.

Overall, *The Esoterrorists* encourages an episodic procedural mode of play, in part to give your players a break from the sometimes punishing dynamics of the interactive environment mode. By breaking your series down into self-contained episodes, this model keeps the players from feeling overwhelmed by an accumulation of ongoing plot detail or an ever-accumulating collection of potential threats to their well-being. Your doughty band of Ordo Veritatis agents parachutes into a dire situation, figures out what's going on, solves the problem, and goes home. Although you can still add the occasional recurring villain or homefront attack, the characters don't have to constantly worry about attracting the ire of a dozen powerful foes at any one time. The sharp mission focus of this mode appeals to tacticians and to reactive players who prefer to work on tasks inherent in the storyline, without having to generate their own agendas. Even players who normally prefer interactive environment campaigns often find the relative simplicity of the episodic procedural refreshing for the stylistic change of pace it offers.

The downsides of the episodic procedural fall more heavily on the GM. Coming up with a continuing stream of entirely new storylines is harder than simply elaborating existing plot threads or building them from relationship diagrams. The procedural part can be even more daunting. Inventing an airtight mystery is a challenging exercise in logic. Because all of their key elements must integrate with one another in a way that allows the players to make eventual sense out of them, they can't be generated with random charts or other short cuts. Good plotting is hard.

That said, the following ways of thinking about the problem will help you in your quest to master this difficult skill set. Once you get the knack for it, you can feel secretly superior to all those GMs who can create storylines only in the comparatively easier interactive environment mode.

Finding Your Premise

The first step to the creation of a compelling mystery is to choose a defining element that drives the story and differentiates it from your other episodes. Look for something that gives the players an emotional or intellectual access point into your story. Ideally your defining element draws on some image or occurrence that they're already familiar with, and hence invested in, and then puts a new spin on it. The twist keeps the scenario fresh and unpredictable.

This is why *The Esoterrorists* relies heavily on story premises ripped from the headlines. They create a shock of recognition for your players, and a reference point allowing them to engage immediately with the narrative. Not only does this technique places the standard images of modern horror in a new, and therefore startling context of real news events. It also gives you a ready supply of premises from which to build your episodes. Think as your daily newspaper as the replacement for the ongoing plot elements and relationship maps of the interactive environment series model. These are where you get your ideas.

Scan the headlines for stories including a a horrific, surreal, or absurdist element. For variety's sake, mix up the episodes based on well-publicized events with the occasional obscure but irresistible story. Many news headline services on the Internet are customizable, allowing you to create home pages with sections devoted to particular keywords. For example, I've customized my Google News page to return stories including the keywords *weird*, *paranormal*, *surreal*, *Fortean* and *ghost*. Many of the stories returned use these words in mundane contexts that don't much relate to the themes of *The Esoterrorists*. Occasionally, though, an ideal obscure headline pops up.

To maintain an element of surprise, you may wish to mix elements from more than one well-known news stories. Maybe the scenario at first seems to be inspired by the O.J. Simpson Las Vegas armed robbery charges, but later draws on elements of the Phil Spector murder trial.

Needless to say, you can also use source material presented in this book as inspiration for story hooks unrelated to the day's headlines. Each entry is salted with unanswered questions, allowing your premise to be as open-ended as "find out what's happening at Camp Pata" (p. 102) or "The Colombo cell (p. 71) has killed another child; this time we're going to shut them down for good."

Once you've chosen your defining element(s), find a source of horrific personal engagement with the material. What about it appalls you, makes you angry, or might push your players' buttons? In a horror game, strive not only to terrify the characters, but to create unease in your group. What is the most horrifying expression of your chosen idea? Your answer might be simple visceral horror, drawing on our quite reasonable primal fears of death and dismemberment. It could equally be a more philosophical or intellectual dread. Ideally, you'll hit all of these notes over the course of a series.

Your emotional trigger point will probably inspire one or more key images, which in turn lead to scenes in which the heroes confront them. Perhaps they include a series of scenes, in which the horror of the central idea is developed and amplified. Jot these down for later reference.

A SPRINGBOARD, NOT A BOX

The scenario generation method shown here is just one way to do it. These suggestions are meant as a springboard to show hesitant or uncertain GMs one way through the sometimes-daunting puzzle that is scenario creation.

You may already be a whiz at constructing investigative horror adventures. Maybe you've already learned to do it by emulating published scenarios, including the rule book's *Operation Slaughterhouse*, which is intended to serve as a template for that very purpose. Don't fret if your creative process differs from the one outlined here.

Developing Your Backstory

Armed with your premise, construct a chain of events that explains what happens prior to the PCs' arrival on the scene. This is called your backstory, or, if you want to get fancy about it, the *antecedent action*.

Your backstory will usually be an account of an Esoterrorist cell plotting and partially executing an evil scheme. Establish what deeds attracted the attention of the Ordo Veritatis, who performed them, and why. Ask yourself what your culprits hope to gain through their scheme. (In other words, create your investigation trigger and sinister conspiracy, as laid out in the scenario structure given on pp. 62–64 of *The Esoterrorists*.)

Often the scheme is ongoing even as the investigators attempt to uncover and disrupt it. This choice allows you to confront the PCs with active opposition. It faces them with disruptive scenes which, unlike investigative sequences, carry an ever-present threat of failure.

In other instances, the enemy operation may be complete as the PCs enter the scene. For example, the Esoterrorists might have succeeded in assassinating a key target or committing a psychologically destabilizing act of sabotage. Here the team's investigation will not lead them into a scheme in progress, but instead into an Esoterror cell. The team must apprehend (or kill) its members and destroy its assets, to prevent other cells from making later use of them.

Mystery scenarios, whether for roleplaying or for books, movies or TV episodes, require you to plot in two directions. First, you figure out what happened. Then you figure out how the investigator, working backwards, reconstructs these facts from a trail of clues.

What Happened Here?

Go through the process of what your conspirators had to do to achieve their physical objectives to date. In the case of a murder, they need to gain access to the victim, overcome his defenses, commit the grim deed, and escape unnoticed. If it's a theft,

they have to gain access to the object, overcoming security measures, and again escape undetected. Acts of sabotage require similar chains of events.

(In many scenarios, the conspirators engage in a series of crimes, so you have to account for all of them in this fashion. Dramatic interest generally dictates that the first crime is committed as part of the antecedent action, and that the others unfold while the investigators are already engaged in the case. Under this model, each successive crime scene reveals something new that brings the team ever closer to the culprits.)

At each stage of the crime—gaining access, overcoming defenses, performing the act itself, and making the escape—the culprit(s) may leave behind bits of physical evidence which will eventually lead the investigators to them. As you break down the crime, note these clues. Look especially for core clues, which can lead the investigators to other people or locations, where they can then gather further core clues to keep the story in motion.

You can read more on structuring GUMSHOE adventures see Fear of Structure I and II in See Page XX: Vol 1.

If you can establish multiple avenues by which the characters can move through the storyline and solve the mystery, so much the better.

Unless your players are whipping through your scenarios with head-spinning speed, don't worry about making your clue trails too easy to follow. Count on your players to supply their own complications, by speculating wildly, fixating on immaterial facts, and by generally double-thinking you when you're only single-thinking.

In scenes where the evidence is primarily physical, clue trail design is largely a matter of visualization. What series of actions occurred? Which useful clues might have been left behind at each stage?

Account also for what clues are not present at the scene, and why. If a clue would be too useful, taking the investigators immediately from introductory scene to climax, you want to ensure its absence from your crime scene. Clues can be missing for various reasons:

- The culprit, especially if he's a seasoned Esoterror operative, may have been savvy enough to clean it up, or not to leave it in the first place.

- Conditions may be unfavorable to the leaving or preservation of clues. Surfaces may not take fingerprints. Track marks might be wiped away by a storm. The security camera might be old or faulty.

- Evidence may be unwittingly lost or destroyed between the time of the crime and the arrival of the PCs. Janitors and cleaning crews can remove crucial trace evidence before they know a crime has occurred. Well-meaning but naïve witnesses can displace items. Inexperienced local officials can obscure esoteric evidence during their early evidence collection efforts. Guns and weapons may be stolen from crime scenes by third parties, as often happens in real life.

Who Knows What?

In scenes where evidence is primarily testimonial in nature, figure out what each possible witness would logically know about the conspiracy. Create your witnesses and informants for maximum variety of outlook, personality, speech pattern, and intentions. Give everyone a distinct reason to withhold information, or an emotional barrier the investigators must overcome through the use of interpersonal investigative abilities. Reasons for innocent parties to initially withhold information include:

1. Embarrassing personal secrets they don't want revealed

2. Dislike of authority figures

3. Fear of arrest for unrelated offenses

4. Aversion to hassle

5. Lack of time

6. Reflexively difficult personality

7. Insecurity

8. Fear of reprisal

To prevent plot logjams, give yourself wiggle room to allow investigators to succeed with credible but unexpected uses of interpersonal abilities. If the motivation for withholding is embarrassing or damaging, the witness will provide misleading reasons for failing to cooperate, or will falsely claim not to have the desired information. These will likely trigger investigators' **Bullshit Detectors**, ensuring that not all witnesses who do so turn out to be actual culprits.

Where team members interview true conspirators but are not meant to discover their guilt right away, establish why their deceptions fail to register with the **Bullshit Detector** ability. They may be conscienceless, trained in deception, or telling a transparent lie to disguise the fact that they're also engaged in a deeper misdirection.

Set Pieces and Endings

Having designed your clue trail, look back to the scenes of unease and terror that came to mind when you first selected the hook. Knowing now where the investigators are likely to go, and the most likely ways they might move through the series, consider ways to bring them into these scenes. Identify the most terrifying or disturbing sequence you've imagined and plan ways to make that your climactic scene. It may occur after the investigators solve the mystery, or might be a prerequisite scene to the final clues allowing them to piece it together.

Find Additional Avenues

You now have a map of your scenario, with at least one likely path the investigators will follow to complete their mission. As a final step, review it and look for possible logjams, where the plot may stall, or railroad points, where you've moved the story forward by removing choices from your players.

When you find a logjam scene, think up alternate ways for to get out of (or into) the situation at hand. Prepare also to accept unexpected moves they may make in play.

Consider ways to inject meaningful choice into your railroad track sequences. Plan additional possible plot branches that keep the characters within a satisfying story even if they take actions you find inconvenient.

Finally, see if you can't find more than one route for the characters to complete their circuit of the necessary scenes in the clue trail.

BUILDING A SERIES

It is more than possible to run a lengthy and satisfying series of *The Esoterrorists* in a completely episodic manner. In this model, each scenario stands happily on its own, with no shared narrative threads except those the players choose to build into the storyline through their development of their own characters. This approach suits mission-oriented groups and those whose members attend unpredictably.

If, on the other hand, your group boasts stable attendance and a core of players with story-oriented or immersive tastes, you may find it rewarding to wrap your various episodes in the mantle of an ongoing story arc which builds to an exciting climax.

To do so, first devise a loose possible storyline for an entire series, or set of episodes within a series. The classic solution to this creative challenge is to give the Esoterrorists a grand scheme, which the characters slowly stumble onto as they solve each episodic case. By busting up these sub-schemes and subjecting them to veil-outs, the PCs disrupt the overarching conspiracy somewhat, but never enough to derail its juggernaut momentum. When the series reaches its conclusion, all is revealed, and they must overcome their biggest threat ever, with possibly world-shaking results.

Alternately, you can go for a more personal story arc, in which the threat is to the characters' emotional well-being. The heroes might be trying to recover a kidnapped mentor or loved one, or seeking collective redemption in the wake of a spiritual crisis.

The first choice is bolder and easier to pull off, and allows for characters to shuffle in and out of the series when and if PCs are horribly killed. The second is tougher to execute because it's subtler, yet also suffers less from over-familiarity.

Whatever your story arc, you have several structural options at your disposal when deciding how to integrate it into your series.

In an integrated structure, it is clear to the players from the outset that every single episode connects into a wider narrative. Episodes and sessions needn't coincide; the team can go off on countless small missions as they work to crack the wider conspiracy. A micro-case might take up a few linked scenes. Other cases might string on for many weeks at a time, possibly with sidetracks in between. Look to the TV series *Alias* as a model for this structure.

The intermittent model plays as a series of discrete episodes, some of which advance the broader plotline, and others of which are standalone events. This model allows you to occasionally loosen the tension with a tonally distinct standalone episode, then dive back into the overall continuity. On the other hand, you have to make it consistently credible for the team to heads off in pursuit of offbeat cases with a more pressing mission hanging over their heads. The series that established this classic structure is *The X-Files*. It's a popular choice on TV because the story arc episodes coincide with ratings measurement periods.

The retroactive continuity model presents a series of apparently disconnected episodes which, when the earth-shattering climax arrives, turn out to have foreshadowed its dramatic events. It's tricky to pull off, because you have to carefully seed lead-up episodes with clues that both serve their own episodes, and then can be folded into a big reveal at the end. Because you can't use flashbacks like a TV show does, this relies on your players to have good memories for small details. The model can be seen to good effect in the revived *Doctor Who* series.

ON CONCEITS

A conceit is a literary device necessary to satisfying storytelling. It is often a departure from strict realism, which the audience must simply accept in order to enjoy the story.

Procedural TV shows are rife with conceits. In one very common example, the detectives have access to incredibly sophisticated equipment. Their forensic departments are never hampered by budget constraints or bureaucratic snafus. The long backlogs for lab work that plague real-world cops are never an issue in the typical TV cop show. Having characters wait for months for lab results, or see their cases derailed by shoddy low-bid contract work, would reflect the reality of contemporary police work. It would also stop the story dead—the teleplay equivalent of failing to get a core clue into the characters' hands. Therefore, except in the rare show like *The Wire*, which takes institutional breakdown as one of its major themes, you simply don't see this happen.

Another standard example, seen on almost every show, is the *conceit of primacy*. The main characters, even when established as ordinary, workaday law enforcement officers, appear to be assigned to every major case their agency is confronted with. Cases which in real life would be handled by giant task forces are routinely closed by our familiar cast of hero cops. In the course of a year, they work about two dozen hugely important cases, getting themselves into multiple gun fights, disciplinary procedures, and sundry high-drama scrapes. Over one season they see considerably more action than a real-life top detective would face in an entire career. As viewers, we accept this. We want our main characters to navigate a new story each week, instead of sitting around doing paperwork. The conceit of primacy is so universal that we scarcely question it.

Another nearly universal procedural conceit is that of *chronological unity*. In the *Law and Order* franchise, entire cases unfold from commission of crime to completion of sentencing in what seems like a few weeks. Here the writers fudge questions of timing to collapse what in the real world might take several years into one discrete episode.

Perhaps the best example of a conceit, because it departs so egregiously from reality in order to make the show's premise work, fuels the various versions of *CSI*. There, forensic scientists take the lead in investigations, going so far as to conduct interviews with witnesses. This contravenes a cardinal rule of evidence control. In the real world, lab techs aren't allowed any contact whatsoever with suspects. This protocol protects their objectivity, allowing them to testify in court free of accusations that their personal feelings toward the defendant have colored their scientific conclusions. However, since the protagonists of the *CSI* shows are forensic scientists, the show's basic conceit allows them to do perform any task a regular cop character would get to do on a standard procedural show. This can be seen as an extreme example of the conceit of primacy.

GUMSHOE procedural series require their own conceits in order to keep the story moving in an entertaining manner. Like the CSI conceit, or chronological unity, they require the audience's complicity in looking the other way. Here GM and players handwave certain elements that break the rules of realism in order to keep the game running smoothly. Just as the aforementioned devices arise from the requirements of TV drama, GUMSHOE's conceits grapple with the limitations of a roleplaying session.

The major device you'll want to adopt, needed for all but the smallest groups, is the conceit of *elastic participation*. Roleplaying is traditionally a group effort; cop shows tend to focus on small teams of investigators. When an ensemble cast tackles a big case together, they split into partnerships to split up necessary tasks. The scriptwriters make sure that obstacles are always matched to the capabilities of the characters in a given scene. In a roleplaying game, where responsibility for the obstacles lies with the GM and task splitting is determined by the players, some additional fudging is required to match the two elements.

GUMSHOE works best when you assume that everyone is kind-of sort-of along for every scene—without squinting too hard at any resulting logic or staging absurdities. That way, the group continues to enjoy collective access to all of the investigative abilities needed to gather core clues. Perhaps even more importantly, the concerted minds of four to six untrained roleplayers are often needed to replicate the deductive skill of a single professional investigator.

Much of the time, you can collaborate with the group to come up with ways to conceal the breaking of the fourth wall that occurs when six people pile into an interrogation room or examine the same piece of physical evidence. Two-person teams can be dispatched to perform particular tasks, while keeping seamlessly in touch with the rest of the team. Assume, for example, that suggestions given by players whose characters aren't present in a scene represent cell phone conversations. Team members might wear ear pieces so that the good and bad cop in the interrogation room can receive prompts from other PCs on the other side of the one-way mirror. A technical expert can lend his ability to another PC by watching a video feed on his laptop. When necessary, you can establish that an absent character with a specialized ability briefed the PC on the scene, telling him what to look for. In many cases, one detective can bag and tag evidence and let the technician look at it later. A suspect can be left to cool his heels while the investigator with the right interpersonal approach makes his way to the interview.

Most of the time, you can just let the group sort through the clues without constantly justifying the use of the elastic participation conceit. That's what a conceit does: it says, "Let's not worry about this annoying bit of realism."

Try to guide the group so that the splitting into teams trope occurs during non-investigative sequences. A stake-out that leads into a chase scene needn't occur under the assumption that everyone is "sort of there." By finding ways to break it every so often, you hide the conceit.

Enlist your players in maintaining it. Convey to them justification given here. Explain that what at first seems to be a departure from police procedural practice is in fact an extension of the same principle, adapted to the needs of a roleplaying session.

(Elastic participation is not unique to investigative games. Most groups playing a classic dungeon delve campaign allow characters of absent players to be present to use minor, exotic abilities. At the same time, the characters are typically not treated as present when a big fight breaks out.)

You probably make regular use of other conceits, even if you don't use the term:

- *The conceit of climactic pacing*: The degree of spotlight time you give to a story branch depends on where it appears in the course of an episode. A scene that you might fill with complications if the players choose to engage with it in the early going is best disposed of in a few sentences if it would prevent you from placing the big finish near the end of a session. You'll probably drop the complications entirely if the players only think to engage with the scene after the climax.

- In roleplaying, the *conceit of primacy* requires PCs to solve a scenario's central problems themselves, rather than expecting supporting characters to take risks for them. Only tasks which are meant to be accomplished offstage can be effectively delegated. For example, in the introductory OPERATION SLAUGHTERHOUSE scenario, the team is expected to enter the island base, but can detail its later destruction to the SSF, during the veil-out.

Operation
Whirlwind
Reaper

Operation Whirlwind Reaper

Operation Whirlwind Reaper serves as a sample scenario for an Special Suppression Forces series. (See Chapter Three for more on this series structure.) It allows the PCs ample opportunities for gritty military combat in a hostile environment. Investigative sequences, including the opportunity to learn a unremitting horror creature's Special Means of Dispatch (SMD), provide tactical advantages in the fight scenes.

As should go without saying, don't read this if you're a player whose GM plans to use this scenario in your series.

MISSION BRIEFING

This is the scenario precis you're used to, with a few heading changes to reflect the flavor of an SSF game. Strategic Objectives replaces the Investigation Trigger. The Trail Of Clues becomes Recon & Intel, while Antagonist Reactions is slightly modified to Enemy Actions.

Strategic Objectives

A month has passed since Cyclone Nargis slammed into the southeast Asian nation of Burma. Misery escalates as the attention of the international community drifts from disaster aftermath. The country remains tightly in the hands of its notoriously corrupt and repressive military junta. Only a few foreign relief organizations have been granted visas to operate within its borders. Among these is Child Hunger Action Network (CHAN), an NGO recently revealed by Ordo Veritatis investigators to be an Esoterror front. The incalculable horror of the catastrophe has doubtless weakened the membrane throughout the nation, particularly in the affected Irrawaddy Delta region. This weakening could be leveraged to unknown and disastrous ends by Esoterror operatives working under the CHAN banner.

Assignment desk has therefore dispatched a team to identify and neutralize this enemy team. As any activity in Burma is classified as a DEO (Dangerous Environment Operation; see p. 43), an SSF detail has been chosen for this purpose.

The Sinister Conspiracy

The Relief Action Worldwide team is led by the group's Executive Director, a Mexican national named Chavela Ferraz. For years Ferraz has cultivated assets within Burma, waiting for a large-scale natural disaster to strike. Now that it has, she has used the ensuing membrane breach to summon a meatgrinder, an Outer Black entity that gorges itself on the psychic agony of disaster victims. Although it feeds mostly on free-floating human distress, it must consume a flesh-and-blood person every few days to remain on this plain of existence. The victim must be a young orphan—of Nargis has left a plentiful supply. The CHAN team occupies itself with the collection of suitable sacrificial victims as the meatgrinder slowly doles ritual secrets to Ferraz.

Recon & Intel

The squad must get its bearings after a covert landing in the Irrawaddy Delta. They head to The Village Of Misery, where SIGINT picked up the last electronic trace of the CHAN team's whereabouts. This leads them to the Solidarity Depot, where regime officials hoard needed supplies. After a fight there, the group can capture and interrogate corrupt functionary Mr. Tin, who sends them on to meet The Meatgrinder. In this climactic combat sequence the group confronts Ferraz's CHAN team and her pet creature of unremitting horror.

Enemy Actions

Ferraz remains unaware of the team until they make their move, and places no active obstacles in their path. However, commandos must remain alert to the possibility of enemy patrols throughout the mission. Depending on travel choices, they may encounter checkpoints, natural hazards, and the disturbing consequences of a membrane breach.

SCENES

Irrawaddy Landing
Scene Type: Action / Pursuit

The scenario begins *in media res*, as the team parachutes into a storm-swept rice paddy under cover of darkness. An expanse of half-flattened jungle, dominated by palm trees, encircles the paddy to the north and east, granting the team quick cover as they rush from their landing zone. Team members are equipped with compact night vision goggles and carry full packs containing their gear. Any character may specify that he has a sidearm strapped to one leg and a knife strapped to the other.

Landing: The first order of business is to land in the rice paddy without incident. This requires a Difficulty 6 Athletics test. On a failure, the character takes one instance of unmodified damage, reflecting a sprain, twist, or minor other landing injury.

Failed landers must also make Difficulty 4 Preparedness tests to see if they lose anything. On a failure, characters with Preparedness ratings of

3 or less lose one non-weapon item of the GM's choice from their pack contents. Characters with Preparedness ratings of 4 or more suffer a +1 modifier to all Preparedness Difficulties for the remainder of the mission.

Escaping Notice: Once the landings have been resolved, the characters must slog quietly through knee-deep water through the muddy rice paddy to reach the trees.

Ask if anyone wants to make a **Military science** spend. On a 1-point spend, the character's battle-honed ears pick up the muffled but telltale sounds

Pack Contents

Any character on this mission has the following gear in his pack without recourse to a Preparedness test: a long gun (such as an assault or sniper rifle, broken down; must be reassembled), two grenades, compass, regional map, GPS receiver, untraceable local cell phone, single-use encrypted SMS message sender, insecure short-range walkie talkie, basic first aid kit, water, and a week's worth of MREs (meals ready to eat.)

Each character has, in convenient denominations, $250 worth of the local currency, the kyat. As of the scenario date, one USD equals about 1150 kyat, so a kyat is worth a little more than a penny.

One character has, in an watertight envelope taped to his torso, a photograph of their quarry, Chavela Ferraz. If you're having trouble deciding who should be carrying it, award it to the PC with the highest Bureaucracy rating, with Military Science as a tiebreaker.

Also included on each team member's person are their cover identity documents: see "Briefing Flashback," below.

Cell phone reception is spotty at best and completely insecure. A Difficulty 6 Preparedness test gets a few bars for the length of a single short vocal communication.

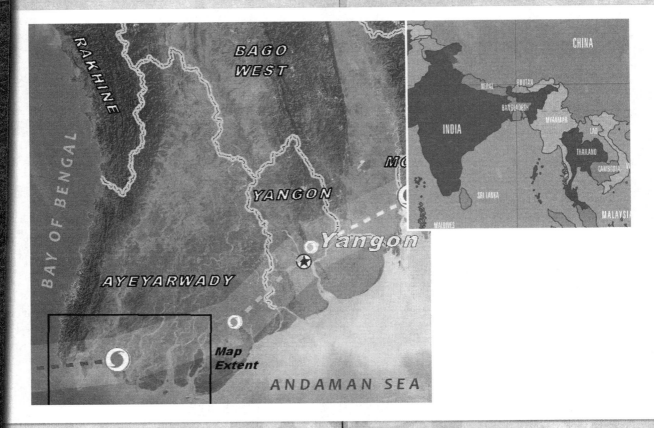

of an approaching patrol, coming in from the stand of battered palms to the north.

Otherwise, the group finds itself with a choice between two areas of covering forest: to the north or east. Going north lands them in an automatic fight with the patrol.

Most groups will spend the **Military Science** point, allowing them to make a squishy run for the eastern forest. Getting there quietly before the patrol emerges from the treeline requires a separate Difficulty 6 Infiltration test for each PC, no piggybacking allowed.

And... scene! The briefing flashback triggers either when the group makes it to the trees unnoticed, or when the group is discovered, but before the first shots are fired.

Briefing Flashback
Scene Type: Introduction

The scene now flashes back to the group's mission briefing. This occurs in a ready room on a French aircraft carrier in the Bay of Bengal.

(If this is the inaugural edition of your series, you might want to back up a step further to have each player describe what his character was doing when suddenly called to duty.)

This time, Mr. Verity is a slim, tall woman in her late forties. A severe haircut frames her angular face. She speaks with a slight Spanish accent.

Languages (Spanish) identifies the accent's regional color: it's Catalan.

"This is where you're going," she says. She pulls down a screen to reveal a power point slide, showing the country of Burma (or, as its cadre of dictators prefers, Myanmar.)

Now reveal the date of the scenario: June, 2008. The characters are all familiar with Cyclone Nargis from media reports. Remind the players of the timing: it's now a month since the disaster.

In your own words, preferably interspersed with player questions, Mr. Verity provides the following basic background information:

  • Official estimates by the infamously

corrupt and oppressive ruling junta put the death toll from the disaster at 134,000. Outside observers agree that this figure is a gross underestimation.

- Death toll aside, two million people have been displaced or suffered other significant hardship due to the disaster.

- Initially, the regime completely blocked independent relief agencies from entering the country. Under international pressure, including a one-on-one visit from UN Secretary General Ban Ki-Moon, the secretive junta relented—to a degree. They issued visas to some NGO representatives, but continue to hamper their efforts.

- Through its Union Solidarity and Development Association, the government strives to divert any incoming resources to itself.

- The junta's actions have only intensified the public's hatred and mistrust of the regime, which only months ago staged a successful and brutal crackdown against a pro-democracy movement.

- No matter how discontented they may be, the disaster-stricken populace lacks the wherewithal to foment a rebellion. Their focus now is on simple survival.

- The suffering caused by a disaster of this magnitude would have weakened the membrane in any case. That the government is using it as an opportunity to prey on its own people is all the more damaging.

- The team's mission is to intercept an Esoterror cell acting under the guise of aid workers. They belong to Child Hunger Action Network, an enemy front organization.

- Their primary target is Chavela Ferraz, the Executive Director of CHAN. [Here Verity flashes a recent headshot of Ferraz taken from the CHAN website.] As photographed, Ferraz is a glamorous, well-coiffed woman in her mid-40s.

- She is accompanied by six to ten CHAN employees, all of them presumed Esoterrorists.

- Ferraz's success in securing visas at a time when all other international aid was being refused strongly suggests that she may be aided by elements of the Burmese regime.

- Her team arrived in country three days after the cyclone. Their presence was only detected by the Order two days ago, during an investigative operation that identified CHAN as an enemy front.

- Ferraz's mission goals in Burma are not known, but whatever she's planning must be stopped.

- Although the Ordo is naturally interested in any intelligence materials the group might gather as it stops Ferraz's scheme, information acquisition is only a secondary priority.

- The mission will begin at a selected drop point in a rural area near the last confirmed sighting of Ferraz and her relief team. This occurred three days ago, in a village named Pandabali.

- Once safely landed at the drop point, they can make their way to the village where Ferraz was spotted. Their GPS trackers have been programmed with its coordinates.

Verity also lays out the following rules of engagement:

- Burma is considered a Dangerous Environment. Its regime is hostile to the west, and perhaps to the Order as well.

- However, the team is to take care not to precipitate an international incident.

- When confronted by local forces not clearly affiliated with Esoterror, the team may defend itself from attack with lethal force but may not initiate hostilities. It may evade apprehension, which may in turn provoke attack with lethal force.

• The team is not to intervene in the local political situation or participate in disaster relief, except where directly necessary to achieve its primary mission.

• Team members been provided with cover identities portraying them as international mercenaries. If captured and interrogated, they should confess to having been hired by eccentric Texas oil billionaire R. Willard Purdum to hunt for his niece, an aid worker with Doctors Without Borders who disappeared a week after her arrival in Rangoon. They should put up enough resistance to make this confession seem believable. (Purdum exists and has been known to hire mercenaries before. The niece is fictional.)

• Cover names for team members include: Joe Faucher, Jason Melendez, Lisa Hickman, Ashley Bullen, Adam Scott, Phyllis Terrones, Troy Dorsey. Characters of obvious ethnic background are assigned surnames suitable to their apparent heritage.

• Team members must follow the OV code of ethics at all times. The area's weakened membrane state exacerbates the usual metaphysical risks of ethics-breaching behaviors.

Once Verity's briefing has covered the above information, describe the team bundling into a C-130 transport plane. They check and double-check their parachutes before being flown high over Burma and dropped into the sky.

Back to the present: If the team completed "Irrawaddy Landing" without being spotted, go to "Hostile Territory." If the patrol has seen them, go to "Rice Paddy Firefight."

Speaking Burmese

To succeed in this scenario, the characters must be able to communicate with the locals. Give two PCs a free point in Languages: Burmese.

Award these, unless the players object, to the characters most heavily invested in Interpersonal abilities. A player may feel that this free language ability completely contravenes his character concept, in which case you should give it to the next qualifying PC instead.

Burmese has two forms, high and vernacular. 1 point of Burmese allows the characters to communicate in the colloquial form and understand the formal version. A character who has an additional build point to spend and wants to do so can, with Languages: Burmese 2, converse in either and write skillfully in the high form. A parsimonious player may realize that the ability to speak Official Burmese (or Myanmar, as the generals insist) won't be worth the expenditure, unless you stage sequels to this scenario.

Rice Paddy Firefight
Scene Type: Combat
Follows "Briefing Flashback" if team was spotted by patrol in "Irrawaddy Landing."

If spotted by the Burmese patrol, the team is plunged into immediate combat. Faced with armed foreigners, the local soldiers open fire without further formalities. There is one more patroller than there are PCs.

Burmese Patrollers
Abilities: Athletics 4, Fleeing 4, Health 4, Scuffling 6, Shooting 4.
Damage Modifiers: 0 (machete), 2 (AK-47 assault rifle), 2 (grenade, 1 each; see below)

"Bully" Patroller
As above, except Health 12, Scuffling 10, Shooting 8.

Half of the patrol's grenades are inoperative and deal no damage even if successfully thrown. Before the scene begins, randomly choose which of the soldiers carry bum grenades.

They avoid stepping into the rice paddy, where their Hit Thresholds decrease by 1. (The PCs, presumably trained in multi-environment warfare, do not suffer this drawback.)

One of the patrollers, the "bully", is taller and more muscular than the others. He is not the one shouting orders. If the bully is injured or worse, the rest of the patrol routs.

If they are routing, a Burmese-speaking character shouting at them and making a 1-point **Intimidate** spend causes them to surrender instead.

This fight offers the opportunity for in-combat fact-finding (see p. 56.) If you haven't done so already, explain the rules for this before proceeding.

The following abilities, arranged here in character sheet order, yield tactically relevant information.

Anthropology: From their body language, you can tell that these guys were born and raised in a city. They're probably not that good at fighting or moving in a rice paddy.

Forensic Accounting: This area has suffered widespread food shortages, and rank and file soldiers are probably starving, too. Their morale will be poor.

Forensic Psychology: The one shouting has the highest rank, but the one all of them furtively look to for signals is the big guy.

Explosive Devices: [Reveals which of the soldiers are carrying dud grenades.]

Forensic Anthropology: These guys are badly malnourished.

Post-Fight Information: If somehow captured and interrogated, the bully (whose name is Kwin Kei Tun) angrily defies any attempt to get information out of him. To capitulate to enemies undermines his sense of manhood. **Cop Talk** identifies him

as the kind of guy who'd rather die than admit defeat.

Any other surrendering soldier, including the putative commander, Shan Pyin Ya, becomes cooperative under **Interrogation**, but has no useful information to spill. He reveals the following:

- He's just a loyal soldier, following orders.

- He loves the regime, as does any good citizen of Myanmar. (This triggers **Bullshit Detector**.)

- The people are recovering quickly from the cyclone. (Ditto.)

- He hasn't seen the lady in the photo. (**Bullshit Detector** registers this as an honest reply.)

After several of these answers, it should be apparent that these guys are just ordinary grunts who have no bearing on the team's mission objectives.

When the team starts wondering what to do with them, **Military Science** or **Cop Talk** shows that they're too terrified of their superiors to admit being defeated by foreign commandos. They can be expected to go about their business as if nothing happened.

(As an alternate choice, if Kwin Kei Tun has been captured, you may decide that he's so humiliated by the experience that he attempts to attack the team again as soon as they cut him loose. This may force them to into an appallingly one-sided slaughter. If the group winds up mowing down these clearly outmatched, pathetic soldiers, they face a potential 5-point Stability loss.)

Hostile Territory
Scene Type: Travel / Logistics
Follows either "Briefing Flashback" or "Rice Paddy Firefight".

The team's GPS receivers show that the village where Ferraz was last seen is three kilometers to the northwest of the rice paddy. Their current map shows a winding country road leading from their approximate current position to the village, Pandabali.

If the players speculate on the current conditions of the road, **Natural History** reveals that the cyclone has probably washed out portions of it out, rendering vehicle traffic impossible.

Military Science or **Cop Talk** further suggest that travel by road increases their chance of encountering patrols or checkpoints.

The group may nonetheless decide to look for a vehicle. **Archaeology** allows a character to follow the patterns of destruction and to find likely piles of debris in which trucks or cars might be found, and then to dig through quickly to penetrate the wreckage mounds. The time it takes to secure a potentially suitable vehicle decreases with a spend: 3 points gets one in half an hour; 2 points takes an hour, 1 point takes two hours. With no Archaeology spend, the group can find a vehicle in three hours.

The first vehicle found is an old flatbed truck. The cab holds a driver and passenger. The rest of the team will have to sit on the wooden flatbed. If the group rejects this or is unable to get it working, the second vehicle they find is a small school bus. No working third vehicle is readily available.

During the vehicle search, check once per hour to see if the group encounters a patrol. Roll a die; on a result of 6, a patrol appears. Add 1 to your roll if the group avoided the patrol during the "Irrawaddy Landing" sequence. Add another 1 for each hour the vehicle search has taken so far.

If a patrol shows up, refer to the sidebar of that name.

Once the PCs find a vehicle, a Difficulty 5 Mechanics test is required to get it working. If the difference between Difficulty and result exceeds 3, the vehicle faces no further mechanical interruptions. Otherwise it breaks down at an otherwise uneventful moment between each scene, and requires another Difficulty 5 Mechanics test to get started again. Only a high result on this initial Mechanics test allows the group to forestall future breakdowns.

Driving to Pandabali

If the group drives to Pandabali, it encounters three obstacles, plus (if not already forestalled) a vehicle breakdown at a dramatically appropriate moment between the three sequences. They are presented in alphabetical order. Order them as pacing demands, or to put the spotlight on players who haven't had a chance to do much recently.

Anguish: The vehicle passes an encampment of displaced flood victims. They huddle in makeshift tents and shanties on both sides of the road. Seeing the vehicle, the displaced swarm it from both

If a Patrol Shows up

The group can talk its way out of an apprehension attempt by pretending to be aid workers (2-point Impersonate spend) or by offering a bribe. The latter requires a Negotiation spend plus a cash payment. The more cash the group offers, the lower the Negotiation spend. It can get off the hook for a 3-point spend plus $100 in local currency, 2 points plus $200, or 1 point plus $300 or more.

Any attempt at Intimidation results in an immediate arrest attempt.

If the patrol leader decides to apprehend the group, the only way out is to fight.

If the group skipped the Rice Paddy Firefight, the first apprehension attempt uses the characters and tactical situation from that sequence—minus the rice paddy terrain element.

Otherwise, the patrol comprises a number of soldiers with the same equipment and statistics as the ordinary patrollers from that sequence, minus the grenades. If one or more PCs is hurt or worse, the base number of patrollers equals the number of PCs less one. Otherwise, there is one more patroller than there are PCs. Add 2 to the base number for each previous patrol encounter. The Rice Paddy Firefight proper does not count as a previous patrol for this purpose. If the group encounters those same characters as their first patrol, it does count.

sides. Taking the PCs for aid workers, they cry out for food, water and medicine. Rag-clad and clearly malnourished, the victims reek of filth and gangrene. **Forensic Anthropology** reveals that many of them will die within days if not given help. Several of the women carry dying infants.

The villagers stand aside, slightly mollified, if given money (1-point Negotiation spend.) Cash does nothing for them in the short run, but, as they explain to the PCS, they can use it to buy supplies from corrupt officials. Reassurance plus Impersonation (1 point spend of each) gets them to move aside if the speaker deceives them into believing that help is on the way. Intimidation (no spend necessary) gets them to move by threatening to run them over.

Having to ignore the pleas of dying survivors may cause team members to lose 5 Stability. Base Difficulty is 4; add 1 if Impersonation was used on them and 2 if Intimidation came into play.

Checkpoint: Rounding a bend in a heavily forested road, the team finds itself mere meters from a military checkpoint. Determine composition of the forces manning the checkpoint as per the "If a Patrol Shows Up" sidebar. The team can talk its way through the checkpoint, as per the sidebar, but checkpoint soldiers are a tougher sell: add 1 to the cost of any interpersonal spends.

If the soldiers decide to detain the commandos, they can elect to evade a firefight by driving through the checkpoint, or by throwing the vehicle into reverse. In either case they do so under a hail of automatic weapons fire.

Driving through exposes the driver to one instance of damage +2, and requires him to make a Difficulty 4 Athletics test to avoid a second instance of damage. (Give the driver the choice of swerving into one of the soldiers firing at him, or driving evasively. If he picks the swerve, he takes another instance of damage while running him over and killing him.) If the vehicle is the flatbed truck, and a passenger is in the cab, he also takes an automatic instance of +2 damage and makes the Athletics test to avoid the second. Other passengers make two Athletics tests (Difficulty 3 in the truck; Difficulty 4 in the bus), with each

failed test resulting in damage.

Backing up exposes the driver to one instance of damage, and requires all passengers to make one Athletics test each (Difficulties as above) to avoid an instance of damage.

All instances of damage from gunfire on the vehicle are at a +2 modifier.

The team's maps show them that there is no alternate road to Pandabali. If the group backs up, it must travel the rest of the way to the village on foot. They encounter obstacles given in "Humping It" until they have reached a total of four obstacles from both that section and this one.

Washout: The vehicle reaches a portion of road that has been rendered completely impassable by storm damage. Fallen trees cover a morass of mud. A 3-point Architecture spend allows the group to construct a viable bridge from the fallen trees which holds just long enough to drive across. So long as one Architecture point is spent, Mechanics and

Preparedness points may be spent as Architecture points, at a rate of 2 to 1. Multiple characters can contribute points, including Architecture points, to the collective effort.

Once the bridge has been built, a Difficulty 5 Driving test is required to get the vehicle safely across it. On a failure, the vehicle rolls sideways into a gully. Anyone in the vehicle at the time must make a Difficulty 4 Athletics test or suffer an instance of damage (-1 modifier.) The vehicle winds up firmly lodged, upside down, in a muddy gorge. It can't be moved without heavy equipment, which the team has no access to. If the vehicle is lost, the group must travel the rest of the way to Pandabali on foot. If Wash-Out is their third obstacle, they walk the rest of the way without incident. Otherwise, they encounter obstacles given in "Humping It" until they have reached a total of four obstacles.

Humping It

These obstacles confront the PCs if they travel to Pandabali on foot. Place them in order as pacing or character spotlighting mandates. To arrange them in order of escalating nastiness: go with Patrol, Corpse Dump, and Membrane Breach.

(If the group decides to look for a vehicle before confronting all three obstacles given here, allow them to do so, as per p. 7. If they get the vehicle, they undergo enough obstacles given in "Driving To Pandabali" to bring their total number of obstacles up to four.)

Corpse Dump: As the team traverses a densely vegetated ravine, a horrible stench assails their nostrils: the smell of putrefying corpses. They then hear the distinctive beeping sound of a truck backing up. Parting the foliage for a better look, they see a truck dumping dozens of corpses into the ravine. **Forensic Anthropology** pegs times of death as ranging between four weeks to several days. Characters with the ability spot bloated drowning victims, dead for a month, to starvation victims who might have expired as early as this morning.

Another dump truck, this one full of debris and muddy earth, stands ready to dump its contents onto the bodies once they fill the ravine.

The work is performed by civilians, some of them armed. **History** identifies the workers as members of the Union Solidarity and Development Association, the government bureaucracy in charge of disaster relief. It labels the armed men as belonging to the Swan Ah Shin militia—another arm of the junta. (Where possible, divide these two facts between two characters possessing the History ability.)

This sight occasions tests against a 5-point Stability loss.

Patrol: Ask the group to specify who's taking point as it machetes its way through heavy tropical underbrush. Allow that character to make a Difficulty 4 Surveillance test. On a success, he hears an approaching patrol. The group can hide from the patrol on a Difficulty 4 Infiltration test (piggybacking permitted.)

If the point man fails the Surveillance test, the group comes face to face with a patrol (see "If a Patrol Shows Up" sidebar), literally bumping into each other in the jungle. The soldiers panic and immediately commence a firefight; no interpersonal ability use is possible.

If the group fails the Infiltration test, the patrol sees them but barks a challenge at them rather than moving straight to the shooting phase. Interpersonal ability use may proceed, as given in the sidebar.

Everything else about this patrol encounter conforms to the situation given in the sidebar.

Membrane Breach: In the midst of a jungle clearing, the group finds a large expanse of recently spaded ground. **Archaeology** identifies this as a mass grave.

The character with the lowest Stability pool feels a low, metallic grinding noise ringing in his head. Everyone else gets a general skin-crawling feeling about the place. Simply being here brings the risk of a 2-point Stability loss. **Occult Science** says this is a place of particularly thin membrane strength in a region that right now is one massive LSML (see Chapter Six.) That's why they're here—to stop the whole storm track zone from turning into a place of near-palpable evil, like this one.

After chewing over this insight, the group member with the highest Surveillance pool spots a series of strange pulsing black spots in the air, hovering over the grave. **Occult Science** suggests that the group might want to clear out of there immediately. Anyone who draws closer to the spots realizes that they function as peepholes into another reality. This realization prompts a test against a 4-point Stability loss. Anyone looking through the peephole sees into the Outer Dark—and sees a million burning, hungry eyes blinking back at him. The character must test against a 9-point Stability loss. Whether successful or not, he suffers a +2 increase to all Stability Difficulties for the rest of the scenario.

Village Of Misery
Scene Type: Core
Lead-In: Hostile Territory

The village of Pandabali is only slightly less desperate than the evacuee camp the group may have encountered if it came here on foot. In contrast to those desperate souls, the people of Pandabali stir only listlessly as the team approaches.

Forensic Anthropology affirms that they're in no better shape than the tent village residents. (Without the point of comparison, the group simply knows that the people here are profoundly sick and malnourished.) On a 1-point spend the character also spots bruising and lacerations on the village's able-bodied men and women, consistent with their having been beaten. A 2-point spend can tell from the relative age of the injuries that this happened on at least three separate occasions, many days apart.

Forensic Psychology notes the signs of severe collective depression—more so than one would expect even from disaster victims.

When the team comes close to anyone, most villagers either respond with dull-eyed catatonia. A few pathetically extend their necks or bare their chests, as if meekly submitting to summary execution.

Villagers who might eventually respond to verbal cues include:

- a young, once-pretty woman, Wa Nyein Thir.

- a skeletal, toothless woman in her sixties, Kha.

- a big-framed but clearly starving man in his thirties, Zaw Hnin.

Any of them can provide roughly the same information, in response to **Reassurance** that the team is here to hurt whoever has harmed them. Whoever speak does so dully, responding exactly to the question asked without further elaboration. PCs will have to keep probing to get the whole story.

- Yes, the woman in the photograph was here, along with other foreigners.

- They were escorted by armed men from the Swan Ah Shin militia. (If the players haven't already learned this fact, **History** or **Military Science** explains that this is a government paramilitary force.)

- The woman instructed the Swab Ah Shin to take children with them.

- They forced the villagers to tell them which of the children were orphans.

- Of course there are many orphans in every village around here, because their parents were killed in the cyclone or flooding. Or by the famine and disease that followed.

- They only took those we identified.

- Those children never came back.

- A week later, the soldiers came back, without the foreigners. They demanded more orphans. By that time, there were more of them, because more parents had died.

- Some tried to fight back, but were beaten

for our troubles.

- They came again a week later and took more children.

- They have taken fourteen children in all. The villagers fear that they will soon be back.

- (core) Zaw Hnin later saw one of the soldiers who took the children at an emergency depot set up by the government's relief agency. (**History** names this as the Union Solidarity and Development Association.)

- The depot is the place where regime officials hoard medicine, building supplies, food and other necessities, releasing them only to those willing to pay.

If the SSFers ask questions of a tactical nature about the depot—number of guards, secret entrances or the like—the villagers suddenly clam up.

Reassurance suggests that they're clearly terrified by the prospect of contributing in any way to a raid on the depot. They fear, not irrationally, that the PCs will be captured and tortured into revealing who helped them. Then they'll all be brutalized and killed.

Combined 1-point spends of both **Reassurance** and **Military Science** (may be undertaken by separate characters) convince Zaw Hnin that the team is more than equipped to hit the depot and get away clean. He then tells them that many of the soldiers sneak out in the late morning hours to smoke and gamble in the jungle. If they hit the depot then, they'll face less resistance at the site, and are less likely to run into patrols on the way there.

(Zaw Hnin has no way of knowing the reason why: the militia commander on duty at that time accepts lets his men slack off in exchange for gifts and cash bribes.)

Solidarity Depot
Scene Type: Combat
Lead-in: Village of Misery

If the team attacks at any time other than the late morning, it encounters a patrol on its way from Pandabali to the depot. The encounter goes as given in "If a Patrol Shows Up" sidebar, except that pool point and cash costs of evading a fight are doubled this close to the militia's commanders. Also, add an extra soldier to the mix.

Devise suitable additional obstacles to a successful raid on the depot if the group is turned back by a patrol encounter.

Assuming it evades or deals with the patrol, the team can use **Natural History** to find a promontory overlooking the complex. It sits in a depression of newly cleared jungle. **Natural History** suggests that its builders cleared out a section of palm forest already flattened by the cyclone. The main structure is three hundred feet long by twenty-five feet wide. **Architecture** shows that's a hastily erected pre-fab building. Though made of cheap materials by first world standards, it's the newest, most secure structure the commandos have seen during this mission.

New construction materials, mostly lumber and tin roof sheets, are stacked outside the complex. More materials can be seen through its open warehouse doors. **Forensic Accounting** suggests that these are donated supplies sent as part of the international aid effort. A close binocular reading (Difficulty 4 Surveillance test) confirms it, picking out stencils on the lumber from Italian, Canadian and Indian relief agencies.

History explains that a peaceful approach to base personnel would result in an immediate attempt to arrest them. The junta's paranoid obsession with the maintenance of its supposed reputation is all too well known.

Chain link fencing roughly encircles the lumber yard, topped by razor wire.

Architecture indicates that the fencing has been poorly installed into wet ground. A good shoulder hit directed at any of the fence posts knocks it over, allowing the assault team to essentially run through the fence.

Military Science estimates that there are four times as many people manning the base as there are PCs. A 1-point Military Science spend says that only three quarters of these are armed fighters, and that they're an ill-disciplined, poorly-trained militia force prone to rout in the face of a convincing assault.

None of the defenders wear the uniform of the regular Myanmar army.

Attacking the Depot

The group succeeds here if they take out one third of the armed soldiers, prompting the others to rout. Certain tactics cause some soldiers to flee early in the fight.

Explosives: Though not given explosives as part of their mission packs, a character may have smuggled a suitable supply of them into his pack on a Difficulty 6 Preparedness success. One or more team members can make a Difficulty 6 Infiltration test (no piggybacking) to get inside the structure, and can plant them on a Difficulty 4 Mechanics test (character undertaking test must have **Explosive Devices**.) If all tests are successful, one third of the forces flee during the first round of the fight, and the Hit Thresholds of all other soldiers are reduced by 2 during the first round and by 1 during the second round.

Sneaking In: If more than half the group sneaks into the compound (Difficulty 6 Infiltration, no piggybacking) and then starts the fight by surprise, PCs inside the compound treat targets as if their Hit Thresholds have been reduced by 2 during the first round and by 1 during the second.

Improvise appropriate responses to any other credible plans the PCs deploy to skew the odds in their favor.

Compound Militiamen

Abilities: Athletics 6, Fleeing 6, Health *, Scuffling 6, Shooting 6.

Damage Modifiers: 0 (machete), 1 (Tokarev), 2 (AK-47 assault rifle)

Any militiaman hit by a PC attack during the first round of the fight drops immediately. Any militiaman missed by a PC attack during the first round or hit during the second round is a leader type with a Health score of 6 who fights unrelentingly until killed or incapacitated. All other militiamen drop when hit. On close inspection (or a distant glance by a character with **Forensic Anthropology** or **Military Science**) easily-dropped characters prove to be playing dead. They do this out of self-preservation and are never brave enough to launch sneak attacks once down.

Ordinary militiamen surrender or flee after two thirds of their total force is down or fled. Leader types keep fighting until the group kills or incapacitates them.

(core) During the second round of the fight, one of the commandos sees a man in a suit flee into the jungle, carrying a briefcase. Try to pick a moment when the character is otherwise occupied—under fire from a leader type, for example. This is Mr. Tin, who features in the next scene. He's short, paunchy, wears glasses, and is the victim of a terrible haircut.

Although the scenario as written assumes Mr. Tin is found in a separate location soon after the fight, let the team capture him during the fight if they take credible, tactically sound measures to grab him. If they wind up killing this important witness, have the contents of his briefcase include a secret journal which can be decoded via **Cryptography** and translated with **Languages: Burmese**. This provides the information given in the next scene.

Mr. Tin
Scene Type: Core (Interview)
Lead-in: Solidarity Depot

Evidence Collection allows a commando to track Mr. Tin from the depot to a spot in the jungle, where he has collapsed from exhaustion. They come upon him in a tangle of fallen trees, his pant leg entangled in the splintered wood of a split trunk. As they arrive, he is being menaced by a very large and hungry boa constrictor. A Difficulty 4 Shooting test or Difficulty 5 Athletics test (with thrown machete) dispatches the beast.

Kyin Aun Tin is a mid-level official of the Union Solidarity and Development Association. He cooperated with Chavela Ferraz out of greed. Now that the commandos have blown apart his depot, he is motivated chiefly by fear. However, getting his most useful bit of information requires an appeal to his overarching motivation, avarice. Until he realizes that it's Ferraz they're really interested in, Tin defiantly parrots the junta party line, excoriating the PCs as colonial aggressors. When he switches gears, he plays down his involvement in, or knowledge of, Esoterror.

Tin's briefcase, found a few feet from his trapped body, is stuffed with bundled 1,000 kyat bills. **Forensic Accounting** sees that the notes are crumpled and worn, deducing that this money is the proceeds from the government's efforts to sell reconstruction supplies to the cyclone-stricken at extortionate prices.

Tin speaks fluent, if heavily accented, English. **Interrogation** or **Intimidation** get him to spill the following, in response to specific questioning:

- (core) Ferraz and the CHAN team are holed up nearby, at a self-sufficient base camp located on the bend of a delta tributary. (On further prompting, he provides the coordinates.)

- Tin has been a sleeper agent of Ferraz's group for over a decade. They helped him get his well-paid job in the development association.

- They never gave him any instructions until Nargis hit.

- These came as coded messages left at a dead drop near his apartment building in Yangon (Rangoon.)

- He had never met anyone from the group until he was called upon to help CHAN during the first days of the reconstruction effort.

- Tin always assumed he was working for the Chinese, American, or Indian government. If pushed, he acts as if he's only at this moment realizing that he's an agent of some far stranger group. (**Bullshit Detector** identifies this last bit as performance.)

- The money in the briefcase belongs to the government. Tin is not stealing from the junta. He's stealing *for* the junta. (He makes this point very heatedly, clearly more afraid of his civilian superiors than he is of either the Ordo or Esoterror.)

- Ferraz was accompanied at all times by three heavily armed bodyguard types, and by several others who seemed more like civilians. She never introduced anybody, and Tin didn't ask.

- Ferraz spoke to him in Burmese and to her people in English or Spanish. She didn't realize until a week into their collaboration that Tin could understand her when she issued instructions in English.

- Yes, he helped Ferraz gather orphans. He

doesn't know what she wanted with them, but whatever it was, she kept needing fresh ones.

- During this time, he overheard several references to something called meatgrinder. At times this seemed like the name of her secret project, but at other times it seemed like Meatgrinder was a person.

- Regarding this Meatgrinder, she called it an "incarnation of consumption." Mr. Tin has no idea what that might mean.

As the interrogation continues, a smug grin creeps across Tin's face. **Bullshit Detector** shows that he's holding something back, as if they're failing to ask the right question. (Skip this hint if a player asks him about any odd behavior Ferraz may have engaged in.)

(tactical clue / special means of dispatch) **Negotiation**—and the agreement that he gets to take the briefcase full of cash with him—scores a decisive reveal: Ferraz, strangely, refused to let anyone bearing paper currency to enter her base camp. Everyone coming near was subjected to a search, and any cash placed in a guarded locker a mile off.

Meatgrinder
Scene Type: Tactical
Lead-In: Mr. Tin

Using their GPS devices, the group can home in on the location of the base camp. Getting into the camp requires that the commandos overcome the camp's defenses.

The camp offers two approaches: through heavily damaged rain forest, or from the river. The camp can be reconnoitered from the river . On land, it is obscured by half-toppled palms.

Having inflatable dinghies on hand requires one Difficulty 6 Preparedness success per two-person vessel.

The camp consists of a circle of armored, converted

motor homes, plus several jeeps and all-terrain trucks. **Electronic Surveillance** and a video camera (requires Difficulty 4 Preparedness) shows a heavy padlock on one of the campers. A child's face briefly pokes up into the window, and then disappears, as if someone has pulled him out of sight.

Three skilled combatants patrol the camp, raising the Difficulty of any Infiltration attempts into it to 7. The commandos must overcome them to get to Ferraz and her fellow Esoterrorists. They are:

Gwynedd Neal
A florid-faced, blond Welsh-American whose yellowed eyes reveal alcohol-related liver problems if observed with **Forensic Anthropology**.

> General Abilities: Athletics 8, Fleeing 4, Health 8, Scuffling 8, Shooting 8.
> Damage Modifiers: 0 (combat knife), 1 (handgun: Mk23 .45-cal. ACP), 2 (9mm Heckler & Koch MP5 machine pistol)

Wesley Nampa
This British-Italian mercenary-turned-occultist hopes that the creatures of the Outer Black will facilitate his dreams of rock stardom.

> General Abilities: Athletics 6, Fleeing 6, Health 8, Scuffling 6, Shooting 6.
> Damage Modifiers: same as Neal, above

Gabriel Toscanos
Chavela Ferraz's cousin would still be stuck in a dead-end job in a dusty small town if she hadn't introduced him to the exciting world of international Esoterror.

> General Abilities: Athletics 6, Fleeing 6, Health 6, Scuffling 4, Shooting 8.
> Damage Modifiers: same as Neal, above

While Neal and Nampa actively patrol, Toscanos practices archery, shooting at a makeshift bullseye with a high-tech bow. Two other bows hang from a nearby tree, as if Nampa and Neal practice the sport, too.

Once the three bodyguards are taken out of commission, it is an easy matter to round up the rest of the conspirators. It does not occur to them to flee; they're sedentary types who know they won't survive long in a disaster-stricken jungle. They are:

Water purity expert Claira Mandujano, 43, (Mexican) was initiated into worship of the Outer Dark by her stepfather. After briefly escaping into aid work as a means of redemption, she has succumbed to her early training.

Tyler Middleton, a 36-year old American logistics specialist who lost his moral moorings after seeing wild dogs feast on the corpses of famine victims in Africa. His formerly callow handsomeness is slowly giving way to a middle-aged plumpness around the edges.

Nutritionist Janna Quartz, 25, (German) has burned out on altruism and hopes that Esoterror connections will fund her line of expensive, charity-themed T-shirts.

Fund-raiser Jose Salinas, 64, (Mexican) introduced Chavela Ferraz to international aid work and followed her down her dark path out of unrequited lust for his protégé.

Vehicles specialist Paul Siluwe, 29, (Zambian) makes a habit of sexually exploiting the disaster victims he's employed to protect.

Chavela Ferraz cuts an impressive figure in her immaculate jungle gear. She bravely maintains composure when captured. She offers the PCs unimaginable power if they will merely let her complete her occult researches. **Bullshit Detector** shows that she doesn't really expect them to say yes, but is very frightened and is temporizing until a better option presents itself. She responds to **Interrogation**, drawing out her answers in hopes of rescue.

- She is the leader of the CHAN cell.

- She knows no members of other cells by their real names and has no current means of contacting members of other cells.

- The orphans are food for an entity she has summoned.

- The entity is called Meatgrinder: it is consumption incarnate.

- It took a massive incident of metaphorical consumption—Nargis' tear through the Irrawaddy Delta—to weaken the membrane enough to summon it.

- Ferraz has been prepping for over a decade for just the right cyclone to hit here.

- Myanmar is the perfect place to bring an unremitting horror entity into the world— the isolated regime keeps foreigners at bay, and is corrupt enough that its thoroughly conscienceless functionaries can be easily rented.

- Meatgrinder's tie to this realm is tentative. As the horror of Nargis recedes, he must literally eat an orphan child every two to four days in order to remain here.

- It is teaching Ferraz occult rituals, which she hopes to one day use to reshape human flesh. She wishes to resculpt herself into a hybrid being exhibiting the immortal physicality of an unremitting horror entity.

- Meatgrinder has dribbed and drabbed the information out to her, as if trying to ensure it gets to eat as many children as possible.

The OBE known as the Meatgrinder appears either when the PCs release the children from the locked camper, or when they attempt to drive the camper away. It contains four terrified, maltreated orphans.

If the PCs are already engaged with Ferraz as they go for the camper padlock, a character with **Bullshit Detector** might note that her expression changes from fleeting panic and then to eagerness—and finally to a poker face. (She's momentarily scared of the meatgrinder's sudden appearance, until she realizes that it will chew up her captors. What she is about to discover is that her first response is the appropriate one.)

The entity manifests as a gigantic torture machine,

arranged throughout the camp like a series of interlocked fence pieces (see creature description.) It places itself so that these pieces zig-zag around the camp, close to each of its current inhabitants.

The PCs immediately perceive it as an intelligent, self-willed entity of inexpressible malignity.

The meatgrinder's Scuffling pool equals the number of PCs times 6. It can attack once per round per opponent. It attacks with Scuffling, spending 2 points on each roll against targets who have not harmed it, and 3 against those who have. Handle its attacks on supporting characters by fiat. At first, the meatgrinder attacks only one child, taking two rounds to kill it. Only when it is reduced to 8 or fewer Health does it go on an orgy of devouring, attacking all of the four children and any surviving Esoterrorists. For each bad guy it attempts to hit in a round, roll a die. On an odd result, the Esoterrorist is torn immediately to shreds.

By forgoing an attack action, PCs can thwart the creature's attempt to harm other characters. A called shot (p. 46) against one of its grabbing arms has the desired effect of preventing the grinder from feeding a victim into one of its various flesh-ripping devices—in game terms, removing its next attack against that character.

Note the meatgrinder's special means of dispatch. PCs can use the kyat they were given on assignment, or perhaps the contents of Mr. Tin's briefcase as the paper money. They may devise their own ways of delivering money-laden attacks, or use the the bodyguards' archery equipment to fire arrows with kyat affixed to the shafts.

None of the Esoterrorists survive the meatgrinder sequence. Once it realizes that it's about to be banished to the Outer Dark, it starts eating everyone in sight.

Potential Stability loss from a confrontation with the meatgrinder is 7 if no orphans or PCs die, or 8, if one of them does.

If the SSFers open the camper before interrogating Ferraz, they may be able to find the information given above on her laptop.

Meatgrinder

Game Statistics

General Abilities: Athletics 12, Health 36,
Scuffling 24-36.

Damage Modifier: +3

Hit Threshold: 3

Armor: 2

A meatgrinder manifests as a gigantic torture machine. This consists of a series of interlocking metal walls, ranging in thickness from 10 to 30 cm and in height from 2 to 3 meters. When it appears, it arranges its pieces in a zig-zag pattern, placing a wall section next to every available victim. Wall pieces might loop around obstacles or encircle victims entirely, imprisoning them in doorless rooms. A meatgrinder's size is fungible; it could fill a football field with labyrinthine wall pieces, or compress itself into a modest back yard.

Each wall piece bristles with saws, blades, screws, loops of razor wire, and complicated torture devices. Every ten feet or so, a bag of chain mail protrudes from the wall like an empty stomach. The meatgrinder seizes a victim, tears it to shreds with its various implements of death. Articulated metal hands grab the chunks of meat and bone and feeds them into its chain mail guts.

While predominantly machine-like, the meatgrinder also evokes a living organism. Its metal surfaces sweat and breathe. When a single blow deals 6 or more points of damage, a wound opens up in the machine, bleeding an oily ichor. When hurt, it grinds its gears in fury. When it kills a victim, it purrs with obscene pleasure.

Although the meatgrinder more resembles a building than a creature, its Hit Threshold represents the difficulty of hitting a vital spot. It uses its many arms and implements to parry incoming blows and bullets.

All That Remains:

Architecture: The creature's wall sections leave behind a maze-like pattern of depressions in soft ground. The depth of the depressions suggests that the weight of each wall section approached the ten tonne mark.

Chemistry: A dark, greasy residue is found where wall pieces touched ground. Its chemical composition, when analyzed, matches no earthly material but combines the qualities of oil and blood.

Evidence Collection: Blood spray analysis indicates that a victim was subjected to some unspeakable high-pressure industrial process, as if placed inside an incredibly sophisticated woodchipper.

Forensic Anthropology: When a meatgrinder fully devours a victim, it leaves behind only tiny dots of blood and a few microscopic shreds of muscle fiber. If the meatgrinder dematerializes in mid-consumption, the corpse left behind shows signs of tearing, sawing and pulverization by multiple blunt and sharp implements.

Where They Come From: Meatgrinders are machine entities resident in the clanking, steaming nightmare cities of the Outer Dark. Eternally ravenous incarnations of the principle of consumption, they endlessly disembowel and masticate the spent spiritual essences of captive mortals. They lust for the chance to incarnate in the material world, where they feed on greed and desperation.

Continued residence on the earthly plane is difficult to maintain and dependent on two factors. First, desperation and greed must be widespread among hundreds of thousands of people, as happens in the wake of a natural disaster. Two, the creature must be provided with sacrifices of the weakest and most vulnerable — specifically, orphan children. It is the sociopathic avarice of the sacrificer, even more than the distress of the victim, that keeps the meatgrinder's blood-fired engines humming.

In its unearthly habitat, the meatgrinder is an inextricable component of a belching, hellish factory city.

On Earth, the meatgrinder spends most of its time in an incorporeal, invisible state, preserving its psychic energy, so that it is not swept back to the world where it belongs.

Intelligence Level: Meatgrinders retain a spark of intellect from every sentient creature they devour. Although capable of great feats of memory, including a vast knowledge of occult ritual, they show little aptitude for anything that can't be bought, measured, or consumed. Perceptive observers of the worst of the human soul, they skillfully manipulate the greedy and conscienceless.

Reconfiguration: The meatgrinder does not move conventionally, but can reconfigure its sections on the fly in reaction to the movements of its victims. However, all of its pieces must form a single structure; it can't divide itself up into separate sections.

Paper Money Vulnerability (Special Means Of Dispatch): As an incarnation of consumption, paper money—the ultimate symbol of expenditure in the modern world—takes on a talismanic significance for the meatgrinder. The act of destroying paper money instead of using it to consume harms its earthly structure. Any successful attack that can be delivered in a way that distresses or ruins paper money does a minimum of 12 points of damage if it hits. Possibilities include cash-wrapped explosives or money taped around blades.

Extraction
Scene Type: Denouement
Lead-In: Meatgrinder

Destroying the meatgrinder ends the mission. The team can then send an encrypted message to Mr. Verity, who dispatches choppers as needed for the extraction. It may take any surviving orphans or cell members back with them. Cell members are whisked away for interrogation. Mr. Verity assures the group that the orphans will be relocated, given counseling, and placed in supportive homes.

APPENDIX

GLOSSARY OF ACRONYMS

CASIE — Case Analysis Schematic Interpretation Engine; data sifting software suite provided to station agents

DAS — Debby Ann score; numerical expression of the likelihood that an MTA report reflects actual Esoterror activity

DEO — dangerous environment operation; an investigation to which SSFs are assigned because it takes place in a war zone or other conditions necessitating paramilitary-level equipment and personnel

DRU — demographic research unit; indirectly monitors membrane strength by collating results of specially devised public opinion polls

EFA — Electronic Forensic Accounting; desk officer team dedicated to detecting money laundering and financial malfeasance

EMA — enemy media asset

ETS — Electronic Traffic Sifting; monitoring of signals intelligence for signs of Esoterror activity

FMA — friendly media asset

IAMA — ideologically allied media asset; a media contact who supports Ordo goals but is no way affiliated with, or even aware of, the organization

MOT — Media Outreach Team

MTA – Media Threat Analysis; duty performed by network of internationally distributed desk assets, in which publicly available media reports are scoured for signs of potential enemy activity

OCT — ongoing complex threat; tactical designation calling for the establishment of a station assignment

ODE — Outer Dark entity

ODIS — Outer Dark influenced subject

NNA – non-agent asset

PPU — Psychographic Profiling Unit; team of experts in criminal psychology

PRG — Preliminary Review Group; first adjudicators in a disciplinary board procedure

RO — Rescue Only; refers to an extraction team without means to engage or defend against enemy forces in combat

RPBD — Recruitment Branch (Paramilitary Division); division of recruitment responsible for assembling SSFs

SIA — Signals Intelligence Analysis; Ordo department tasked with analyzing electronic communications intercepts for signs of enemy activity

SDC — Surveillance and Deep Cover; field agent wing responsible for active monitoring of potential Esoterror threats

SMD — special means of dispatch; a way of slaying or otherwise neutralizing an OBE unique to that particular creature (or creature type)

SPM — soft psychological means; acceptable techniques for extended interrogation which do not damage the membrane

SSF — Special Suppression Forces; commando team equipped and trained for heavy combat

TET — Tactical Euthanasia Team; security personnel trained to quickly and safely neutralize agents determined by a psych evaluation to be possessed or infested by OBEs

UF — uniformed friendly; a person whose goals coincide with ours, but who is unaware of our existence

UO — unaffiliated operative; person aware of the Outer Dark and the supernatural underground who owes allegiance neither to us nor to Esoterror

INDEX

ESTERROR FACT BOOK